RED FLOWER OF CHINA

翟振华

ZHAI ZHENHUA

SOHO

Published in the United States of America by
Soho Press, Inc.
853 Broadway
New York, NY 10003

Published in Canada by
Lester Publishing Limited.

Library of Congress Cataloging-in-Publication Data

Zhai, Zhenhua, 1951–
Red flower of China / Zhai Zhenhua.
p.   cm.
ISBN 0-939149-83-4 :
1. Zhai, Zhenhua, 1951–   . 2. Hung wei ping—Biography.
3. China—History—Cultural Revolution, 1966–1969.   I. Title.
DS778.Z47A3   1993
951.05′6—dc20

[B]   92–44047
                                                CIP

Manufactured in the United States

10 9 8 7 6 5 4 3 2 1

To Danny, with love
To China, with hope

CONTENTS

Prologue vii
Acknowledgements ix

PART ONE: CHILDHOOD

The Older Generation..3
Childhood in Shandong Province...8
A Taste of Hardship..16
Living in Legendary Worlds...22
Primary School..26
Dragons Bear Dragons?...31
Middle School 34
Fables of Revolutionary Heroism..39
"I Want to Be Progressive!" 43
Walking along the Class Line..47

PART TWO: THE CULTURAL REVOLUTION

The Origin of the Cultural Revolution 55
"What Is Going On?" 57
A Working Group Comes to School..61
The Anti-Working-Group Movement...66
Becoming a Red Guard 73
Bedevilling Devils...79
Chairman Mao Receives the Red Guards...83
Destroying the Old Four and Raiding Homes 91
The Capitalists and the Privileged...101
Fighting the "Sons of Bitches"..104
The Great Contact...110
Punishing the Pickets and Joint Action 116
Purging the Red Guards..119
Watching the Revolution from the Sidelines.......................................125
The Unfettered Life 129
The Impact of the Revolution...133
The Other Half of the Family 137

PART THREE: LIFE AS A PEASANT AND WORKER

Walking the 5/7 Road and Joining the Brigade 145
Farewell, Beijing 155
Yan'an — "The Sacred Shrine of the Revolution" 158
In the Stone Quarry 166
Spring in the Fields..172
The Peasants 178
Troublesome Students in Dates Garden 182
Summer Work and News..190
Interlude in Beijing..194
Back in Yan'an 198
The Easier Second Year...205
The One Crackdown and Three Combats Campaign............................213
A Dream Shared by Two Generations...218
The Knitting Mill..222
Treading the Boards 226
Fighting for University 231
My New Life Begins 238

Postscript 242

PROLOGUE

I was born in China in 1951, a little more than a year after the Communist Party took power on October 1, 1949. My generation was called the Socialist New Generation. Older people used to tell us how lucky we were, never having had to taste the bitterness of the dark, old society and the war. "You are born on sugared water and brought up on sugared water; when you grow up, you are going to have a much better life than we had," they said. I felt full of hope.

But before we grew up, the Great Proletarian Cultural Revolution (1966-1976) erupted. My education was interrupted and my entire life was altered. I became a Red Guard, attacked people ruthlessly, and in the end was attacked myself. In 1969 I was sent to the countryside to be "re-educated" by the poor and lower-middle-class peasants. There I did back-breaking labour and ruined my health. It wasn't until 1972 that I managed to get into university to continue my education.

When the Cultural Revolution finally ended my generation had an unofficial new title: The Destroyed Generation. Older people now shook their heads, some with pity and some with spite; they believed that we had learned nothing in life but revolution. In a sense, they were right. But why were we destroyed? How did it all happen?

This book tells my story. From my idealism and patriotism before the Cultural Revolution to my excitement and frustrations as an active participant in it to my disillusionment with Mao Zedong when I was exiled to the countryside, I recount my eventful early life in China. Many people in the West know of the Red Guards. Few, if any, are familiar with their backgrounds and motivations, and what ultimately befell them and their generation. I have written this book so people will know the whole story.

ACKNOWLEDGEMENTS

My greatest and deepest thanks are due to my philosopher-husband, Danny. Without him I would never have dared to start this project, and without his persistent urging and support this book would not have survived its many crises. He was my reader, critic, and first editor. For the hours and hours he put in, for the painstaking efforts he has made, he truly deserves the dedication.

I am in debt to Professor Robin Skelton, now retired from the Creative Writing Department of the University of Victoria. He read an early draft of the book, assured me of its value, and provided some professional hints about writing that were very helpful in later drafts.

I also owe my agent, Denise Bukowski, and my editor, Nancy Flight. Denise's enthusiasm for the book brought about its publication, and Nancy's skill in editing and right-to-the-point comments and suggestions brought it to its present state.

Finally, my gratitude is extended to my sister-in-law, Judy G. Daniels, for her encouragement and suggestions, and to all my relatives in China who have given me their support.

PART ONE

CHILDHOOD

THE OLDER GENERATION

I KNOW LITTLE ABOUT MY GRANDPARENTS. THEY LIVED IN the countryside in Shandong Province, which runs along the centre of the east coast of China, and died early, except for my father's mother, who died in 1974 at age eighty-two. She came to visit our Beijing home twice, once in 1961 and again in 1962. That was all I saw of her.

The first time we met she was sixty-nine. Her teeth were gone, her mouth shrivelled, and her hair silver-grey. She was a small woman, five-foot-one and weighing no more than ninety pounds, with delicate features and fair skin. She wore her hair in a bun at the nape, and her attire was that of a typical countrywoman in the old days: her body was deeply hidden in a loose, dark-coloured Chinese jacket buttoned at the side, and she wore loose, black slacks string-tied at the bottom even on the hottest summer day. Her bound feet were packed in many layers of white fabric and fitted into a special pair of triangular-shaped shoes. In old China women's feet were bound to reduce their length. Before a young girl's feet were grown all her toes except the big one were bent under the sole and her insteps were folded. Her feet were then swathed tightly with long cotton bands to keep them in that position. For months she had to endure the pain as she walked. The deformation then became permanent and the pain diminished. A woman with natural, "large" feet was considered ugly, while a woman with a pair of three-inch golden lotuses was considered beautiful. Although not quite the ideal three inches, Grandma's feet didn't miss it by far.

Everything about Grandma seemed odd, not just her appearance. When I asked what her name was she said: "Fan Shi," which means "maiden name Fan." I had to think for a while before I understood. In old China all married women were referred to that way — Zhang Shi, Li Shi, or whatever Shi. I had only read names like that in novels. We were now in the sixties, some ten years after Liberation. Grandma couldn't be so old-fashioned as to keep using that kind of name. "Maybe she has two names," I thought. I asked again: "What is *your* name? Your *own* name?"

She repeated "Fan Shi." Then, seeing my still-incredulous look, she asked for paper and pencil. I took her to the writing-table where they were. She sat down and, with much ado, drew two barely recognizable characters in extra-large size — Fan Shi. It was her *only* name.

Every morning before getting up Grandma sat on the bed, combed her hair, made the bun at the nape, and then patiently wound the long, long strips of cotton tightly around her feet. The winding was essential to keep her bound feet in shape. Some days the ritual was completed smoothly. Other days it wasn't, and she would untie the binding and begin again and again until it was absolutely comfortable.

In those days Grandma's style of clothing and triangular shoes were available in department stores. When my parents went shopping for her, Grandma would go along to make sure that everything fit. She couldn't keep up but didn't want us to wait for her, so inevitably she trailed way, way behind. I joined them on a couple of these outings and saw how she walked, splay-footed, in tiny steps, hurriedly moving her legs at almost a run. After a few hundred feet, she would become exhausted and have to find somewhere to sit down and rest.

A Chinese who was lucky enough to visit Beijing never missed a chance to see its many historical sights. Grandma came twice, each time for more than two weeks, but she never saw anything. Whenever my parents proposed sightseeing, she would say she wasn't interested. It was too tiring.

My father, Houren, was born in 1917 in a village in Qufu County, Shandong Province, the home of Confucius. Father seldom talked about his birthplace and never took us back to his home. The Communists didn't think very highly of Confucius because of his feudalist doctrines — his belief, for example, that sons should obey fathers, wives should obey husbands, and everyone should obey the emperor — and Father was a Communist. Whenever I filled out a form, however, I always wrote "Qufu" under "Native Place" (one's father's home town) with pride, as if I were related to the great saint by sharing his home town.

Father was his parents' last child, and he was much younger than his two older brothers. Smart and good-looking, with bright, piercing eyes, a straight nose, and a nicely shaped mouth, he was the apple of the family eye. They weren't rich, but it was decided that he should go to school so he could have a brighter future. Everyone — his parents, his two brothers, and their wives — was willing to work in the fields to support him.

In the 1920s getting to school in the countryside was not easy. It was miles from Father's home to the school, and he had to cross a swift river with no bridge over it. When he was too small to ford the river by himself, the task of carrying him over fell to his second sister-in-law. He never forgot this. More than forty years later, one day in the seventies, I walked into my parents' bedroom and saw Father searching the drawers of their chest. He was wearing one of his usual suits, navy-blue cotton with a high Mao-style collar. Both the top buttons on the suit and the white shirt inside were open.

"What are you looking for?" I asked.

"I'm looking for the last letter from Peiquan," he answered. Peiquan was the eldest son of this sister-in-law. Several times recently Peiquan had asked my parents for money.

"He's a pain," I said. "Why don't you ignore him? Why don't you ignore them all, now that my second uncle is dead?"

"What do you know about them?" he said sharply. "I wouldn't have got through school if it weren't for my second sister-in-law! Many times in summer and winter, in rain and snow, she waded through the river carrying me on her back. She's like my second mother."

I stood there stupefied. Father was a reserved person, and he almost never talked about himself. This was the first time he had ever told me anything detailed about his childhood and his relatives.

"Since your second uncle died, I've sent her money from time to time." Father put the pile of letters in his hand back into the drawer and continued in a softer tone. "Not long ago, when I was in Nanjing for business, I went to visit her and left her more money. I really want her to live well in her old age. Unfortunately, she never spent the money on herself. She gave it away to her children," he sighed.

Father was a high-ranking officer. In the Chinese administrative system there were twenty-six ranks. Ranks one to thirteen were classified as high-level, fourteen to seventeen were middle-level, and the rest were low-level. Father was in rank eleven. He started his revolutionary career in 1937 and became a Communist Party member in 1938. I always marvelled at the force that drove him through the dangerous years, and I used to pester him to tell his revolutionary stories, expecting to hear earth-shaking plots. But he rarely talked.

"What do you want me to say?" he would ask.

"Tell me why you joined the revolution in the beginning."

"To beat the Japanese devils," he replied.

During the Japanese invasion in the Second World War, Chiang Kaishek's ruling party, the Kuomintang, had a policy of non-resistance, which was very unpopular. Maybe the Chinese weapons weren't powerful and the Chinese troops weren't well trained, and maybe we wouldn't win, but most Chinese thought we ought to fight — better to die than to become a slave without a country. In contrast, the Communist Party was determined to fight the Japanese to the end. "Only the Communist Party can save China" became the common view among students. Many people joined the revolution then without knowing what Marxism was, as did my father, who was studying in a teacher's college at the time. He became a Communist afterwards.

In the twelve years from 1937 to 1949, Father worked underground for the party, sometimes as a teacher in a village, sometimes as a grocery store owner in another small town. He changed his name frequently. Right before Liberation he was called Zhu Yun, which means Red Clouds.

My mother, Xiutian, was also from a peasant family in Shandong Province. Her village was in a different county from my father's. In Mother's youth the tradition of binding feet was still in force in the countryside. But Mother didn't want her feet bound. No matter what her parents said — that she would grow up ugly, that no man would marry her — she wouldn't allow them to touch her feet. "It isn't up to you!" her mother said, then pushed her down on the bed, grabbed her feet, and bound them. Mother couldn't stop that, but whenever she was alone tending cows on the hill, she loosened the bindings to release her feet. Before going home, she would wrap them up again just tightly enough to pull the wool over her parents' eyes. Her feet never became as small as they should have. In early 1945 the Communist Party liberated her village. All young women were called on to abandon foot-binding, and Mother's feet finally went free.

Mother wore normal shoes and walked like a normal person. But I had seen her feet and the legacy of the binding when she washed them in a basin. Her insteps were higher than normal, and only her two big toes could stretch out naturally. "Was it painful when your feet were bound?" I once asked. "How can it not be? Each step was a heart-stopping agony!" were her exact words.

Father met Mother while he was working in her village. She wasn't a stunning beauty. Her face was broad, and her eyebrows drooped and thinned at the end, but she did have large eyes and a fair complexion. The real thing that attracted Father to her, however, was her revolutionary fervour.

Mother's family was lower middle class. They didn't have enough land to live on and had to sell their labour. When the Communists liberated her village, she learned that the revolution was to benefit the poor people and she was naturally in favour. She became active in revolutionary work to support the front where the Communists were battling the Kuomintang. She sewed shoes and clothes for the soldiers, like many other women in the liberated areas. To celebrate each Communist victory, she joined the team that performed Yang Ge, a simple dance popular in northern China, in which the dancers hold up the ends of the wide red sashes that bind their waists while twisting their hips and performing certain steps. "You don't know how well your mother twisted Yang Ge!" I heard Father say several times. Mother always blushed and told him to be quiet.

My parents got married in 1945. Soon after that the two of them left home to live and work in the "enemy-occupied regions." "I never got one good night's sleep in the days we were in the underground," Mother used to tell me. She was not as reticent as Father and didn't mind reminiscing about their earlier days in the revolution. "We never knew when the devil [the Kuomintang forces] would find out where we were staying and attack. Often I was awakened by a guard shouting, 'The devil is coming, quick, get up!' I jumped up, picked up my small package, and ran. The package contained all our possessions. We had no home, no furniture, no trunks, only a little clothing. Bombs and bullets flew around us, but I wasn't afraid. The worst was to die, and we were all prepared to do so any moment."

Every time the western New Year or Chinese New Year holidays approached, groups of children would begin setting off firecrackers in the streets. I hated the sudden explosions and always tried to avoid them, even if it meant taking a longer route. But Mother marched right through the crowds of boys lighting firecrackers without blinking. "Aren't you afraid?" I asked her. "No. I've heard too much bombing and shooting. This is nothing!"

She also liked to talk about an unfortunate older brother of mine who didn't survive the war: "He was a big, well-built boy who ate a lot, a good boy who never gave us any trouble. 'Mama, mama,' he'd call me sweetly. Your father and I should never have taken him with us in that environment. One day he became sick with pneumonia. His little face was crimson from fever, his windpipe blocked by phlegm, and his breath rasped. Although our team had a nurse, we had little medicine. There was nothing we could do but watch him suffer and unconsciously grasp the air with his hands. Poor child. In a couple of days, he was gone."

CHILDHOOD IN
SHANDONG PROVINCE

IN 1949 THE PEOPLE'S REPUBLIC OF CHINA WAS BORN. MY parents became "cadres," or civil servants, in the new government. In China people are divided into workers, peasants, soldiers, students, merchants, and cadres. White-collar workers, administrators, civil servants, teachers, and engineers are all classified as cadres.

At the beginning of the Communist regime civil servants received no salaries, but were provided with the necessities of life under a special distribution system. When a new child was born, the family would get an increase in supplies. In a way it was as if all the children were supported by the government. This helped to stimulate a higher birth rate for several years. My parents had five children, two girls and three boys.

My older sister Aihua, which means Loving China, was born at the end of 1945 during the civil war. For her sake and their own, my parents entrusted her to a peasant family. There must have been some arrangement between my parents and this family, but I don't know what it was. Quite a number of revolutionaries did the same thing. Some told the peasants that the arrangement was only temporary; some said they were giving up their children permanently. The revolutionaries had little choice at the time. After Liberation, however, when they assumed power, many went to take their children back.

My mother reclaimed Aihua after compensating the peasant family with a sum of money. At first the peasants didn't want to let Aihua go because they had grown very fond of her. But under Mother's persistence they took the money and gave their permission. When Mother approached Aihua, she ran to the peasants, clung to them, and started to cry. To her, the peasants *were* her parents. Who was this strange woman? "Don't be silly. It's for your own good!" Mother plucked Aihua free and put her on the back of a donkey. Ignoring her kicking and blubbering, the little animal bore her off. Aihua's homecoming was not a happy one. For many years to come she didn't accept our parents.

As a general rule in China, the older the child, the shorter he or she is. Aihua was the eldest and shortest, only five-foot-one as an adult. Like my mother, Aihua was of medium weight and a bit short-legged. But she had a beautiful round face, a nice mouth, and large bright eyes. She always wore her hair in two braids at the back.

While Aihua was the problem child in my family, my older brother, Xinhua, was the model. He was born before the Republic's birthday, hence his name — New China. In early 1958, when we lived in Jining City, a small city in the south of Shandong Province, two cadres I had never seen before came to our home one evening to talk with my parents. It turned out that Xinhua, eight years old at the time, had done a good deed that brought honour to the family. He found a purse on the street that contained eighty yuan, a large sum in those days, took the purse to the police, and helped them to find its owner. The two cadres were from the city municipality and they had come to my parents to praise Xinhua and arrange for him to be received by the mayor at a meeting of all primary school students in the city. Soon all the children in Jining knew Xinhua's name. For a while, when I walked down the street I kept my eyes peeled for lost items, but to no avail.

Not only was Xinhua an honest child, but he also had a talent for making speeches, attracting people to him, and getting along well with them. He was a leader all his life, starting in primary school. No wonder my father favoured him. In Xinhua, Father saw his successor.

I was born February 16, 1951. My name, Zhenhua, means Vitalizing China and is rather a common one for boys. In old China girls were often named after flowers or jewellery, but my revolutionary parents weren't about to follow the old traditions. In their eyes, boys and girls were born equal and should all be raised to be revolutionaries and patriots.

I was an ordinary-looking girl. Looking at myself in the mirror, I sometimes felt my face was a bit too wide, my eyebrows needed a bit of thickening at the ends, and my eyes could have been larger. But other times I felt pleased with my appearance — at least my smile was nice.

According to my brothers and sister, I was my mother's favourite because I was "clever" and had a "sweet tongue." I am not sure about this, but I do remember when I was about six Mother often took me, and me alone, to work with her. During her breaks she would feed me fruit juices or other treats.

The elder of my younger brothers, Weihua, or Defending China, was born in February 1952, during the Korean War. Most Chinese supported the government when it sent troops across the Yalu River. The slogan

"Fight the Americans and Help the Koreans, Protect Our Homes and Defend Our Country" was seen everywhere and seemed right. US imperialism was overrunning our neighbour before our front gate. Would we be next?

Weihua had a distinctive mole below the centre of his eyebrows. Auntie Wang, a middle-aged countrywoman who was our nanny from 1954 to 1959, used to say that it would have been a very auspicious thing had the mole been just a bit higher. As it was, Weihua's fortunes were in no way exceptional. He didn't talk much and didn't attract too much attention. Of the five children Weihua remained the most anonymous.

My youngest brother Jianhua, or Building China, was born in the peaceful times of 1954. My parents thought that from that time on the main task facing the Chinese was to build China. Jianhua was the tallest and best looking of us all, blessed with both of my parents' good points. He had long legs, wide shoulders, a narrow waist, and big, wide, and bright eyes. If his eyebrows were only a little thicker, I would declare him perfect in looks.

Everybody liked Jianhua. My parents doted on him, Auntie Wang spoiled him, and even the often ill-tempered Aihua humoured him. In the adoring competition to see to his needs, Auntie Wang even went so far as to steal eggs for him from my father's rations. This was later discovered and Auntie Wang chastised, but Jianhua was so moved that he made a five-year-old's pledge to her: "When I grow up I'll take care of you. I'm going to send you five yuan every month, I promise!" Now thirty-seven, he is easily making enough money to fulfil his promise, but he cannot. Our family lost track of Auntie Wang when she moved from Shandong Province to the northeast of China.

In the early fifties, my mother attended a special government school set up for illiterate cadres from worker-peasant backgrounds. Being a female from a lower-middle-class peasant family, Mother was uneducated. Now she had her chance to study, and she threw herself into it with enthusiasm. It took her two and a half years to finish primary school and another two and a half years for junior and senior high school. She and my father, who was also working hard, were seldom home and had no time left for their children. All of us except Aihua were raised by nannies at home and in boarding nurseries.

My mother told me I was the most unlucky child in the family. Apparently I had three nannies. The first was halfwitted, the second was lazy, but the third seemed all right. Mother fired the first nanny right away, after she caught her clapping her hands and laughing as she watched me crawl crying through my own urine. During most of my childhood I was skinny and weak; I never became very strong.

Teng County in Shandong Province was my birthplace, but I have no memory of it. After Liberation my father was frequently assigned new positions, each time in a bigger city. Our family moved often. Teng County and our second home flitted in and out of my life without leaving a trace. My first memories are of Jining City. There, at the age of three, I was put in a boarding nursery. Every Monday morning my mother took me there and handed me to the "aunties" for the entire week. In the yard there were rocking horses, tricycles, and slides. But most of the time the aunties kept us inside — we were allowed out only at play periods. They taught us singing, dancing, and paper-cutting. Life there was not bad, but I was unhappy. I liked to run wild, and I missed my family.

As Saturday afternoons approached, I would cheer up. It was won-derful to go home. The compound we lived in belonged to the prefec-tural Party Committee where my parents worked. It was vast, with an orchard, gardens, fields for crops, and rows and rows of one-storey buildings. Our home was in one of these rows at the edge of the com-pound. It had three rooms side by side, one used as both living-room and kitchen, one for my parents, and one for all five children and Auntie Wang. Our only pieces of furniture were three large beds, a number of stools, a couple of desks, and some trunks. The apartment had electric-ity, but no plumbing. We shared the water tap in the centre of the front yard with the other families, and used public toilets during the day and a chamber-pot at night. The first task each morning after getting up was to empty and clean the pot.

At home I rarely saw my parents, even on Sundays when they were supposed to take time off. They worked long hours, ate most of their meals in a communal dining-hall with their comrades, and sometimes even spent the night at their offices, which had adjoining dormitories with beds. I wish they had spent more time with me; nevertheless, home was home, I loved to play with my siblings. In the fields we chased grasshoppers and in the bushes surrounding our home we turned over stones to catch crickets, prized for their singing and the way they would fight each other when put together in containers. Once we even saved a frog from a snake's mouth by beating the snake with sticks until little by little it vomited up its prey and slithered away. The poor frog lay on the ground motionless for a while. One of its hind legs was now pink because it had been down the throat of the snake and was partly digested. We thought it might be dead, but eventually it sat up and slowly crawled off into the darkness without thanking us.

For much of my childhood I was closest to my older sister, Aihua, who was five years my senior. As far as I was concerned, she knew everything about everything and had endless new ideas to thrill me. I followed her everywhere. She would take me to a garden full of flowers, brilliant scarlet cannas, white-and-blue morning glories, and red double-blossomed garden balsam, which we called nail flowers because they could be used to dye fingernails. We would put a mixture of alum and smashed petals on our nails and wrap them for the night with pieces of cellophane from candy wrappers. The next morning our nails would be completely red.

Aihua also took me to the peach orchard in the compound and told me to climb the trees and pick peaches while she stood guard. Despite my best efforts half the peaches turned out to be unripe, sour, and puckery, so what we ate was always less than what we threw away. After two visits I started to wonder whether our mischief was worthwhile. Then one day a boy began shouting, "Aihua's sister is stealing peaches!" Aihua's sister — that's me, I thought. In a sweat, I prayed no one heard him, especially my parents, and decided to quit stealing right then.

When I was six years old, my parents tried to send me to a local school. But the school refused to take me: I was too far from the official age of seven. Seeing Aihua and Xinhua go off with their book bags over their shoulders made me curious and envious. I gathered a group of my little friends and went to the school gate. We timidly peeped in and imagined what it would be like to be inside.

I entered primary school on September 1, 1958, when the Great Leap Forward and the Great Steel Smelting were at their peak. These were the major events of 1958, although they later generated violent controversy within the party. Until 1957 the country had done well, making a solid economic recovery from the ruins of the Japanese occupation and the ensuing civil war. Believing the conditions for realizing the ideals of Communism were ripe, the party launched the Great Leap Forward at the end of that year. Peasants were organized into communes, and overconfident and unreasonably high industrial goals were set. The foundation of all industry was steel — thus the Great Steel Smelting campaign. The whole country, peasants included, was mobilized for steel smelting and grand construction projects, and agriculture was neglected. In many villages one saw only women and children working the fields. The weather in 1958 was very favourable. Had all the crops been collected it would have been a bumper harvest, but much was left in the fields to rot.

From the very beginning my education was abnormal. Like many other schools in the country, mine erected small iron-smelting furnaces. My classmates and I were sent to the fields to search for hunks of pink iron ore, which we put into our baskets and brought back to school. We then smashed the ore into small pieces with hammers. The teachers and older students fed these into the furnace and operated the iron smelter.

In October the heat of the Great Leap Forward began to dissipate. I finally got to sit down in the classroom and learn to read and write our square Chinese characters and discover that $1 + 1 = 2$. Before long, however, my father was made Associate Party Secretary of the Chemical Industry Bureau of Shandong Province in Jinan City, the provincial capital. In December of 1958 my family moved to Jinan to join my father, who was already there.

Jinan was a big city, beautiful, clean, and well planned. It was laid out like Washington, D.C., with numbered avenues traversing numbered streets. Because of its many springs and geysers it had another name, the Spring City. My parents often took us out to see them. I was too young to view them with real interest, but walking on streets paved with large, flat stones wet with spring water and breathing the balmy fresh air did leave an indelible impression.

In Chinese schools students did their homework in groups. They would meet at one student's home one day and at another student's home the next day. I liked these study sessions because they gave us an opportunity to see different homes. Most of the students in my class lived as I did, in a few rooms in a compound that consisted of three or four rows of houses in a quadrangle around a courtyard. To this day, my family has never lived in more than three rooms.

Sheng Qiang's home was something else entirely. Her father was a military leader for the Shandong Province region. Their home was surrounded by red-brick walls, and the front gate was guarded by an armed soldier, indicating the special status of those who lived there. Inside the wall I saw an enormous yard of several acres with a three-storey concrete mansion standing in the centre. The grounds were covered by an evenly cut, lush, green lawn. There were no tall trees, perhaps for security reasons, but here and there throughout the yard were clumps of wide-leaved bushes. No flowers were in sight either, but still I was amazed. I couldn't help but compare this with our three rooms and the small shared yard outside. And until now I thought only landlords and capitalists lived in big houses!

As I walked into the hall, Sheng Qiang bounced down the wide stairs to meet me and immediately led me to a room at the end of the building, perhaps a servant's room, which was simply furnished with a large bed and a desk. I guessed that there were at least eight rooms on each floor and wondered what they looked like, but Sheng Qiang gave me no chance to look around.

One by one the students arrived. We did our usual homework, memorizing the multiplication table and composing sentences. When everybody had finished, Sheng Qiang brought out some illustrated story-books, letting on that she had many more. "Now you can go out and play on the lawn if you like," she announced. Everyone else went out, but I stayed inside, reading the illustrated books.

I loved picture books — *The Snow Queen*, *The Girl with Ten-Foot Tresses of Gold*, and all the stories adapted from the famous *Dream of the Red Mansion*. I couldn't get enough of the exquisite drawings. We had few such books at home. Several years earlier the distribution system had been changed to a salary system, and my family's financial situation deteriorated. There was no money for luxuries like illustrated story-books, so I read those belonging to others whenever I had the chance.

While my family was living in Jinan an important political event happened: the change of the chairman of the People's Republic. In December 1958 Mao Zedong proposed to relinquish his chairmanship and governmental responsibilities and to let his second in command, Liu Shaoqi, take over. The party and the whole country responded to his wish.

One day many primary school students were assembled in a huge hall. We first-year students were at the front. A city leader mounted the stage and spoke to us. Chairman Mao, he said, had too many titles and too much to do. If he could retreat from the front line to the second line, he would then have more leisure time to consider the party's organization and to write theoretical articles, which would benefit not only us but generations to come. I was then barely eight years old and didn't understand much the man said, so I didn't pay strict attention. In the end, when he asked those of us who supported Mao's retreat to raise their hands, I didn't know what to do. Looking back through the hall, though, I saw a forest of senior students' hands raised. I raised mine. Thus, with my permission, Chairman Mao resigned.

On April 20, 1959 Liu Shaoqi was elected chairman of the country. The situation he inherited was difficult. From 1959 to 1961 China suffered the disastrous economic consequences of the Great Leap Forward and many natural calamities as well — some provinces were deluged with floods and others scorched by drought. Peasants returned to their crops, but the slogan "humans can conquer nature," seen often during the Great Leap Forward, didn't hold true. An already-empty grain reserve in 1958, and the three lean years following, put the country's food in unusually short supply. Aside from certain basic rationed provisions, food prices sky-rocketed and money became devalued.

Our life in Jinan was affected. My brothers, who needed more food than I did, started to experience hunger. Before a real crisis set in, though, my father was appointed associate party secretary in a bureau of the Agricultural Machinery Ministry in Beijing. We left Jinan on New Year's Day, 1960.

A TASTE OF HARDSHIP

WHEN MY FAMILY FIRST MOVED TO BEIJING, WE LIVED IN a big compound with a two-storey former office building standing in the centre and thirty or so additional rooms along the side walls. Two dozen families lived there, from directors of bureaus, chiefs of sections, and retired military leaders to common cadres who worked in my father's ministry. On the average five families shared one water tap and one water-closet with three toilets.

Once again our new home consisted of three adjacent rooms, each about twenty square metres in size. They were on the second floor of the office building, facing north. Two were connected by a door. The inside room was used as my parents' bedroom, and the outside one was the living-room, dining-room, and kitchen. The third room was for the five children. It was partitioned into male and female quarters by a floor-to-ceiling curtain.

The furnishings were better than any we had ever had. Our children's room had two wooden trunks, one desk with three drawers, one wooden chair, two high stools, and several little stools made of bamboo. The little stools, which weren't much more than ankle-high, were indispensable. We brought them out into the yard to sit on, and we perched on them to wash our clothes in a basin and to do our homework, using the beds as desks — one desk was hardly enough for five children. My parents' bedroom had a wardrobe equipped with a mirror and a good wooden desk with a cabinet attached to its right side. In our living-room, we had a low dining table and even two upholstered chairs with a coffee table between them.

All the furniture, except the trunks and little stools, were on loan from my parents' work unit. They were not expensive to rent, a few yuan a month, but nor were they in great shape. The dark green corduroy chairs were so dusty that one slap would produce a powder-storm, and our beds, though not my parents', were badly infested with bedbugs. At first we put benzene hexachloride on them. This controlled them for a while, but they slowly became immune to it. Lifting the bedding I'd see them swim freely in the ocean of poisonous chemicals. Finally, my father came up with a brilliant idea: kill them with boiling water. He helped us carry the beds outside, stand them up, and pour boiling water along the seams. That did it. The bugs and their eggs were eliminated, and they never came back.

Our first two years in Beijing, 1960 and 1961, were hard ones for us and for many Chinese. In hard times like those the more mouths in a family, the more severe the crisis. I thought my parents had only their five children to feed, but during these two years I learned there were more. My parents had to support not only my grandmother but also Shuxian, my father's first wife, and her two daughters.

Shuxian's existence came as a great surprise. My father had had an arranged marriage in the thirties, before leaving home for the revolution in 1940. When he married my mother in 1945, he was still legally married to Shuxian, who lived with my father's family in their home. He and Shuxian had two daughters, Fuxiang and Fuzhen, fifteen years and ten years older than me, respectively.

Father and Shuxian divorced after Liberation. In the divorce agreement Father stipulated that he would support my two half-sisters through college and Shuxian herself until they graduated. He wanted to make it up to the two girls by providing them with a bright future. Very few Chinese went through college but, despite having grown up without a father, both my half-sisters did. Fuxiang graduated from a college of engineering in Tianjing (about eighty miles from Beijing), and Fuzhen from a military college in a suburb of Beijing. My parents had always tried to keep this unpleasant truth from us, but it came out when my two half-sisters visited.

So there were eleven of us sharing my parents' salaries, which would have provided adequately for a normal family of five. Auntie Wang, the housekeeper who had worked for us for years, was dismissed. Every day our parents worked late and ate in their refectory. We children were left to fend for ourselves. Headed by Aihua, the five of us, aged five to fourteen, had to clean the house and wet-mop the cement floor, wash our clothes, do the daily shopping, light the coal stove, and cook food for ourselves. Our cooking was inventive but not always successful. Once we boiled some large balls of unrisen rice-flour, one per person, which turned out as hard as rocks. Even these had to be eaten because we couldn't afford to waste anything.

Beijing was arctic cold, although its lowest temperature was only about 0°F. We had no warm outerwear and lived in a room facing the north and heated only by a stove that burned rationed briquettes. Every winter my hands and feet were frostbitten and swollen like pink steamed buns. The frostbite on my right hand once got so bad that the scar is still with me.

One ordeal was to buy briquettes and wheel them four long blocks home in winter. The cylindrical briquettes were made from compressed coal dust. Each was about five inches long and four inches high, with a dozen or so holes punched in it to let oxygen in. The workers at the coal yard took our money and counted out the briquettes and then returned to the warmth inside. It was up to us to stack the ice-cold blocks on the borrowed wheelbarrow. My hands in their thin gloves gradually became stiff with cold. When my turn came to push the barrow, I could hardly hold onto the handles.

We had no milk or milk products and would have forgotten what meat tasted like if it were not for the once-a-week dumpling dinner. The dumplings were filled with Chinese cabbage and ground meat. As we gobbled like wolves, each of us had to keep count of how many dumplings he or she ate so as not to exceed the fair share allotted. Years after the crisis when my family had dumplings, my father still chastened us. "How many have you had now, children?"

But for me, with my sweet tooth, the most unbearable thing was not to have dessert. My parents *never* bought candies or desserts for us. Even the sugar, which was rationed to two ounces per month per person, was locked away. When our neighbours' children enjoyed their once-a-week indulgence, or even just steamed buns sandwiched with plain white sugar, I could hardly take my eyes off them.

One day when my parents were at work, Aihua took me into their bedroom. There was a look of conspiracy on her face as she squatted down to open one of the wardrobe drawers below the mirror. A stack of ten-yuan bills (less than two US dollars each) lay prominently in sight. My jaw dropped. I never knew my parents had hoarded so much money! Aihua looked up at me, smiled, and then pouted her mouth towards the bills. "Take one," she said. "I can buy sweets!" was my immediate reaction. I giggled, but my hands wouldn't move. It was wrong to take the money without my parents' permission, wasn't it? And a ten-yuan bill was too large.

Several days later, Aihua held out a five-yuan bill to me. She was determined to share her fortune with her beloved little sister. I weighed the pros and cons for a while, and then my desire and Aihua's persistence got the better of me. It was *just* a five-yuan bill. "It's Aihua's money, not my parents'," I rationalized.

Money hot in hand, my eagerness to spend it grew by the minute. The next day was Sunday. On Sundays my parents often worked overtime or went shopping. The next morning, after breakfast, I tried to learn their plans for the day but didn't succeed. Had I bided my time until Monday I would surely have been safe, but I couldn't wait. Flinging caution to the wind, I ran out to the closest pastry shop.

In the shop I dithered over what to buy. The prices weren't marked. I knew how much coal or salt cost, but I had no idea what five yuan could buy in pastries. Burdened with a guilty conscience, I didn't dare ask either, afraid of eliciting the saleswoman's curiosity and an interrogation about where I got the money. Several customers came in, did their shopping, and left. I finally settled on one type of crude moon cake. Standing on tiptoe, I handed my money to the young saleswoman behind the high counter and asked for one jin's worth (slightly more than one pound). She weighed the cakes without paying any attention to me, wrapped the pieces in paper, and put over two yuan in change on the counter. I felt vastly relieved.

As I neared home I hid the package carefully under my jacket, worried about the appreciable bulge it made. The moment I stepped into the gate of our compound I caught sight of my mother, sitting on the windowsill cleaning the windows of her room. Our second-storey windows all overlooked the yard. My heart pounded. I averted my eyes, pressed hard on my jacket, and scuttled across the yard. The problem was that I had to pass her room to reach ours. Before the door I stopped for a second and listened. Not a sound. I flew past it as inconspicuously as possible.

Mother had been affectionate to me in Jining, but in the hard years of hunger and malnutrition nobody seemed able to keep an even temper. She was apparently already annoyed by my absence for the morning. I had never gone anywhere without her knowledge before. "Zhenhua, where have you been? Where are you going?" came her loud voice from the room behind me. I kept running. My last ray of hope was that she wouldn't break off her work to follow me. When I reached my room, my brain was numb. Had I acted quickly I might have hidden the package in a drawer, but I stood petrified. In a fraction of a second Mother appeared behind me and snapped: "What's wrong with you? Why didn't you stop when I talked to you?"

I turned back mechanically and saw her framed in the doorway. She was wearing a light grey jacket. The sleeves were rolled up to the elbow, her forearms bare. A cleaning rag was in her hand. I glanced at her face — not a hint of a smile. Unwittingly, I pressed harder and harder on the bulge under my jacket. The paper package tore, and fourteen or so moon cakes dropped onto the floor and rolled away in all directions. Mother instantly caught on. In a rage she stepped up and cuffed me on the head. I burst out crying. She demanded a full confession and I told all.

On Sundays we usually ate two meals. When the time for the afternoon meal came, I shuffled into the living-room. The dining table was set. In the centre was a large bowl of stir-fried tomato and eggplant, a plate of sliced cucumber in soy sauce, vinegar, and garlic, some steamed cornflour buns, and four moon cakes beside four sets of bowls and chopsticks. Xinhua and Weihua were already sitting on their little stools beside the table. After I sat down, Jianhua entered. We ate in silence. I kept my head lowered and dared not look at anybody. What did my three brothers think, especially my older brother, Xinhua, who had once been honoured for returning the lost purse and money? Now his sister had become a thief. I was so ashamed. Yet, if it weren't for me, they wouldn't be eating moon cakes, I thought.

My parents' absence at the dining table was not unusual, but the fact that Aihua did not show up troubled me. She must have been punished very hard. I hated myself for being so stupid, spoiling the whole thing, and plunging her into hot water with me. But I also blamed her for drawing me into this shame. For her part, she detested my cowardice in betraying her. The event damaged our relationship. After that I was forced out from under her wing and had to make my own way.

Aihua had been unhappy ever since my mother had taken her back. She felt my parents had deserted her at birth, even though they had had compelling reasons to do so. She believed they should have left her with the peasant family, since she had been happy with them.

Schooling had not been a problem for my brothers and me, but it was for Aihua. She hated every minute of it. She didn't get along with the other students and she often failed tests. Eventually, she began to play truant. My parents were so angry they beat her, further alienating her.

Study was probably hard for her; she had had no pre-school training, and she hadn't entered school until she was nine. She was ashamed to have to sit in a class where all the other children were younger than she was. Older students in a class were usually the ones who had had to repeat a grade, though that wasn't always true. My oldest half-sister,

Fuxiang, was years older than the others in her class from primary school through college. She did well in her studies, was always a student leader, and joined the Communist League in school and the Communist Party in college.

After we moved to Beijing, things went from bad to worse for Aihua. As the eldest child, she had more of the household duties. The peasant family had never made her do chores, and it seemed to her that my parents had only taken her back to be a servant. Aihua became more and more defiant. She argued violently with my parents and twice ran away from home. Once she was away for three days. I admired her courage and asked her about life on street, but she shook her head sadly and said the free life wasn't as nice as I thought. She had slept in parks and had been afraid at night. She never did it again, but her will to leave my parents hardened. Her eyes were always open for opportunities that might allow her to escape.

LIVING IN
LEGENDARY WORLDS

IN THE COMPOUND WHERE WE LIVED ALL FAMILIES KNEW each other, and everybody knew everybody else's business. I knew why beautiful Ling was unhappily married to ugly Luo. "She's the daughter of a capitalist in Shanghai. Who wants her? And actually the match isn't bad. No matter what, Luo *is* a university graduate!" my mother explained to me. I also knew the disappointment the Chu family felt when each of their girls came into this world. In the end, after six unwanted daughters, they were rewarded for their perseverance with a son.

In the hot summer evenings many of us would ascend to the large patio (at least 6,000 square feet) on top of the office building. All the families brought little stools to sit on and mats to lie on. While the adults waved their large palm leaf fans and chatted, we children would play. We sang songs newly learned from movies, skipped with an elastic rope made of rubber bands, guessed at riddles, and had team tug of wars.

When there were no other children to play with, I would stay with my family. Father was never there, but Mother sometimes came up late in the evening. When she was in the right mood, she would tell stories and jokes; otherwise, she would ask how we were doing in school. I knew she only wanted to hear good news, so that is what I reported, if there was any, and kept my problems to myself.

In a day-to-day sense, Mother was in charge of us. She checked on us, talked with us, and scolded us when we did something wrong. Father was rarely heard from. He intervened only when absolutely necessary — when Mother lost control of Aihua, for example. Several times he had long conversations with her, and afterwards I noticed that Aihua's behaviour improved, although it usually didn't last very long.

There were also quiet evenings when I was left alone to play on the patio in my own dreamworld. To lie down in the open under the summer night sky was wonderful. The dark blue sky was mysterious, with twinkling stars, the gauzelike Milky Way, and the two constellations, Vega and Altair, on either side of it. The Milky Way, Vega, and Altair reminded me of a Chinese legend, *Nulang and Zhinu*. In this legend the Milky Way is a celestial river. Vega is the heavenly Zhinu (Weaver Girl), whose job is to weave the colourful clouds. The big star in the centre of Altair is Zhinu's earthly husband, Nulang (Cowherd), and the two smaller stars on either side of Altair are their two children.

Just as all humans are curious about the immortals in heaven, they too are curious about humans. Zhinu and her girlfriends often watched humans from behind the clouds. There they saw the adversity against which Nulang struggled. His parents died early, so he lived with his older brother and his shrewish sister-in-law. They mistreated him, letting him slave in the fields while keeping all the good things at home for themselves. Finally, when Nulang grew up, they decided to throw him out altogether. The family property was divided and Nulang only got an old cow, while his brother took the house and all the land. Zhinu saw how industrious and kind Nulang was, and her heart went out to him. She flew down from the sky and they were married. Nulang tilled the land, Zhinu wove silk for sale, and their lives were happy.

Seven years passed — in heavenly terms, a day. The gods learned that Zhinu had left heaven and they were angry. Celestial troops were sent to bring her back for punishment. By then she had given birth to a boy and a girl, and Nulang's cow had died. Before it died, however, the cow told Nulang to save its skin, which one day would enable him to fly. When Nulang came home from the fields one evening and found his wife had been taken away, he put the children into two big baskets, lifted them at the ends of a pole onto his shoulder, drapped himself in the cow's skin, and soared into the sky in pursuit.

As he flew closer and closer, Goddess Wang Mu stood forward to stop him. She took off her hair clasp and drew a line behind Zhinu. In no time at all the line widened to become the Milky Way, a wide, celestial river with turbulent waves, which parts the lovers to this day. Because Zhinu was persistent in her entreaties, she and Nulang are allowed to meet once a year on the seventh day of the seventh month in the Chinese calendar, on a bridge made by the world's magpies. Each time they meet, Nulang brings all his clothes and the children's clothes for Zhinu to mend and wash! It is said that in the dead of night one can hear the sounds of their cooing and sobbing if one stands quietly under a grape trellis and maintains an absolutely empty mind.

The Chinese also have a legend about the moon, *Chang'e Flying to the Moon*. Long, long ago there were ten suns in the sky. The land was scorched and people perished. Houyi was the greatest archer in the world. He shot down nine of the suns and saved the earth. For this, Goddess Wang Mu rewarded him with two magic potions, which were to keep him and his beautiful wife, Chang'e, forever young. He carefully hid them away.

Houyi was always working for the people and he had little time to spend with Chang'e who grew lonely and unhappy. From boredom she started to hunt for the magic potions and eventually found them. "What would happen if I were to take them?" she thought. One evening when Houyi was just arriving home, he saw Chang'e flying away into the sky. He immediately went where he had hidden the two potions, but they were gone. Chang'e had taken them both.

Chang'e had expected to fly all the way to Paradise and live there happily ever after, but the potions only had enough power to get her to the moon. The moon, it turned out, was a desolate place that was home to only a magnificent, spacious, cold palace (the Vast Chilly Palace), a thousand-year-old osmanthus tree, and a jade rabbit who stood under it and ground divine medicine in a huge jade mortar. To her great regret, Chang'e was doomed to live an even lonelier life on the moon.

On a night when the moon was full, my neighbours called me over to their quarters and asked if I could see the Vast Chilly Palace, the osmanthus tree, and the jade rabbit. They said they did. "Look carefully," they urged me. I wanted to believe that a beautiful goddess was living in her chilly palace on the moon. I tried hard but all I could see, or more correctly, imagine, was the big tree, not the palace or the rabbit.

My mother worked for a time for the Union of the Agricultural Machinery Ministry. In China a union is just another government branch under the leadership of the party. It doesn't organize strikes or bargain with a company on behalf of the workers. Its main function is welfare. I remember seeing my mother and her comrades in the union issuing soap and working gloves to the staff and arranging movies, performances, dances, and New Year's parties in the ministry's large hall.

I saw many of these movies. Tickets were very cheap — often only one American cent and, at times, even free. My brothers liked fighting movies but I didn't. The heroes always died and I was frightened throughout waiting for it to happen. I remember seeing one called *The Electric Wave That Never Disappeared*. It was about an underground revolutionary in Shanghai before Liberation. He collected information from inside the Kuomintang and sent it in cipher by telegraph to Yan'an, where Chairman Mao and the party were. The day the Kuomintang secret police went to arrest him, he sent out his last telegram: "Farewell forever, comrades. Farewell." In the end they killed him. I left the movie crying and regretted coming.

I much preferred watching the traditional legends and the bizarre fox spirit stories, in which a fox spirit falls in love with a man and performs all kinds of magic deeds to win him. The women in these films wore their hair in high coils and sported beautiful ancient Chinese costumes. Goddesses flew through the air with long, wide silk ribbons, colourful silk skirts, and long sleeves fluttering and waving gracefully behind them. I felt intoxicated just watching them, and imagined myself living in legendary worlds where the true, the good, and the beautiful always won.

Later I learned to appreciate other movies, but fairy stories always occupied a special position in my heart. When the Great Cultural Revolution broke out, all such movies were banned as feudalist "poisonous weeds." I missed them terribly.

The dance parties the union sponsored drew me too, although I was never allowed in. "Can't I stay in a corner just to watch?" I begged. But my mother was firm: "These dances are meant to give young people in the ministry a chance to mix with others from outside, not for children like you to monkey around." As I waited in my mother's office to accompany her home, I heard the music, including my favourite, "La Paloma," wafting out from the ballroom. The life of the adults seemed so romantic! I wanted to grow up quickly and join the fun. Yet when I grew up during the Cultural Revolution dancing parties were unthinkable, and love songs were condemned as "sickening," foreign ones most of all.

PRIMARY SCHOOL

MY PRIMARY SCHOOL IN BEIJING WAS RIGHT ACROSS THE street from where we lived. All five of us went there. There were better schools, but at the primary stage convenience was more important.

On my first day, as I timidly approached the school gate, I saw two boys nine or ten years old guarding it. They stood beside the stone lions, turning away those who didn't have flyswatters. China was forever having campaigns and "Eliminating the Four Pests" was the present project. The four pests were rats, bedbugs, flies, and mosquitoes. My school decreed that all students had to carry flyswatters so they could do their part in eliminating whatever flies and mosquitoes came their way.

I retreated to our compound and hid myself behind the gate. I was already nervous about attending a new school. My move from Jining to Jinan had not been smooth. There seemed to be an invisible wall between my classmates and me throughout my stay in Jinan. I would watch them cluster around Sheng Qiang, whose father had the highest rank and whose family was the richest, and I felt very lonely. But who was I to them? An outsider from Jining, a small country town. Wouldn't Beijing children, the children of the number-one city, be even more snobbish? At least in Jinan I spoke the language, the Shandong dialect. Now I had to learn to speak the Beijing dialect, Mandarin

Every province in China has its own dialect. Some — for example, Cantonese and Shanghaiese — are very different from the others. People who speak these dialects won't be understood outside their own provinces. For a vast country like China, a standard language is a must, and Mandarin is the standard. It is close to the dialects of many of China's provinces and is taught in schools all over the country, so most young Chinese know how to speak it. Shandongese isn't as far from Mandarin as Cantonese, but it was still a big change for me to shift from my mother tongue to another language. At the beginning I inevitably mispronounced a word or two and showed a definite accent.

I didn't have a flyswatter, and it was too late for me to find my parents to get them to buy me one. I watched the boys through a seam in our gate, hoping they would leave as class time drew near. But they didn't move. In the end I gathered all my courage, crossed the street again, and presented myself. "I'm . . . a newcomer," I said slowly and awkwardly, then turned my eyes down and waited. I expected laughter, or at least, "You'll have to bring a flyswatter tomorrow!" But instead they said, "You're excused as a new student."

This was an auspicious start in my new school. The school turned out to be fine, with no cliquishness. I got along well with everyone and enjoyed all the courses: arithmetic, Chinese language and literature, history, geography, nature, abacus, calligraphy, singing, painting, and physical education. There were two marking systems in China: in one, 5, 4, and 3 counted as passes while 2, 1, and 0 were failures; in the other, percentage marks were used, with 90% and above equal to 5, 80% to 90% equal to 4, 68% to 80% equal to 3, and so on. In my markbook there were many more 5s than 4s. When I turned nine and was eligible, I became one of the early Young Pioneers.

Every May, a beautiful time when all the flowers bloomed, the school held its Red May Singing Contest. Each class from grade four up would perform a chorus of revolutionary songs in the schoolyard. In 1962, when my class was first eligible for the contest, I was lead singer. In my navy blue pants and white blouse, with the red scarf of a Young Pioneer around my collar and my class behind me, I sang:

Along the bank of the surging Gan River,
There are the places where Comrade Fang Zhimin* fought.
In the forest of white snows,
There is the thatched hut where General Yang Jingyu lived.

(Chorus)

How many martyrs, how many brave fighters,
Were faithful to the revolution and the party?
For the sake of Chinese people,
Their blood was shed on the motherland.
For the sake of Chinese people,
Their blood was shed on the motherland.

*Fang Zhimin (1889-1935) and Yang Jingyu (1905-1940) were revolutionary martyrs. Fang died fighting the Kuomintang reactionaries in Jiangxi in southern China, and Yang died fighting the Japanese invaders in Manchuria in the northeast.

Today we wear our Red Scarves,
And happily walk through the schoolyard gate.
It is all because countless martyrs
Exchanged their lives for our joys.

(Chorus)

Step into the footprints the martyrs left,
We continue to march forward.
To these respected and beloved martyrs,
We vow to carry on your cause to the end.
To these respected and beloved martyrs,
We vow to carry on your cause to the end.

My class didn't win the contest, but I won the attention of Mrs. Zhang, our music teacher and the instructor of the Young Pioneers organization. She was a fashionable middle-aged lady. Most women teachers in my school had plain short hair or braids, but Mrs. Zhang had a permanent. The fluffy hair made her large head look even larger. She always wore lipstick on her large mouth — sometimes blood-red, sometimes pink. She wore colourful western clothing and she loved foreign music. Often she locked herself in a room and listened to recordings of foreign songs by famous Chinese singers. When she told me she would give me voice training, I was elated. I loved singing and thought I would be able to listen to her records.

Shortly after the Red May Singing Contest there was an inter-school solo competition. Mrs. Zhang decided that I should enter it. The song she selected for me was "Chairman Mao Came to Five Finger Mountain":

Chairman Mao
Came to Five Finger Mountain.
Under the Hero Tree
He rested his horse.
Before leaving
He cast a dipper of water at the root.
Hence the tree
Was laden with brilliant red flowers.

This was a simple song of the Yi people, one of China's fifty-five minority tribes. At the end of each sentence, there was a long note.

Normally I could sing it with ease, but not after Mrs. Zhang's coaching. She accompanied me on the organ, raised the pitch higher and higher until I reached my limit, and fixed that for my performance. She made me practise at that level until I was exhausted and intimidated.

About twenty contestants from different schools turned up for the competition. One after another they went on the stage to sing children's songs eulogizing Chairman Mao, the party, the people, and the motherland. All the contestants had sweet voices, and many sang well. In comparison, my singing was strained. I knew I would be out, and I was.

According to Mrs. Zhang, my singing lacked emotion. To correct this, I had to learn how to "express myself" through story recitals. As part of her new regimen, I recited a short story called "Mother" over the school's loudspeaker system. It was about a young girl before the Liberation who thought her mother was cold and uncaring. Afterwards she learned the truth. Her mother was secretly a revolutionary, and at times her role as a spy didn't allow her to acknowledge her daughter. Sitting in the tiny studio, I spoke loudly into the microphone, yelling from time to time: "Mama! Mama!" To my mind I was overacting, but Mrs. Zhang insisted I do it that way. Throughout my reading, she paced around the schoolyard and listened. When I emerged, she told me the effects were "quite satisfactory." "Now you are ready for interschool reciting competitions."

After that I went from one competition to another. I had to memorize revolutionary stories a few pages long and try for emotion when reciting on the stage. I kept reminding her that I wanted to learn singing, not reciting, but she paid no attention. She just kept passing me short stories to learn, often rather insipid ones, and informing me when competitions were scheduled. I finally got sick of it. Why should I give up my playtime to this nuisance? My textbooks already provided me with enough to remember.

Sometime in the middle of grade five, she handed me a short story that was longer than any I had tried before. I flung it in my drawer in disgust. Two days before the contest, I took the story out and tried to memorize it. When the time came for the contest, I knew I wasn't ready.

The moment I mounted the stage I saw Mrs. Zhang sitting alone in the last row of the large competition room. I started in on my story, searching my brain for the right words and giving no thought to expression or emotion. I tried to look everywhere but Mrs. Zhang's direction. The more nervous I became, the more glances I shot at her, and the more irritated she looked. She shook her large head and sneered at me with her big, red lips. Halfway through, I got completely lost and couldn't recall another word. After a long, awkward pause, I stepped down from the stage. There had been many bad reciters, but in all the competitions I had been in, I had never seen one leave the stage before finishing. After this disaster, I was never again bothered by competitions. But I also never learned the secrets of good singing or had the opportunity to listen to Mrs. Zhang's records.

DRAGONS BEAR DRAGONS?

"**D**RAGONS BEAR DRAGONS; PHOENIXES BEAR PHOENIXES; and moles bear sons accomplished in digging holes." So goes an old Chinese saying. In my class, the painter's son did paint the best, and the intellectual's daughter did write most beautifully.

I didn't do badly in painting. One of the girls in my compound loved to paint. Her older brother, who was learning Chinese painting in the Central Arts and Crafts College, had taught her and she in turn taught me. We drew ladies in ancient costumes, Chang'e flying to the moon, or Zhinu standing on the road waiting for Nulang to pass. In school my painting assignments often got 5s and were exhibited in the school gallery. But Lin, a plump boy who was the son of a painter, painted better than any of us. His assignments were, of course, exhibited often. My pieces pleased me but they paled beside Lin's. The difference showed especially clearly when we drew the same subject. His lantern would look fuller and brighter than mine, and his figures more vivid. He showed me his pencil drawings of generals in full armour on horseback. I thought they were masterpieces.

Grade six had just started when I found a new girl standing in front of me in the school assembly. Her braids rested on her shoulders and her creamy short-sleeved blouse was tucked into a skirt with white dots against a burgundy background. She had beautiful legs and a small waist. I tapped her on the shoulder and asked her who she was. When she turned around I saw she had a delicate oval face, a small, feminine mouth, large, kind eyes, and eyebrows so trim they looked as if they were painted on. "I'm Liu Wenhui. I just joined your class today," she said with a smile. I liked her.

In class, when I sat down at my seat and took out my pencil box, textbook, and notebook, I noticed that the girl who used to sit in front of me was gone. In her place sat Wenhui. Before I could say anything, she turned her head and asked, "Am I welcome here?" I said, "Very." Later she told me that our teacher-in-charge, Zixiang, put her there on purpose. He wanted the two of us to become friends.

Wenhui was a good student. Her grades were as good as mine and she was better in calligraphy. We had one calligraphy lesson a week, when we all brought our brushes and ink sticks and slabs to class. Under the teacher's eye, we made the ink, then copied a page of characters. Wenhui always finished hers faster than I did, and they were always better.

We did become good friends as Zixiang wished, sharing secrets and showing each other things we wouldn't show to our classmates. At midterm she showed me her literature exercise book with Zixiang's remarks in red ink in it. She hadn't wanted anyone else to see them. The book was filled with graceful penned script. I had thought she only wrote well with a brush. "Why do you write so well?" I asked. "It's my parents. They've made me practice calligraphy every day ever since grade three. They know that if one writes well with a brush, one also writes well with a pen."

Most Chinese appreciate beautiful handwriting. To me, reading good handwriting is just like looking at good paintings. I wished I could write like Wenhui, but I didn't have the parents she did. Both were intellectuals — her father was a physician-in-charge in a big hospital in Beijing and her mother was a doctor there. Only people like them could provide their children with such direction and training at home.

When a group of students went to study sessions in Wenhui's home, they were allowed to use one of the rooms her grandmother and her two pairs of twin brothers shared. When I was there alone with her, however, she would take me to another set of four rooms she and her parents occupied. The windows there were always closed and the knitted white curtains drawn. On our way to her bedroom we passed the living-room, the study, and her parents' bedroom. On one side of the living-room two burgundy sofas sat facing each other with a wooden tea table in between, and on the other side stood a display cabinet with glass doors. The study had two bookshelves filled with books, a large desk, and a couple of soft chairs.

On the way out, as we passed the living-room again, I approached one of the sofas and planned to try it. "Don't!" Wenhui stopped me just in time. Frozen halfway there, I asked why.

"Because if anything is moved or rumpled, my parents will grumble. I don't want that." She frowned.

Wenhui dressed well. Most of my clothes didn't fit; they were either too big or too small. But everything she wore looked as if it were specially tailored. One day a beautiful emerald-green T-shirt showed in the neck opening and below the short sleeves of the blouse she had on. The material was so shiny and smooth that I suspected it was silk. Having never heard of silk underwear, I asked her in disbelief, "Are you wearing a silk T-shirt?"

"Yes, but it's not mine," she explained quickly. She didn't want to stand out from the rest of us. "None of my underwear was dry this morning. My mother lent me this."

"Wow! Can I feel it?" She nodded. I slipped my fingers into her sleeve and felt silk for the first time in my life.

To my eyes, Wenhui's life was perfect. She had a nice home, decent clothes to wear, and even a bicycle to ride. I was sure that her parents provided her with tutoring at home, besides giving her calligraphy lessons. Material abundance and a good education. What else could a child want? But for Wenhui there was something she didn't have. She thought her parents were boring. "They only talk to me about my studies. Nothing else about me interests them. Do they care whether I have friends or am happy? No. Sometimes I think they don't have any feelings for me at all."

MIDDLE SCHOOL

DURING THE LAST FEW MONTHS OF GRADE SIX NOTHING new was taught. Teachers spent this time preparing us for the middle school entrance examination. To do well in this examination and get into the best school, a "key school," was of the greatest importance because this was the first step towards university.

For thousands of years the Chinese believed that "the educated are superior, all others are inferior." Although Chairman Mao and the Communist Party repeated time and again that in our socialist country all jobs "served the people" and were equal, deep in the Chinese mind those who were good and smart became scholars and were superior. Even during the Cultural Revolution, when the intellectuals were called the "stinky ninth" behind such other villains as capitalists and landlords, the Chinese also called them "preserved beancurd," a cheese-like Chinese condiment that smells foul but tastes delicious. A woman's ideal bridegroom was still an intellectual.

Most young Chinese dreamed of a university education, but few made it. The difficult nationwide examinations eliminated all but a few candidates every year. Those who were not in key schools had little hope of attending university at all, much less a good one. My life's goal, instilled by my parents, was to graduate from a top university and become a scientist. I wanted very much to get into a key school.

A month before the exam, Zixiang handed each of us an application form. We had to give a ranked choice of three middle schools and declare, if our marks were not good enough for these, whether we were willing to go to another school, usually an awful one, assigned by the government. A student who didn't do well had the right to take the examination again another year. I carried the form home to ask my parents' advice. They favoured the Twelfth School for Girls in Beijing. It was a key school and it was only five blocks from home. They also liked the idea of a girls' school. I didn't have much of an opinion myself, so I made it my first choice. Wenhui also ranked it first. Her home was close to mine, and her parents thought the same way.

Teachers could have some say, although not a decisive one, about students' selections. After we turned in our forms. Zixiang commented on them and encouraged us to be brave and apply to the better schools. Then he called some of us into his office for private talks about our applications. Wenhui and I went in one after the other. He advised us both to apply to the Second School for Girls in Beijing, another key school that had an even better reputation than the Twelfth. But the Second was far from home, so neither Wenhui nor I followed his advice. Still, we were happy about his suggestion, which we took to mean that he thought better of us than we did. A teacher knew how his students had done in the past and could often predict what school they would get into.

The examination day came at the end of July and the tests turned out to be quite straightforward. When I came out of the arithmetic examination room and checked the results, I knew I had gotten everything right. In the literature exam I had filled in all the blanks correctly. The composition topic was "My Family," one of those Zixiang had chosen several times for us to practise. Nonetheless, we waited anxiously for the notice announcing which school had accepted us. It finally came in mid-August. Both Wenhui and I were admitted to the Twelfth School for Girls.

Wenhui always remained on good terms with Zixiang. She went to see him and found out we had both received double one hundred per cents in mathematics and Chinese literature. With these marks we could have gotten into any school. She also learned that no one else besides us had been accepted by a key school. Other good students, like Lin, didn't do well in the exams. He had to go to the second school in his ranking, not a key one.

The Twelfth School for Girls was originally a private missionary institution, founded with money from an American woman, Mrs. Bridgeman, more than 120 years earlier. Before Liberation it had been a school for girls from rich families and was referred to as "the young ladies' school." After Liberation it became one of the ten key schools in Beijing, but the nickname stuck since now it was for daughters of high-ranking cadres. Its most distinguished graduate was Li Na, the daughter of Chairman Mao and Jiang Qing. Occasionally while I was there I would see a striking senior student with fair skin and blue eyes. People told me she was the daughter of Li Lisan, a famous figure in the party's history, and his Russian wife.

Middle schools were divided into junior and senior sections. After three years of junior middle school, students had to pass another exam to get into senior middle school. The chance for us to get into our own senior school was very high, since we had the advantage over graduates from elsewhere. After another three years' study in senior middle school, it would be time for university exams. Students from the Twelfth School for Girls had a university acceptance rate of eighty per cent. I was full of hope. The road towards my goal of becoming a scientist seemed to be smooth and clear, my future seemed bright.

On the designated day, I went to school to register. I thought school officials would notice that Wenhui and I had been in the same class in primary school and would put us in the same class in middle school. It would be much nicer to enter this new environment with a friend. On the wall inside the school gate was a large piece of paper assigning the new students to four classes of about forty girls each. Wenhui was in class two and I was in class three. Had the teachers failed to notice that we were from the same school? Or did they want to discourage close personal ties between students? I wasn't sure.

The class was subdivided further into six groups. In mine, Guomei was the shortest so she sat in the front. She was a plain-looking girl. Her father was A Lao, a famous painter. I had often seen his sketches in China's most important newspaper, *The People's Daily*. Guomei never talked with us about her father. She tried to avoid the subject even if we asked directly.

Behind Guomei was Jiamei, the daughter of a capitalist family and the class beauty. She had rosy skin, dark eyebrows that arched like the new moon, large, pitch-black pupils, and a shapely figure. Her hair was cut short in "the athlete style," and her feet were always clad in white runners.

She was good at sports, especially at gymnastic rings. In the summer she played on them almost every day. Wearing a white short-sleeved blouse and a pleated apple-green short skirt with suspenders, she would swing high with her body bent back and turn 180 degrees in the air. None of us could do that. We imagined that she must dance well, and she said she did indeed like dancing. "Why didn't you apply for a dancing school and become a professional?" we asked. "I did!" Jiamei answered. "But the school wouldn't accept me. They thought I would become a little fat when I grew up." Her disappointment was undisguised. Jiamei was sweet and she was one of our three squadron leaders, the highest rank in the Young Pioneers in our class.

Immediately in front of me was our group leader, Yi, who was originally from Canton. Her family moved to Beijing when she was very young. The Cantonese are known to be short, but Yi reached five-foot-six when she was grown up. She had a slender body, long arms, long legs, and high cheekbones. From cheek to chin her face narrowed quickly. Her skin was very fine, though slightly dark. She was also beautiful.

Yi's father was formerly a high-ranking cadre, but in the anti-rightist campaign of 1957 he was labelled a rightist. That had its effect on her. She matured earlier than most of us, was always sensible and self-constrained, and was well liked by the students. In my class no one insulted her because of her father's situation. Most of us felt sympathy.

In primary school studying had been a piece of cake for me, but in middle school I found I had to work harder to get good marks. The teachers' standards were high and the competition was strong, since the level of achievement was fairly even. Only Yixie stood out. Like Wenhui, she was from an intellectual family. Both her parents were professors at Renmin University in Beijing, and her grandfather was Mao Yisheng, a famous bridge-building expert. We even found one of his articles about the history of stone bridges in China in our textbook. Yixie apparently had special tutoring at home and kept way ahead of us. By the time we reached the third lesson, she was already finishing the textbook.

Yixie excelled not because of any superior natural ability but because she worked exceptionally hard — too hard. Excessive studying had ruined her sight and she wore very thick glasses. It had also bent her back. One could hardly believe she was just thirteen. I didn't think it was worth the pain to study so hard and kept wondering how much harder she could push herself if one day she went to university.

As much as Yixie moved ahead of us in studying, she lagged behind physically. Nobody knew who gave Yixie the nickname Old Bear, referring to her clumsiness. Once, when we were learning the high jump in P.E. class, everyone but Yixie passed the starting height of two and one-half feet, and she was one of the tallest girls in class. Time and again she dashed to the bar and failed to jump at all.

Yixie wasn't popular. She was smooth, perhaps too smooth. Old Bear is not a pretty name for a girl, yet Yixie never showed any resentment on hearing it. She never offended anybody, and even helped students with their studies. But we thought that beyond her smiling mask she was conceited.

In middle school more social activities were added to our agenda. One such activity was participation in the National Day parade. Every year China held this parade to demonstrate to the world, and to the Kuomintang in Taiwan, of course, the strength and prosperity of socialism. Great amounts of money and effort were expended, and thousands of people took part.

At 6:00 a.m. on National Day, October 1, we assembled at the school and by 7:00 a.m. our team had arrived in its appointed place on East Chang'an Street. Chang'an is wide, with eight automobile lanes and two bicycle paths, as well as pedestrian walks. It runs straight through Beijing from east to west, passing through Tiananmen Square. The celebration started at ten. Either Chairman Liu Shaoqi or Premier Zhou Enlai would deliver a speech, eulogizing the accomplishments of the past year and never forgetting that "we are determined to liberate Taiwan!" at the end.

It was usually noon when we, the "flowers of the country," the Young Pioneers, passed through Tiananmen. In white blouses and red skirts (on loan) we marched and danced to drumbeats and music, all the while streaming long, wide silk ribbons in unison from our arms. To dance and to march forward in a straight row of one hundred people is no easy thing, and we had practised long hours beforehand.

The parade was supposed to be viewed by Chairman Mao and other leaders on the Tiananmen rostrum, as well as all the representatives attending the National Day celebration, my father sometimes among them, on the two lower stands that flanked the sides of the central rostrum. But we didn't know whether Chairman Mao saw us. We couldn't see anything beyond ten feet. A whirlwind of flying ribbons completely blocked our view. For all we knew, Chairman Mao might have been off taking a break.

After passing the square, we went a mile beyond before being dismissed. There were no buses running because of the parade, so we had to trudge the long miles home. To me, this event was not much fun. It was exhausting and occupied the better half of the first day of a two-day holiday. In China the working week has six days, and there are only four official national holidays a year. But I put up with the parade as my sacrifice for my country and its people. I was learning that one shouldn't live just for oneself.

FABLES OF
REVOLUTIONARY HEROISM

IN MIDDLE SCHOOL OUR POLITICAL EDUCATION ACCELERATED. This wasn't an extreme change, however, since revolutionary education was constant throughout our lives. It came to us through the media, our texts, our teachers, our parents, and the workers, poor and lower-class peasants the school invited to give us talks. It took root in us gradually and imperceptibly.

In history classes we learned to take pride in our ancient civilization and its four great inventions: papermaking, printing, gunpowder, and the compass. We also learned to be ashamed of the humiliations of recent Chinese history. Well before the invasion by the Japanese devils, almost all the capitalist countries had carved up and enslaved China. The ramshackle and corrupt Qing government couldn't do anything to protect its citizens, and the barbarians bullied, burned, killed, and looted wherever they went. They flooded China with opium, turned its people into addicts, and then hypocritically viewed China with disdain as "East Asia's sickman."

Next to the Japanese invaders we learned to hate the Kuomintang government, which had kept China's working people miserable. Capitalists and landlords ruthlessly exploited workers and peasants. Those who made cloth didn't have clothes to wear, and those who tilled the land didn't have food to eat. One year the Kuomintang government, stupidly thinking it would stop the Japanese, even opened a breach in a dyke along the Yellow River and loosed a flood without warning. The water didn't stop the Japanese, but it did kill countless Chinese and forced thousands upon thousands more to wander as refugees. Frequent famines and epidemics forced the peasants, more than eighty per cent of China's population, to struggle for existence on the edge of death.

What we studied most were perhaps the rebellions. Lin Zenxiu burnt opium at Humen against the opium trade, the Taiping Rebellion rose in resistance to the Qing dynasty, the Boxer Rebellion stood up to the western barbarians, and finally the Communist Party led the revolution against the Japanese devils and then the Kuomintang reactionaries. Poor peasants joined the Red Army, one stepping into the breach as another fell, and fought valiantly for a new and brighter China. We were reminded again and again that the happy life we lived today had been paid for in blood. It was ours only because countless martyrs had sacrificed their lives. All Chinese were taught not to forget but to honour and learn from these heroes.

One of these martyrs was Liu Hulan. She was a young member of the Communist Party — perhaps the youngest — who gave her life for the revolution. When she was fifteen, the Kuomintang chopped her head off with a huge hay cutter in the threshing ground as her fellow villagers watched. Despite the threat of death, she refused to renounce her Communist ideals. "Aren't you afraid of death?" they asked. "If I am, I wouldn't have joined the Communist Party!" was her answer. To her, Chairman Mao dedicated the words "A great life! A glorious death!" To do something that sensational by the age of fifteen was my dream.

The idol for girls was Liu Hulan and the idol for boys was Dong Cunrui, a soldier in the Chinese People's Liberation Army. In one battle against the Kuomintang, he was sent to blow up the enemy's strongest pillbox. Approaching the pillbox under a hail of bullets, he found it built on an arch with the main part of it suspended in the air. The only way to destroy the structure was to detonate the dynamite pack against the bottom of the arch, but there were no poles to prop the pack against it. As Dong Cunrui searched for a pole, the bugle sounded the charge, and the pillbox began strafing. Rows and rows of soldiers fell. So Dong Cunrui held the dynamite pack against the pillbox himself and pulled the fuse, shouting: "For victory, charge!"

Stories of war heroes like Liu Hulan and Dong Cunrui dominated in the 1950s. In the 1960s peacetime heroes came to the fore. One was Lei Feng, a soldier who died in 1962 in an accident while on duty at the age of twenty-three. His short life was held to be "extraordinary in the ordinary," and he became *the* everyday hero for people to emulate. Even Chairman Mao himself wrote "Learn from Lei Feng!"

Lei Feng had a terrible childhood in the old China. He came from a family of five. His father worked as a sharecropper and the family never had enough food. During the Japanese invasion his father was killed, and the family fortunes went from bad to worse. His older brother got work as an apprentice in a small machine shop, was injured in an accident, got fired by the factory owner, and died because there was no money for a doctor. His younger brother starved to death. His mother went to serve a landlord family, the landlord raped her and then drove her out, and she hanged herself. At the age of seven Lei Feng was an orphan. To make a living, he tended cattle, fed pigs, and fetched firewood for the rich. He was scolded and beaten. Once a termagant landlady got angry because young Lei Feng didn't fetch enough wood for her. She grabbed the axe from him and severely chopped his hand.

The Communist Party saved him and provided for his education. When his schooling ended, he became a worker on a state-run farm, then a soldier, a Communist League member, and later a party member. He knew that his family had been destroyed in old China, and that he had gained a decent life only after Liberation. Out of gratitude he devoted his life to the party. He did everything the party assigned him, no matter how hard, happily and diligently. In daily life he was utterly devoted to others, with no thought of himself. Lei Feng helped countless people: an old woman from the countryside carrying too much luggage, a little girl crying because she couldn't find her mother, one of his comrades-in-arms whose family urgently needed money. Many of these incidents were unknown until he died, when his comrades discovered his diary.

All students had a copy of *Excerpts from Lei Feng's Diary*. Moving passages in the book expressed a deep affection towards Chairman Mao, the party, and the people. Here are some quotations: "A person's life is limited, but the task of serving the people unlimited. I shall devote my limited life to the unlimited task of serving the people." "Treat comrades warmly like the spring, treat work fervently like the summer, treat egoism like the autumn wind sweeping fallen leaves, and treat enemies cold-bloodedly like severe winter." "Read Chairman Mao's works, listen to Chairman Mao's instructions, and be a good soldier of Chairman Mao."

The "Learn from Lei Feng" movement began when I was in grade five and lasted until the Cultural Revolution. People were encouraged to be like him: to obey orders, to work hard, to do good deeds, to be selfless, and to study the writings of Chairman Mao. The more one learned from Lei Feng, the more "progressive" one was considered.

"Progressive" is a term the Chinese use to characterize someone conscientious and revolutionary. It is the opposite of reactionary — one of the most negative words in mainland China. A reactionary is a conservative and counter-revolutionary. Before Liberation a person who was sympathetic to the Revolution and the Communist Party was called progressive, whereas one helping the Japanese or supporting Chiang Kaishek's government was reactionary. After Liberation nobody dared oppose the Communist Party, at least not openly. Thus a progressive person became one who stayed close to the party and took a lead in the political campaigns as well as in his or her own work, whereas a reactionary was one who said anything at all disparaging about Communism or the party.

"I WANT TO
BE PROGRESSIVE!"

MIDDLE SCHOOL MEETINGS GREATLY OUTNUMBERED those in primary school. Every time the party had important instructions, the school would have a meeting to relay them and to organize study sessions for the students. Once or twice a year the school invited soldiers or model workers to tell of their experiences in serving our socialist country and in studying Chairman Mao's works. They used *Mao Zedong Thought* as the guide to solving problems at work and in life and overcoming selfishness.

As part of our class education, factory workers were invited to tell of their sufferings in the old society. One of these workers had been a child labourer. Driven by poverty and hunger, he started to work in a coal mine at thirteen. Like all other miners, he worked under the constant threat of cave-ins and gas explosions. He was as skinny as a skeleton, and his shabby clothes hardly covered his body. Whenever he didn't dig fast enough, the overseers would whip him. As the miners said, "The coal is black, but it isn't as black as our lives before Liberation."

Every mid-term and term end there were routine school meetings. At these meetings the previous term's work was summarized, new tasks for the next period were proposed, "progressive" students were praised, and the rest were told to emulate them. We were constantly reminded that to be "progressive" was glorious, to be "backward" shameful.

The teachers-in-charge organized their own meetings. Besides giving instruction in one of the major courses, these teachers took care of the ideological education of the students as well. Most did their jobs responsibly. The younger, newly graduated ones, like my teacher, Zhang Yuying, were especially eager. They had been educated in New China and their thoughts were progressive. Many of them tried hard to join the party, and turning their classes into models of progressiveness was a good way to prove their loyalty. In my class Yuying held a meeting every week or two, at which she chose five good students to speak about their political advances.

Each autumn all students and teachers in the Beijing middle schools were sent to the suburbs of Beijing to live and work with the poor and lower-middle-class peasants for a month. Through this activity the government hoped to improve the townspeople's attitude towards labour and the peasants. China was an agricultural country. Eighty per cent of its population were peasants whose living standards were considerably lower than those of city dwellers. The Communist Party taught us that the peasants and workers raised us: the peasants provided us with food and the workers clothes. We shouldn't be allowed to be indifferent to or ignorant about the peasants and their lives.

When we were on our autumn sojourn in the countryside, the commune often held a couple of evening meetings to "recall past sufferings and think over the sources of present happiness." A thousand commune members congregated on a huge threshing ground, and poor peasants went up to the temporary stage in turn to condemn the evil old society. Some hadn't been poor to begin with — their descent into poverty had started in one lean year when they were forced to borrow money at usurious interest rates from black-hearted landlords. The sum grew bigger and bigger until, under the landlord's constant pestering, they had to give up their land in payment. Among the speakers there was often some woman who had been sold by her parents to a rich family as a child bride, the lowest stratum on the social ladder. She had to serve everyone in the family and was dealt with like a slave: beaten, mistreated, and ill fed. Sometimes a speaker became too distraught to continue. Then someone in the audience would stand up and take the lead in shouting slogans: "Down with the vicious old society!" "Keep alive the memory of class bitterness!" "Remember forever the blood-and-tears feud!" We sat on the ground among the commune members, shouted slogans with them, and shed tears if we could.

These periods of working in the countryside were rough. The physical life was hard and the mental pressure enormous. Since we all worked and lived together, everybody was under the surveillance of others. All news, good or bad, went directly to Yuying without delay. Based on what she saw and heard, Yuying gave a summing-up almost every evening to praise "fine deeds and fine people" and occasionally to criticize violations of discipline without mentioning names. At the end of the month there would be a long meeting, at which each of us would report our achivements and then elect four or five model students. From these Yuying would choose one as a candidate for commendation in a school meeting.

The school and the teachers pushed us hard to be progressive. Had we refused to cooperate, there was nothing they could have done. But how could we not cooperate? We all had a revolutionary education, and most of us were conscientious. Before entering my school many of my classmates were student cadres (monitors, Young Pioneer squadron leaders, and so on) and excelled in the three aspects: moral, intellectual, and physical. To respond to the school's call to be progressive posed no problem at all. With these students leading the way, the rest naturally followed. In the country-side we were on our best behaviour: we vied for the heaviest work in the fields, wore old, patched clothes, ate coarse food, and slept little, all without complaint. That my school was nicknamed the Young Ladies' School was ironic. Where would one find young ladies amongst us?

I hadn't been progressive in primary school, but I wanted to be so now. The urging of school leaders, pressure from teachers, and the atmosphere among the students had its effect on me, along with the influence of my family. Since I had entered middle school, my parents kept admonishing me to stay close to the Communist League and to be progressive, and my older brother, Xinhua, kept passing on the revolutionary thought he had just gained. Sometimes he would tell me a revolutionary story and stress at the end that it was a real story, not a fabricated one. Sometimes he introduced me to books. It was his ardour for "Lovely China," an article written by the famous revolutionary martyr Fang Zhimin, that lead me to read it.

Fang had been an important leader in the Red Army and Communist Party in the early days. In 1935 he was caught by the Kuomintang. The reactionaries spent half a year trying to make him betray the cause. Even Chiang Kaishek himself once showed up, but Fang was resolute. During his half year in prison he wrote "Lovely China" and several other articles. On August 6, 1935, by Chiang's order, Fang, then thirty-six years old, was secretly executed.

"Lovely China" sharply reminds the reader of the unfortunate half-colonial state of China in the 1920s. A sign at the gate of a French park in Shanghai read "Chinese and Dogs Are Not Allowed." All over China there were small colonies ruled and policed by foreigners; Chinese were without rights in their own land. Fang travelled from Shanghai to Jiangxi Province on a Japanese boat and saw a fat man directing six thugs to beat three countrypeople who had boarded without tickets: a young soldier, a weak forty-year-old man, and a woman. After beating them hard with rattan and bamboo pieces, the thugs threatened to throw them overboard. The soldier said, "Just because I had no money for a ticket, I don't deserve death!" But they jeered at him and tied his hands and feet to the rail, letting his body hang a foot above the water. The waves beat over him relentlessly. When they began to do the same to the older man, he begged: "Please don't hang me, let me jump into the river myself. Why should I want a life which can't even afford me a boat ticket?" But he was not allowed to jump. They hung him over the side too. When they went to the woman to untie her trousers, Fang shouted: "Beat them!" "Who said that?" the fat man bawled. "Beat them!" dozens of voices chimed in from the spectators. The fat man panicked, and the men ran away.

"My friend," Fang wrote, "this tragic scene I shall never forget! The victims were not just our three countrymen, but the whole Chinese nation. The pain was in their bodies, but the shame was in our faces! Ah! Ah! My friend, is a Chinese really not as good as an animal? Aren't you sad when you hear such a story?

"My friend, later on I experienced many things like this and even worse. If I tell you all, I won't be able to finish for days. Suffering and shame are everywhere in our half-colonial China. But, my friend, each such experience has helped me fortify my determination to bring about the liberation of the Chinese nation. I often think that if it can help further liberation, I shall not begrudge my unworthy life!"

There I cried. His writing and his patriotism moved me deeply. I was also a Chinese. Why couldn't I live a meaningful life like his? Why couldn't I be a revolutionary?

WALKING ALONG
THE CLASS LINE

Yes, I WAS POLITICALLY AWAKE, MY HEART FIRED WITH idealism and revolutionary heroism. But my teacher-in-charge, Zhang Yuying, was as cold as ice to me. China had an official policy called "walk along the class line," which classified people by their family backgrounds and accorded them different treatment. Those whose parents were workers, poor and lower-middle-class peasants, or revolutionaries were considered to be from good families and held higher than all others politically, although not academically. It was taken for granted that students from good families had a genuine and natural love for the party and for their socialist country. Their parents were grateful or faithful to the party, so they had been brought up to feel the same. But if words of loyalty and gratitude came from the mouths of the students of other backgrounds, their sincerity needed to be tested against time.

Yuying's favourites were from workers' families and she was from a worker family herself. Our monitor and secretary of the Communist Youth League, Jiuhong, was the daughter of workers. She was two years older than most of us and already a league member when she entered our school. Yuying had promoted her to these two top positions on the first day. Jiuhong was a good girl who worked very hard in the countryside, but she was also inarticulate.

Next to students from worker backgrounds, Yuying preferred students whose parents were revolutionary cadres, army leaders, or poor peasants. Next were those from intellectual and even capitalist families, like Yixie and Jiamei, since students from these backgrounds often excelled as academics. Even a "rightist" daughter, like Yi, was given proper attention. They all belonged to the list of those to be fostered and trained as the successors of the revolution. On the bottom rung of the ladder were the offspring of common office staff. As parents, they were considered mediocre, so their children were thought to be mediocre too.

When filling out forms in China, students always had to specify their family backgrounds and parents' positions. From modesty, my father told us to put revolutionary office staff instead of revolutionary cadre in the column for family background. Thus, Yuying thought I was from the family of common office staff and didn't bother to read the posts my parents actually held. Besides that, my file from primary school really didn't have much to catch her eye. I wasn't a "student good in three aspects" or a Young Pioneer squadron leader.

Even though I hadn't done well in primary school, I was now in middle school and wanted a fresh start. However, coming from a family of common office staff, I didn't have a chance. At least I had been a group leader in primary school. But in middle school, with more student cadres — three squadron leaders, six group leaders, representives for all the major courses, a monitor, and an associate monitor — there wasn't a post for me. Perhaps it was too much to expect Yuying to promote me as a student cadre, but at least she could have seen *something* good in me. But she didn't. It was as if I didn't exist at all. Once, after working in the countryside, my friend Yi and I were walking home behind all the others. We kept seeing wheat heads scattered here and there on the ground, so we stayed in the field a little longer to collect the heads for the brigade. The next day Yuying praised Yi alone for it. I didn't exist.

To sit in Yuying's routine class meetings was a torture. The speakers were always from a small circle among the student cadres. They talked so frequently I could predict what they were going to say before the meeting started. While listening to Yixie's flat voice bragging about how well she studied, and others' ramblings about their "thought improvement," I yearned to be on stage too. I could tell them of my revolutionary zeal, and I would tell it with passion. How happy I would be if Yuying just asked me once!

At the beginning I had no misgivings about being ignored. A selfless person, like Lei Feng, shouldn't think of personal gain or loss, right? But when it lasted a whole year, I lost heart. Did this mean I would be on the bench for the two more years I was going to be in Yuying's hands? Or, even worse, for the rest of my life if all my teachers and leaders turned out like her? I became pessimistic and moody.

The only pleasure left to me was to lose myself in novels. I *was* one of the two book representatives in charge of returning and borrowing books from the school library for all the students in class. This title was my only success. It didn't make me a student cadre, mind you; the title was mine only because nobody else wanted it. But I did get to read lots of novels. My favourite was Jules Verne's *20,000 Leagues under the Sea*. I hung on every word. Captain Nemo was my idol, with his vast knowledge, unimpeachable character, and insightful views about humankind. He was absolutely right to detest humanity. There was no justice and no goodness. Humans were snobbish, narrow-minded, and prejudiced. Oh, if only I could follow him! If only I could live a life like his when I grew up!

I noticed that Captain Nemo had friends who helped him build and operate the ship and travelled with him. I decided I needed a friend to help me too. I thought of Yi but decided against her right away. She was doing fine, so she had no reason to go with me. Then I thought of Yang Yanping, the class' other book representative. She was a Young Pioneer group leader but seemed inconspicuous enough. Perhaps she felt like me. So I recommended the book to her and waited patiently until she finished it. "Did you like the book?" I finally asked her. "Yes," she said with no great enthusiasm. "I adore it," I told her. "I want to live that kind of life when I grow up. How about you? Would you like to join me?" Yanping was flabbergasted. Her large, large eyes on her small face grew larger still. "Are you out of your mind?"

In December 1965 my father was shifted again. This time he was made the associate director of the Machinery Import and Export Company of the Foreign Trade Ministry. This ministry was an older organization and had accumulated many more dormitory buildings than the Agriculture Ministry. Finally my family moved into a real apartment, with two bedrooms and a living-room. Although we still had no shower or bath, our living conditions were greatly improved. We had our own toilet and a kitchen with a water tap in it. Now self-sufficient, we kept our apartment door shut most of the time. Except at residence meetings concerning security and other district affairs, we didn't see our neighbours. This was modernization.

While Father had only a five-minute walk to work, Mother, one of my brothers, and I took the bus to work or school, forty-five minutes each way. A monthly bus pass for a student was only two yuan, but the bus was usually crowded, especially during rush hours. It would have been nice if the bus trip could have been avoided, but after some discussion, my parents decided that for the time being I should stay where I was. I only had a year and a half before junior middle school graduation. I could apply to a closer key senior middle school when the time came.

Unexpectedly, my father's new job brought a wonderful change. I suddenly realized that it could have been my filling in "revolutionary office staff" on the school form that had turned me into a non-person. My chance had come! I could tell Yuying my father's new position and in doing so correct her mistake while not making her lose face. I felt a prick of conscience. "Shame on you!" I said to myself. "You can't prove your progressiveness on your own merit but have to rely on family." But it wasn't my fault, was it? I had suffered too long. "It isn't a crime to inform your teacher about your father's new job," I decided.

The next day, as usual, Yuying descended from the front platform during class break and walked among the students to answer questions. I watched her closely as she moved in my direction, but several feet away she halted and started to turn. She didn't even want to get near me! "Teacher Zhang," I called out, "I have something to report." For the first time she looked at me squarely and surprise showed in her small eyes — she didn't expect me to address her. "Yes?" she said with a faint smile, as she moved over and sat down on an empty seat in front of me. Before she got herself comfortable, I said my piece. She nodded but said nothing. Then, with the same faint smile, she stood up and strolled away.

The situation changed afterwards. My name was now often heard in class. I was sent to a children's centre to learn radio goniometry; only good students were allowed honours like this. And I was finally given the chance to talk at one of her meetings.

I carefully prepared two full, tightly written pages. Two days before the meeting, I handed it to Yuying. She always read all the manuscripts beforehand to decide the sequence of the talks. That day I was last. On my way to the platform I heard noises from all sides. Someone was leafing through a book, others were gathering their things together to prepare to leave. I had never talked before and nobody thought I would be any good. Beginning my talk, I poured my feelings into my voice and used the skill from my recitals in primary school. The students became attentive. As I went on, the class became quieter and quieter. I had them in the palm of my hand.

"Each day when we come to school and sit in the bright classroom to study, do we ever think of the unfortunate children before Liberation who couldn't attend school? My mother never went to school. She had to tend herds for the landlord. Sometimes when passing a school she would stop a moment and listen. She heard the loud reading of the students and yearned to go in and join them, but she couldn't. School wasn't for her and her kind in old China.

"Each day when we put on warm clothes and eat good meals, do we think of the Red Army soldiers in the Long March? They scaled snow-topped mountains in straw sandals and one layer of clothing. They ate grass roots, bark, and their belts.

"Each night when we go to a comfortable bed to our sweet dreams, do we think of the revolutionary martyrs who spent their nights cuffed and fettered in the prisons of the Kuomintang and American reactionaries? Their sleep could be broken at any time for sessions of torture, to 'sit on the rack,' or have bamboo sticks inserted under their fingernails.

"We all know the stories of many revolutionary heroes like Fang Zhimin, Liu Hulan, Dong Conrui, but do we have any idea how many more there are unknown to us whose lives were also devoted to the revolution? Do you know of the countryboy who led the Japanese devils into a trap and got himself killed? Have you heard of the handful of guerrilla fighters who were under siege in the centre of a bridge and pulled the fuses of their grenades to kill themselves and two dozen reactionaries?"

Before I could finish, the bell rang. Usually the class would be restless, but today nobody made a move. I looked up at Yuying. "Continue," she said.

"For our happy life today, countless revolutionaries died. They died for freedom, they died for justice, they died for the working people, and they died for us. Think of the martyrs. What reasons can we have to quail at difficulties in our studies? Think of the martyrs. What reason can we have to favour our own interest over our country's? Think of the martyrs. What reason can we have not to be the successors of the cause of proletarian revolution?

"My classmates, the revolutionary martyrs gave their lives in exchange for a new China for us! It is now our turn to build on the foundation they laid. What a glorious task it is to build a strong China. And what an arduous task it is to carry the revolution through to the end. Let us study hard and ready ourselves for the day to come! Let us stimulate each other, help each other, and march forward together along the revolutionary road!"

Before I sat down a student asked for my manuscript to copy two paragraphs. "It was like poetry," she whispered. After the meeting another student came to me and asked if it would be all right to borrow my messy manuscript for the night. Apparently she was touched. Her eyes were moist.

I had succeeded. I didn't dare be too jubilant, however. What if Yuying asked me to talk every time from now on? How could I possibly keep on producing material like this? But Yuying didn't ask me a second time. She herself was learning, and from my example she realized there could be others like me in the class, so she changed speakers frequently to give all students a chance.

Under Yuying's instructions, Jiuhong found me for a heart-to-heart talk after school. I knew now the Communist League was thinking about me. Jiuhong's round face was always red when she talked. The more serious she was, the redder her face. I felt sorry for her, so I tried not to look at her face when we talked, but I did listen carefully to whatever she said. Necessary or unnecessary, I accepted all her advice gratefully. I wanted to join the league, and Jiuhong was the league. From January to March my progress was so rapid that I rocketed to membership in the league one month after my fifteenth birthday.

There was a children's revolutionary song I learned from the radio. Its tune was martial and its words vehement. It sums up my childhood revolutionary education and my morale before the start of the Cultural Revolution. The song says it all.

Be prepared, be prepared, be constantly prepared,
To be the successor of the revolution.
Be prepared, be prepared, be constantly prepared,
To fight for Communism.
The revolutionary torch
Lights our path forward.
We revolutionary youth
Kindle our revolutionary spirit from childhood.
Be as brave as Huang Jiguang*,
Be as loyal as Liu Hulan,
Be as strong as Liu Wenxue**,
Be like Lei Feng to serve the people heart and soul.

To love study and manual labour is our duty.
To love the country and the people is our responsibility.
March forward, young companions.
March forward, successors of the revolution.
The motherland's ten thousand li*** await us.
The revolutionary people of the world expect us.
March forward, young companions.
March forward, successors of the revolution.
The motherland's ten thousand li await us.
The revolutionary people of the world expect us.

*Huang Jiguang died in the Korean War. He blocked the gunport of an enemy pillbox with his body.
**Liu Wenxue was a Young Pioneer who died at thirteen in the early 1960s during a fight against a class enemy.
***A li is just under six hundred yards.

PART TWO:

THE CULTURAL
REVOLUTION

THE ORIGIN OF THE
CULTURAL REVOLUTION

FROM 1959 TO 1965 CHINA HAD A RESPITE FROM MAJOR political campaigns. The new government, headed by Liu Shaoqi, put its emphasis instead upon construction. To stimulate the economy, communal lands were divided and lent to the peasants, who were then allowed to keep what was left of their crops after paying the government its share. They were also given their own small pieces of land to grow whatever they liked. They could either consume the produce themselves or sell it in cities in "free markets," street markets free from state control. By 1963 the hardships of the Great Leap Forward and various natural calamities were over, and the country began to thrive again. People were content — except for Chairman Mao.

Sitting on the sidelines, Mao watched Liu's measures with growing displeasure. They went directly against his principles and were leading China onto the road to capitalism, he thought. As time passed, Mao became more and more aggravated. From February of 1964 he started to lash out at the "revisionists" in the party, claiming they were everywhere, from the central seat of government to local municipalities. His tone became sharper and sharper. As he told Edgar Snow, author of the famous *Red Star over China*, Mao decided on January 25, 1965 that Liu Shaoqi must step down. All the many party leaders Mao suspected of belonging to Liu's revisionist camp would have to go as well. Overestimating Liu's sphere of influence, Mao feared that his own power in the party would not be enough to defeat Liu. He decided to use the force of the people, for he correctly believed that the vast majority of Chinese still revered and trusted him. What followed was the nationwide disaster of the Great Proletarian Cultural Revolution.

The curtain rose on November 10, 1965, when a Shanghai newspaper published an article entitled, "Comment on the New Historical Play *Hai Rei Being Deposed*," written by Yao Wenyuan. Hai Rei was a famous historical figure of the Ming Dynasty, well known in China for his loyalty and straightforward advice to the emperor. The writer of the play was Wu

Han, the associate mayor of Beijing and a scholar who was an expert in Ming history. In his article about the play, Yao claimed that Wu Han wanted to "restore the evil rule of landlords and rich peasants." Wu thus became the first pawn to be removed in Mao's chess game, all because he worked under Peng Zhen, the mayor of Beijing, who was considered Liu Shaoqi's ally.

In early April 1966 newspapers began to criticize the Three People Village, a pen name of a group of three writers, which included Wu Han. Towards the end of that month, Peng Zhen was deposed and the Beijing Municipality was reorganized. On May 16 the Central Party Group to Lead the Cultural Revolution (CPGLCR) was officially established. Its head was Chen Boda, assisted by Jiang Qing, Mao's wife, and Kang Sheng.

At the instigation of the CPGLCR, on May 25 a big-character poster, an essay handwritten in brush on large paper, appeared on a wall in Beijing University. Its authors were Nie Yuanzi, the party secretary of the philosophy department, and some of her colleagues. The poster made some none-too-subtle accusations against the Party Committee of the University and the University Branch of Beijing Municipality. This set the precedent for the masses to attack their leaders. On the morning of June 1 radio stations all over China broadcast the full text of the poster, calling it a Marxist-Leninist big-character poster. *The People's Daily* published it the next day, together with an editorial calling for revolutionaries "unconditionally to accept the leadership of the Party Centre under Chairman Mao and fight against the 'Black Gangs' who oppose Chairman Mao and his thought."

"WHAT IS GOING ON?"

WHEN I GLANCED THROUGH YAO'S ARTICLE ATTACKING *Hai Rei Being Deposed*, and the newspaper columns railing at the Three People Village, I didn't think any of this could have anything to do with me. I had never seen the play, and I didn't know who these people were or what they were up to. It was all adult business; I was too young. My job, for the party and the country, was to be a good student, study hard, and be progressive. Even when the text of Nie Yuanzi's big-character poster was broadcast, I paid little attention.

June 5, 1966 was a cloudy summer day. As usual I arrived at school ten minutes early and practised English with Yi until eight, when the first classes met. But when the bell rang, no teacher appeared. Ten minutes passed, then twenty, then thirty. No one came. This had *never* happened. When a teacher was ill, someone else always replaced her. A few students went outside to find out what was going on. They came back with the news that a big-character poster had appeared on campus.

At the end of the first class I went out to see for myself. Zigzagging through two courtyards, I found the wall with the poster on it. It was surrounded by so many students I couldn't get close. I had to stand on tiptoe at the back of the crowd and crane my neck. The writing was obscure, with no beginning, no introduction, and no conclusions. It cited what so-and-so leader had said to students on such-and-such a date and then quoted parts of speeches made by leaders at school party committee meetings, none of which I had even heard of.

After skimming it through, I failed to see what all the fuss was about. "This can't be responsible for the cancellation of classes," I thought. Maybe they had started again. Maybe the teacher had arrived and was counting heads. It wouldn't do to be absent, so I went back to my classroom. But there was still no teacher, and the number of students was dwindling. I sat down at my desk, took out my textbook, and tried to read, but I couldn't concentrate. At ten o'clock I gave up hope and again made my way to the wall with the poster on it.

There was now less of a crowd. I advanced to the front and saw three names — Yingqiu, Yu, and Xubo — on the bottom of the poster. All were from the third grade of our senior middle school. Yingqiu and Yu were in the third class, Xubo the second. Having studied these names for a while, I started at the top and read the article again, this time much more carefully. Still I couldn't understand it. "Are they accusing the school leaders of doing something wrong?" I wondered.

During the following days my classmates and I continued to go to school each morning and sit in our room, but no teachers ever showed up. Even Yuying, the one we thought we could always rely on, wasn't anywhere to be seen. We had a thousand questions but nobody to ask. We were raised to be disciplined and obedient. Now, all of a sudden, we were without guidance.

I was one of the four Communist League members in my class. As a result of Yuying's help and my own efforts, I had a good reputation. I wanted very much to do the right thing, but I didn't know what that was. In the beginning I thought Yingqiu, Yu, and Xubo were wrong. Whether or not the school leaders had made the mistakes they were accused of, it wasn't right to criticize party leaders in public. As young as I was, I knew the outcome of the anti-rightist campaign in 1957. It had started with people, including party members, criticizing the party, and ended with many of them being branded rightists and losing their jobs. What Yingqiu and the others were doing looked dangerous. I anticipated that there would soon be a self-criticism from them and everything would be over. It seemed wise to keep a good distance from this poster business. Later, if the leaders investigated who was involved, they wouldn't find me.

I kept my distance for days, until one of my classmates, Yishu, told me that people were signing their names on the poster. I was very surprised. Could I be wrong? Should I reconsider? Otherwise, if Yingqiu and company were later proved right and I hadn't shown support, my classmates might question my political standing. No, that shouldn't be allowed to happen. I went to visit the poster again and see how things looked.

For the third time I stood in front of the poster. Luckily, as I had hoped, there was nobody around. I could study it and wrestle with my doubts without being seen. Indeed, there were now many signatures written all over it — a hundred by my rough count. If all these people dared put their names on it, they must know something I didn't. Even if things later turned ugly, there would be a hundred others to dilute the punishment. I decided to sign. In a corner I found an inconspicuous place and quickly put my name down, feeling anything but inconspicuous.

Afterwards, I heard rumours about Yingqiu's background. It was said that she was the adopted daughter of an associate mayor of Beijing. Her real father had been a high-ranking general who had drowned while swimming in Zhongnanhai, or Centre South Sea. Zhongnanhai is not a sea but a lake located next to the Forbidden City inside the red walls of the Zhongnanhai enclave, where the country's highest leaders, including Chairman Mao, lived. Our highest school leader couldn't even compare in rank with Yingqiu's adoptive father. It was impossible for her to be called a counter-revolutionary! I began to feel better about signing the poster.

After I had shifted to Yingqiu's side, the upper-level students started to debate Yingqiu's poster and the situation in our school. Usually they did this in their classrooms with the doors tightly shut, but one day Yishu rushed in and announced that there was a debate we could all watch. We scurried to the yard where our music lessons used to take place and saw two students facing each other and arguing. They were ten feet apart, and each had a team of supporters behind her. We quietly joined the crowd of onlookers.

"Do you know who they are?" a student behind me whispered. Someone else answered: "The one with black-framed glasses facing us is Diandian. She's a student in the senior school second grade and she's on Yingqiu's side. Her father is a high-ranking officer. The other speaker is in the same grade but from a different class. I don't know much about her."

Diandian was of average height, with a thin body, thin face, and tawny complexion. She wore dark pants and a Mao jacket, which was buttoned up to the chin. To this day I remember how fast she spoke. The Chinese say that a person with narrow lips has the gift of the gab, and true enough, Diandian had a sharp tongue that cut her adversary to pieces. Even though I understood little of the debate, which involved school events I knew nothing about, I enjoyed her quickness. After half an hour, Diandian tired and began to move away. Her opponent tried to end on a winning note: "You're wrong! The school leaders may have made small mistakes, but on the whole they're good leaders."

Diandian stopped. Half turning back she said: "I don't want to argue with you any more. But I can tell you this: soon everything will be clear. Black won't become white and white won't become black."

"You are black! I am white!" shouted her adversary. As in the West, white represents purity and good, whereas black represents darkness and evil, as in "black heart" (evil mind), "black hand" (evil hand), and a later phrase that came into use in the Cultural Revolution, "Black Gangs" (revisionist or counter-revolutionary gangs).

"You are white! I am red!" Diandian snapped immediately, meaning that her opponent was a reactionary and Diandian was a revolutionary or Communist. The onlookers laughed and some, myself among them, even applauded. But Diandian wasn't laughing. Her opponent silenced, she led her team through the moon-shaped gate at their rear and disappeared behind the wall.

A WORKING GROUP
COMES TO SCHOOL

W HEN THE *PEOPLE'S DAILY* PUBLISHED THE TEXT OF NIE
Yuanzi's big-character poster against the leaders of Beijing University,
they were automatically fired from their positions. That was how things
worked in China at the time. Yet the university needed someone in
authority, so on June 3 the Beijing Municipality sent a working group, a
committee of cadres from different departments of the government, to the
university. The next day a few more working groups were sent to other
universities in Beijing. Hearing this, students from the remaining universities and schools went to offices of the municipal party committee of
Beijing to request working groups for their units.

Mao was still in Hangzhou, and Liu Shaoqui and Deng Xiaoping were in
charge of the party's routine business in Beijing. In the rapidly changing situation Liu and Deng were unsure about what to do, so they flew to Hangzhou
to report the developments to Mao and ask him to return and take charge.
Mao said he wasn't ready to come right away. "You do as you see fit," he
told them. They flew back to Beijing and held an urgent enlarged politburo
meeting at which it was agreed to send working groups to "control the
movement and maintain order in universities and schools." When Liu
Shaoqi informed Mao of this decision by telephone, Mao gave his consent.

From June 5–20 working groups came to most universities and
schools. In mid-June, amid the debates of our senior students, a working
group came to our school. After meeting with the seniors, it established
the Revolutionary Committee, made up of eight members appointed
from the second and third grades of the senior school. Since the working
group wanted to pull the students together, the Revolutionary Committee
included both radical students like Yingqiu and Yu and moderate ones
who opposed them and their poster. Under the influence of the working
group, the students stopped attacking one another.

At a school assembly the working group announced that we were now
in a revolution, the Cultural Revolution. We finally knew what was happening in our school. The working group then informed us about our new

Revolutionary Committee, and asked each class to elect a Cultural Revolutionary Small Group to lead the campaign. When we returned to our
classrooms I was elected, together with two Young Pioneer leaders and
two student cadres. At the first meeting of our small group I was made
leader and Jiuhong was made associate leader.

Thus the Cultural Revolution, which lasted ten years, entered my life.
Important newspaper articles and central party documents were passed to
our small group, and we in turn organized the students to study them. We
learned that during the seventeen years of Communist Party control
China's culture, art, and education had been under the dictatorial
command of "capitalist and revisionist black gangs." Later each student
was issued a pamphlet, *Chairman Mao's Comments on Educational Revolution*, which contained some of Mao's sayings:

> *The examination method now used is an example of how one
> treats enemies instead of the people. Sudden attacks are launched
> and tricky questions proposed for the students to answer.*
> *The students read textbook after textbook, study concept after
> concept. They know nothing else. They are lazy in four limbs and
> unable to distinguish the five grains [rice, wheat, millet, sorghum,
> and beans].*
> *The more they learn, the more stupid they become.*
> *Professors just administer schools and universities.*
> *Schooling should be shortened. Education needs a revolution.*
> *And the capitalist rule over schools and universities must be ended!*

I was astonished to learn that our country was in such bad shape.
Until then I hadn't suspected that the songs I sang, the movies I
watched, and the books I read were unhealthy. I had thought my school
a revolutionary one, maybe too revolutionary. Nevertheless, I swal-
lowed what I was told and didn't raise a single negative question, not
even to myself. I had been chosen leader of this revolution in my class.
If I had problems in understanding these documents, how could I
expect the rest of the class to do so? Besides, what experience and qualifications did I have to judge what Chairman Mao and the central committee deemed right and wrong?

My classmates tried to comprehend too. We all considered ourselves
progressive youth, and we were determined to follow Chairman Mao and
the party centre. If they thought this Cultural Revolution to be necessary,
if they wanted us to participate, we would.

After a few days of studying, it was time to write big-character posters. Everybody was encouraged to write, to expose the capitalist and revisionist deeds of the school leaders, to criticize anything capitalist or revisionist, or at least to show that we had the correct attitude.

In practice, we found our good intentions were of little help. After scouring every nook and cranny of our minds, we couldn't recall anything our leaders or teachers had said that was anti-party or anti-socialist. Had we dreamed that things would turn out like that when we entered the school, we would have kept careful notes on all they said so that one day we could search out their guilty words sentence by sentence! Nonetheless, we did manage to produce one poster every few days. Most of our essays were targetless. We made some general criticisms of revisionism, claimed that we would never allow our socialist country to revert to capitalism, pledged to be pathbreakers in the Cultural Revolution, and promised to transform ours into a red and revolutionary school.

I soon noticed that more and more students were naming school officials and teachers in their posters. It would look good if we could do so too, at least once. Who should we attack? We knew no school officials, only the few teachers who taught us; and the only one we could claim we knew well was our teacher-in-charge, Yuying.

To be honest, Yuying wasn't a bad teacher. She didn't treat us as "enemies," as Chairman Mao had accused many teachers of doing. Indeed, she was never harsh to us. She wasn't capitalist either. She didn't curl her hair like other fashionable young women, and her dress was always simple and plain. I never saw her wear leather shoes or wool pants. On each trip to work in the countryside she worked harder than any of us. She wanted as much as we did to be progressive. Poor Yuying — we just had no choice.

I proposed to several students that we write a big-character poster about Yuying. They all supported the idea and gave me the job of drafting it. I thought for a long time about what "cap" would be proper for her. What counted as proletarian and capitalist? What was Marxist-Leninist and revisionist? I was never too sure. By watching others, though, I concluded that all the good things, such as loving our country and its people, doing one's job well, and being selfless and progressive were proletarian or Marxist-Leninist, and all the bad things one could think of were capitalist or revisionist. Thus to denounce Yuying's capitalist and revisionist behaviour, all I needed was to find a few of her previous faults.

In two days I completed the text. It enumerated Yuying's "mistakes" and put a proper label on each — for example, "teaching in a capitalist way" (not making her lectures novel and interesting) and "being anti-pro-letarian-democratic" (never consulting the revolutionary students in making decisions). The title I picked was "See on What Side Zhang Yuying Stands?" hinting that she might well be with the school revision-ists. My comrades read the text and passed it. Then one of them copied it with a brush onto two large pieces of paper, and we pasted them on a wall. Would Yuying see it? Would she be convinced by my criticisms? Would she be angry at me? I didn't know.

The campaign seemed to develop healthily for a while. In less than ten days all the walls of the school were covered with big-character posters. After that, new posters had to be pasted on top of old ones. To prevent a poster from being buried immediately, it would be marked "To be kept until such-and-such a date."

I found most posters trivial. Many were full of empty phrases like "Hold High the Great Red Flag of Mao Zedong Thought and Carry the Cultural Revolution to the End." Occasionally I saw well-written poems, but I never saw one that provided concrete, forceful evidence that our school system had really been revisionist. Even so, I never doubted the Cultural Revolution and Chairman Mao's instructions just because they failed to apply to my school. My school could be an exception. There were so many more schools of which I had no knowledge.

Meanwhile, after enough "problems" were exposed, school meetings were held. The students sat on the ground of our exercise field, and the working group and Revolutionary Committee members sat in front of them on a wooden platform. Finally I saw Yingqiu, the school heroine. (The working group didn't make her a heroine by singing her praises, but we all knew it was she who had started the whole thing.) Although Yingqiu was a bit plump, she had a beautiful face and the sweetest smile I had ever seen, which could lighten everything around her. Unfortu-nately she seldom smiled; she always looked cold and unfathomable.

Before each of the meetings I would pray that the working group would not call on me to speak. I really didn't know what I should say. Luckily, we junior students were never selected. Because of this I was grateful to the working group and to all those who did speak. No matter how pointless and boring their talks were, they were great — they were doing the job for us.

The revolution kept on like this for several weeks, then the pace began to slacken. Whatever could be written had been written, and the number of new posters put up each day decreased. The working group decided to let us out to see what other schools and universities were doing. We went to nearby schools to read their posters, then to Qinghua and Beijing universities, where the revolution had originated.

I spent whole days in universities reading big-character posters. There were many more of them there, and many more people were studying them. Often the better-written posters attracted more readers. Many stood copying paragraphs down in their notebooks. I wasn't patient enough to wait my turn to read these, so I went to the ones that had fewer viewers but they were uninteresting. I had brought my notebook, expecting to discover and copy down important ideas, but I jotted down little.

Still, I did learn that the universities had produced many graduates who were good only at natural science and not at "proletarian politics." They didn't have sympathy with the working people, and they were "lazy in four limbs and unable to distinguish the five grains." This kind of intellectual was called "white and expert," whereas the party and the people needed "red and expert" ones. There was also an assertion, which ran contrary to my own experience, that students from the exploiting class and intellectual family backgrounds were more biased than those from other backgrounds, because they often got high marks.

I was glad I had read those articles. They revealed the real revisionist side of the universities. Although I accepted Chairman Mao's theories about education systems without really understanding them, I preferred to see facts. The Cultural Revolution was making more sense to me.

THE ANTI-WORKING-
GROUP MOVEMENT

IN LATE JULY I THOUGHT THE TIME TO WRAP UP THE CULTURAL
Revolution had come. School leaders and teachers who backed and fur-
thered revisionist teaching had been denounced and criticized. They
would certainly not do this again in the future. The eyes of the mass of
students were now opened, and they knew how to distinguish capitalist
from proletarian education. The purpose of the Cultural Revolution had
been accomplished. But to Chairman Mao, the Revolution had just
begun. The number-one representative of the capitalist line in the Communist Party, Liu Shaoqi, hadn't even been touched. By hook or by crook,
at any cost, Mao was out to get him.

Liu Shaoqi was kept totally in the dark. He never dreamed that Mao's
Cultural Revolution was directed at him and so never took any precautions
against it. Liu was known to be Mao's successor and it was Mao who, in
1958, had made Liu the country's chairman. While Mao was away in
Hangzhou, plotting how to bring Liu down, Liu tried his best through the
working groups in universities and schools to lead Mao's revolution.

To ordinary people like me, working groups were necessary and
helpful; without them I could never have figured out what was going on.
But to the radicals, the working groups were obstructions. The Beijing
University students were the first to write anti-working-group posters. The
working groups had said students should not put big-character posters
outside of universities and should not hold meetings and demonstrate on
the streets, and the students announced that these strictures "stifled the revolution" and served as "frames that constrained the movement."

On June 18, directly in the face of decisions taken by their working
group, the students of Beijing University denounced the "black gangs"
(their former leaders) and physically abused them. They adopted the
methods the peasants used in the 1920 upheaval against landlords in
Hunan Province, painting ink on their victims' faces, pasting big-character
posters on their bodies, forcing them to kneel, pulling their hair, tearing
their clothes, and cuffing and kicking them. The victims were then paraded

through the streets until the university working group interfered. The students were dispersed and forced to admit their mistakes, which further angered them. The mutinous mood spread, and a few days later thirty-nine universities and colleges in Beijing threw out their working groups.

Liu Shaoqi couldn't allow the working groups to be defied. They represented the party, and to oppose them was to oppose the party. At the end of June he instructed the working groups to strike back. Those students who were most active were called to account and labelled "black hands" and "counter-party–counter-socialist elements." In Qinghua University Quai Dafu, the most defiant radical, was even denounced at meetings of the whole student body. The events at Beijing University were condemned as counter-revolutionary. All the working groups were sent back to the universities and opposition was quelled.

On July 17 Mao suddenly returned to Beijing. The next day he received Liu and others. Despite the fact that he had given his consent to sending in the working groups, he now reversed himself. "Having just returned to Beijing, I feel sad to see that the campaign [the Cultural Revolution] is growing cold. The doors of some universities are closed, and in some universities student movements have even been put down. Who put down student movements in the past? Only the Northern Warlords. Those who put down student movements will never come to a good end. Directional and fundamental mistakes have been made. Reverse course immediately! Smash all the old rules to smithereens!"

Since Mao said the working groups had made mistakes, Liu quickly moved to temper the harshest measures they had used against the students. But he was unwilling to disband them. He believed what the working groups had done was in the main right. What a campaign the Cultural Revolution had become! How could it exist without the leadership of the party? This was what he thought, and he said so publicly.

Mao learned Liu's position and decided to use the students against him. He sent out CPGLCR members to stir up the students. At a mass meeting of university students, Jiang Qing shouted to those who had been disciplined by their working groups, "We all stand with you revolutionaries!" At another meeting Kang Sheng "revealed" that "Chairman Mao didn't send out even one working group!" On July 26 the CPGLCR held a meeting of ten thousand people at Beijing University. At the urging of Chen Boda, head of the CPGLCR, the students drove out their working group a second time.

In my school there wasn't really an anti-working-group movement, but at the end of June we heard that our revolutionary heroine, Yingqiu, had fallen out with our working group. Supposedly she clashed with the group's members and at one meeting even stalked out before it was adjourned. She was once again in the vanguard, but I didn't twig to that. I took it as merely a personal matter between Yingqui and the working group. The media were completely silent about the conflicts between the university students and working groups. Ordinary students like me who didn't have "long ears" remained ignorant.

In late July, a few days before the official retreat of our working group, Yingqiu resigned openly from its Revolutionary Committee to indicate her stand. Something was wrong, I finally realized. On July 28, the same day the Beijing Municipality withdrew all its working groups, ours left school without even a word of farewell.

The substance of Yingqiu's dispute with our working group was finally disclosed: she had insisted that more severe measures be taken towards our school leaders while the working group favoured moderation. The gloomy disappearance of the working group could only mean that Yingqiu had won and that our past attacks on revisionists had been too mild. As a result, students in my senior school started to hold class denunciation meetings at which they fought the "revisionists" one by one, face to face.

In the beginning I didn't think we needed to hold such a meeting in my class. Once the working groups left, the revolutionary committees they had set up disbanded. No one had assumed leadership yet, and nobody was giving orders. If the seniors wanted to do what they were doing, let them. I became concerned only after one class in my grade and then another held denunciation meetings. Their rooms were right beside ours, one on the left and one on the right. Standing at our door, we could hear them shouting slogans.

I was still the leader of our Cultural Revolution Small Group. We had been elected by the students and still enjoyed their trust. If my class lagged behind in the revolution, it would be my fault. Action must be taken, I decided, and once again Yuying had to be victimized. One sunny afternoon I called a meeting of the small group to discuss the matter.

"As you know, the other classes have had denunciation meetings. We must do something too. Have you thought about it? Do you have any ideas?" I asked. My right hand held a pen poised to record anything worthwhile in my little notebook.

An awkward silence ensued. Nobody looked at me. One of the girls sat across from me with her body bent forward, her left forearm lying flat on her knees and her right hand supporting her chin. Her gaze followed her toes, which were pivoting back and forth. Another girl leaned against a pillar and looked upwards. Jiuhong rested her elbows on her thighs and looked into the yard where students occasionally passed. Finally one girl spoke. "What can we do? Do we have enough material to denounce anyone?"

"We'll make do with what we have. We don't want to concede that our class is inferior to the others, do we? If they can do it, so can we! I suggest that we target Zhang Yuying."

Another silence. They all knew that was probably what we would have to do, but who was actually going to denounce her? Who would chair the meeting and bring Yuying to account? Amid fidgeting, some stood up and walked about. To bolster morale and to show I wasn't afraid, I declared, "I'll chair the meeting and deal with her, OK? But we need some speakers. You don't have to go onto the stage if you don't want to, but you must help me find students who will."

The meeting became animated. The girls started to talk and no longer looked away. One came up with one name, another with another. While they haggled about it, I wrote and scratched in my notebook. They named this person and that, but none of them offered to speak themselves. For a moment I had the wicked idea of suggesting Jiuhong, Yuying's favourite, the one who should know Yuying best. But I quickly gave it up. I didn't want to be that cruel!

Finally we agreed on five speakers. Then another problem arose. Who could guarantee the students we chose would accept? Why should they? "Leave it to me!" Jiuhong volunteered. She seemed thankful for being let off herself. "I'll inform them, and persuade them if need be." With all this settled I went to the teachers' office and advised Yuying of the forthcoming meeting.

Two days later, at 8:00 a.m., I called the class to order. Yuying entered. She walked to the platform, stepped up onto the right corner, and turned to face the students, head lowered and back bent.

"Comrades, the purpose of this meeting is to denounce and criticize our teacher-in-charge, Zhang Yuying," I solemnly began. "In the past two years she has carried out a revisionist line in her teaching and filled us with capitalist and revisionist ideas. She has poisoned our thoughts. Today, in this Great Proletarian Cultural Revolution, we shall clear these ideas away. Let us be incisive in our criticisms. This is the only way to help her return to Chairman Mao's revolutionary line and to educate ourselves. But first, before we start, we shall give her a chance to confess. I hereby demand that Zhang Yuying recount all her wrongdoings without reservation, including both the ones we revolutionary masses know of and the ones we don't." I turned to her. "You may now begin."

Yuying took out a pile of paper from her pocket and started to read in her deep, husky voice. I descended from the stage to sit among the students and listen, hoping she would surprise us by revealing some of her dirty capitalist thoughts from her mind's depths. There must be some teachers who were rotten inside, otherwise why would Chairman Mao castigate and pursue them so relentlessly? But Yuying "confessed" almost nothing concrete, just some general weaknesses — for example, that she had made mistakes because her political consciousness wasn't high enough. The bulk of her talk was filled with quotations from Mao and segments from the *People's Daily*. As a revolutionary leader, I should have interrupted her in the middle to reprimand her for making so superficial a self-criticism, but I didn't. I thought it more likely she didn't have too much evil to confess.

As soon as she stopped, I took the lead in shouting slogans to create a strong atmosphere. I made a fist and pounded the sky, and the other students followed my example. The voices of forty girls thundered and filled the classroom.

"Fire fiercely at the anti-party–anti-socialism black gangs!"

"Criticize thoroughly the revisionist education system!"

"Leniency to those who confess their crimes, and severity to those who refuse!"

"Long live Chairman Mao!"

"Long live the victory of the Cultural Revolution!"

I looked at Yuying to see if we had scared her. She was standing still, face blank and dull. Both her waist-length braids were now hanging in front, but she didn't fling them back like she usually did.

When we ran out of slogans, I mounted the platform again and said, "Zhang Yuying has admitted some of her mistakes, but her confession is not profound. Now let us revolutionary masses make our thoroughgoing criticisms!" I called the name of one of our speakers. She mounted the platform, stood behind the lectern, and read her manuscript. One by one, five students came forward to make their speeches. Following each, slogans were shouted. Sometimes when I saw Yuying hold her head a little higher, I would demand, "Zhang Yuying, lower your head!"

It turned out that none of the five speakers had anything sharp to say. Our "thoroughgoing criticisms" were even blander than Yuying's self-criticism. As time went on, enthusiasm waned. The shouting became less forceful and the audience restless. It wasn't a very successful denunciation meeting, I realized, yet I didn't know how, nor did I try, to improve on it. I had been braver than other students, but I wasn't fearless. The meeting had no official sanction, and Yuying *was* our teacher-in-charge. She had held a great deal of power over the students before the revolution, how did we know that she wouldn't get it back when this revolution ended? Wouldn't she then "square accounts after the autumn harvest?" These things do happen in life. Pretending not to notice the growing lack of interest, I waited patiently for the five denunciations to end.

Finally the last speaker came down from the platform. I went up. "Zhang Yuying, I have questions to ask you," I said in the sternest manner I could. She turned towards me, keeping her head low. "What is your opinion of the criticisms the students just gave you?" I asked.

"I accept them."

"Are you going to change?"

"Yes."

"Do you have anything else to confess now?"

"No."

All the poses had now been struck; I could finally finish this business. "All right. That's all for today. You can go." She started to turn and I added, "But we reserve the right to hold meetings to criticize you at any time in the future!"

Yuying promptly left the classroom, carrying away with her a stone from my heart. Our class had finally held a denunciation meeting. We wouldn't be viewed as the tail of the revolution.

On August 5 Mao posted his own "Bombard the Headquarters, My Big-Character Poster" in the Zhongnanhai compound. It was broadcast to the rest of the country on the same day:

> How well written was the country's first Marxist-Leninist big-char-
> acter poster [Nie Yuanzi's poster on May 25] and the editorial on
> it in the People's Daily! Comrades, please reread this poster and
> commentary. But in a span of fifty days, from the party central to
> local precincts, certain leaders have gone in a diametrically oppo-
> site way. They have adhered to the side of the capitalists, exercised
> capitalist dictatorial powers, dampened the fire of the Proletarian

Cultural Revolution, confounded right and wrong, mixed up black and white, encircled and suppressed the revolutionary party, stifled differing opinions, and implemented "white terror." They are very pleased with themselves. But they boast the capitalist morality and suppress the proletarian spirit. How malicious this all is!

As politically insensitive as I was, I knew this was aimed at the working groups and their backer, Liu Shaoqi. I now found it harder to follow Mao's logic. In my own experience, the working group really wasn't that bad. This was the second time Mao had condemned something that to me seemed quite all right. I also couldn't understand why he had to use all those vicious words about Liu Shaoqi. After all, Liu was Mao's comrade and successor, and he had contributed a great deal to the country. Could it be that Mao's bark was worse than his bite?

After the publication of Mao's poster the working groups were criticized in newspapers and at public meetings. They were said to have been pushing a "capitalist reactionary line." Two more subjects were now required in our big-character posters — the working group and the "capitalist reactionary line." The leader of yesterday's campaign became its object today. "What an unpredictable revolution!" I thought.

BECOMING A RED GUARD

THE FIRST RED GUARDS WERE A FEW STUDENTS IN THE MIDDLE School Attached to Qinghua University (MSQU). They were the children of certain high-ranking cadres and had learned through the grapevine that somebody in the party centre was opposing Chairman Mao. On the ruins of Yuanmingyan, burned by the British and French invaders in the Opium War of 1860, these students secretly created the Red Guard organization. It was May 29, four days after Nie Yuanzi's poster appeared at Beijing University.

"We are guards defending red power. The party centre and Chairman Mao are our backers. To emancipate the whole of mankind is our duty. Chairman Mao's Thought is the ultimate principle of our actions." This was the pledge of these early Red Guards. Students from high-ranking cadre families soon learned the news. In early June, one after another, student organizations — Red Guards, Red Flag, and East Wind — were established in other middle schools.

On June 24 the Red Guards in MSQU put out a big-character poster, entitled "Long Live the Rebelling Proletarian Spirit!" It went on to say: "Dare to think, dare to speak, dare to do, dare to attack, dare to carry on a revolution, in a word, dare to rebel. This is the basic principle of the party spirit! Not to rebel is one hundred per cent revisionist! Revolutionaries are Monkey Kings,* brandishing the big stick, applying supernatural power, destroying the 'old world,' 'turning heaven and earth upside down,' and 'throwing men and horses off their feet.'"

The working groups in middle schools couldn't tolerate the existence of such secret organizations. In China the only organizations to have recognized status were the Communist Party, the Communist League, the Young Pioneers, and a few democratic parties that had been accepted

*The Monkey King is a legendary character in a famous Chinese novel, who rebelled in heaven. He turned things to chaos with his magic iron rod, which could grow to any size he wanted. When not in use, he would shrink it to smaller than a needle and hide it behind his ear.

long ago by the party. How dare anybody set up another one! The Red
Guards were ordered to disband. To those who defied the order and
remained active, the working groups were merciless.

In our neighbouring school, the Twenty-Fifth, the working group had
convicted a handful of its Red Guards, all eighteen-year-olds or older, as
a "counter-revolution clique." I learned this when our working group
sent us out to exchange revolutionary information in July. I was shocked.
"What could they possibly have done to make themselves counter-
revolutionaries?" I asked myself. "They are so young! What will their
future be? Lucky for me I'm only fifteen! No matter what mistakes I
make, nobody can brand me a counter-revolutionary yet!"

In late July, when the anti-working-group movement in universities
won, the Red Guards popped up again and put out another comment on
the rebelling spirit. This time they quoted Mao Zedong's words: "The
thousands and thousands of reasoned parts of Marxism can be summarized in one phrase: It is right to rebel." They then pledged, "We, the
most faithful Red Guards of Chairman Mao, infinitely loyal to Chairman
Mao, will most resolutely, most bravely, most faithfully carry out the
supreme instructions concerning the Proletarian Cultural Revolution and
Chairman Mao's supreme instruction about rebelling!"

On August 1 Chairman Mao wrote a letter of support to the Red
Guards at MSQU, praising their revolutionary spirit and saying, "You
have shown it is right to rebel against reactionaries. I give you my warm
support." Proudly they made the letter into a big-character poster and put
it up on the campus.

One day in early August Yishu passed me handwritten copies of
Mao's letter and two Red Guard commentaries on the rebelling spirit. I
read these with interest and then asked her whether we had Red Guards
in our school. She shook her head and told me she didn't know. The following morning our loudspeaker, quiet since the departure of our
working group, came to life again: "Comrades, students, this is an
announcement from Red Guard headquarters. From today we are going
to establish the Red Guard organization in our school. Each class will
elect its own Red Guards. Qualifications include: (1) being faithful to and
loving Chairman Mao and the party, (2) being politically progressive, (3)
being active in the Cultural Revolution, (4) coming from a good family
background (workers, poor and lower-middle-class peasants, revolutionary cadres, army leaders, and revolutionary martyrs). The headquarters is
going to send an inspector to each class during its election. Wait for
further instructions regarding when elections should take place."

The school was again thrown into commotion. People exchanged questions like "What is this Red Guard organization?" "What will the relationship be between the Red Guards and the existing Communist League?" and "What will the Red Guards do once elected?" Nobody knew. But everybody believed it was good to be a Red Guard. Consider who were members at its headquarters: Yingqiu, Xubo, and other children of high-ranking officers or army leaders. Thus far they had been doing all right, stirring up the school and fighting the working group. Nothing could go wrong if one just followed them. Despite the unanswered questions, the entire school obeyed and prepared for elections.

The inspector the headquarters sent to our grade was Sutao, an amiable and soft-spoken girl. When she smiled, two deep dimples appeared on her cheeks. Throughout the election, she sat in a corner of our classroom and wrote non-stop in her notebook.

I presided over the election. First I let the students nominate candidates and give reasons for their choices. Jiuhong took the lead: "I nominate Zhai Zhenhua. She's from a good family, she's progressive, and she's strict with herself. Her political consciousness is high and her love for Chairman Mao, the party, and our socialist country is deep. As the leader of our small group, she acted very responsibly and never pushed hard jobs onto others. I also name Xiao Ping. She's also from a good family and also behaved well."

"I name Zhai Zhenhua, too. She is good at organizing the students."

"I think Zhai Zhenhua meets the conditions. She always leads in the discussion when we study party documents."

"I too agree that Zhai Zhenhua should be a Red Guard. But I have one wish: she should make herself more accessible to students and make more friends."

This way or that, many students mentioned me. At the same time, two other students, Xiao Ping and Wang Xiaonan, were also nominated. Ping had always been a student cadre in class. She was our Young Pioneer squadron leader and also the representative of the mathematics course. Her father was an associate minister of the transportation ministry. Xiaonan was only a Young Pioneer group leader, but her father worked in the logistics department of the army. Ping's and Xiaonan's fathers both ranked higher than mine. Somehow the last requirement the headquarters proposed had been narrowed in interpretation to children of revolutionary cadres or amy leaders. Perhaps the students took to heart the example given by the members of our headquarters.

When I was sure there were no more new candidates, I asked Xiaonan and Ping to say a few words. Xiaonan said nothing, but Ping said she would try to do well if elected. Then I made an earnest speech: "Thank you for your compliments and for nominating me. In the past I have not been as active as I should have been, and actually I have a long way to go to reach the level you say I have attained. If I should be elected as a Red Guard, I would do my best not to disappoint you. As to the criticism of my being inaccessible to some students, I sincerely accept it. I promise to change." In the end all three of us were elected. I got an almost unanimous vote.

One day later the loudspeakers formally announced the names of all the Red Guards and the leaders of the six detachments. I became a Red Guard and, unexpectedly, leader of the detachment in my grade. Only then did I realize why Sutao had come to us. She was helping the head-quarters to feel us out and pick leaders.

The next thing the headquarters did was to announce the establish-ment of a new Revolutionary Committee by election. A list of twelve candidates was passed out to the students for discussion. I was one of the twelve, which caused an uproar in my class. Most of my class-mates did not think I qualified at all for such an important post. "She was completely lost in the beginning of the Cultural Revolution! How can she possibly lead the revolution in our school?" I heard one of them indignantly telling an investigator who had come from another class to gather information about the candidates. The investi-gator was to bring this message back to her own class, and so would other such investigators.

My happiness at becoming a Red Guard disappeared. My foolishness from the time Yingqiu put up her poster until the working group entered our school was a secret pain in my heart. Now my angry classmates had dug it out and broadcast it to the whole world. How could I face anybody again?

I didn't want to become a Revolutionary Committee member. I was not politically creative, nor did I have a father who lived in Zhongnanhai and knew the latest trends and could steer me accordingly. I had known nothing about the revolution when it started, and I knew little about it now. What could I do on the committee? Sit mute and just listen?

Despite my fears and despite the resistance my classmates put up and their propaganda against me, I was elected. My vote was considerably less than that of the winning seniors, but the candidate from the lower grade received even fewer votes.

The committee was never active; I don't remember attending one important meeting. The Red Guard headquarters monopolized everything. My other position, leader of our detachment for my grade, wasn't as great as it sounded either. It didn't make me a policy maker or member of headquarters. In many ways I was just a common Red Guard, except that I felt more heavily weighed down by two titles.

What did make me nervous were the Red Guard meetings our headquarters held. At these, instead of explaining what was happening in the revolution, Yingqiu liked to pose difficult questions and discuss the situation with us. The meetings took on the air of an examination. I was happy to sit in the same room with Yingqiu, my heroine, but I was frightened to hear her questions and be unable to answer them.

Once she asked, "What is the relationship of the Red Guards and the Revolutionary Committee?" For a long time the room was silent as all of us Red Guards thought hard. About seventy of us sat around a huge rectangular table, with Yingqiu in the centre. From one side to the other she looked us over. When her eyes moved towards me I lowered my head. "Nobody has even made it clear to me what the Red Guards are for yet," I thought muddle-headedly. My only hope was that some senior would speak out and save us all.

Finally Danan, from the second class of my grade, raised her hand. She was a robust fatty, with a round red face and big eyes. Her father was a high-ranking cadre in the Propaganda Ministry of the Chinese Communist Party. "The relationship of the Red Guard and the Revolutionary Committee is like that of the Communist Party and the Chinese government. The party leads the government; The Red Guard leads the Revolutionary Committee," she said with assurance.

Shit! Why didn't I think of that? And why couldn't the answer have come from a senior, instead of someone from my own grade? The Revolutionary Committee member and leader of the detachment of my grade didn't know anything!

Because of lack of evidence, the working group at my school hadn't labelled the school administrators members of a black gang. Once the Red Guards came to power, however, their status suddenly became more precarious. A special group was established to investigate their "crimes," and with approval from above, our president and a few others were put into custody in school.

Many student governments tried to convict the former leaders of their schools. The idea behind this was that the worse the leaders could be shown to be, the better the student governments were at fulfilling their revolutionary duties.

Never having had a chance to see the president before, a few Red Guards and I went to where the leaders were being held. Other visitors weren't allowed. When we entered the big room where the library catalogue was normally kept, we saw two elderly women standing in the centre of the room, butting heads. I couldn't tell if they were butting hard, but their heads did collide. Someone pointed at the fatter one, who looked to be in her fifties, and told me that she was the president. Her head had been shaved.

Behind the two women stood about a dozen Red Guards, some on the floor, some on chairs, and some on tables. They waved their arms in the air and shouted, "Come on! Come on! Harder! Harder!" as if they were the directors of a children's sporting contest. Later the president and her partner did work harder. Like penguins they sluggishly waggled their bodies and stretched their arms out to keep their balance. To add to the "fun," one of the onlookers took a Chinese brush soaked with ink and smeared the president's bald head. Perhaps the sensation of the brush on her bald head tickled her; for some reason she grinned.

That was the first time I saw corporal punishment in the revolution. I didn't make a fuss. This was a revolution. As Chairman Mao had said, "A revolution is not a dinner party, not writing an article, or painting or embroidery. It cannot be that exquisite, that calm and unhurried, that urbane, that gentle, fine, respectful, that thrifty and yielding. A revolution is an insurrection, an act of violence by which one class overthrows another." There was bound to be some violence, but I felt uneasy nonetheless. What would they do next? Would they beat the president? I wasn't ready for that yet. Nudging my companions, I whispered, "Let's go!" and led the way out.

BEDEVILLING DEVILS

For THOUSANDS OF YEARS LINEAGE HAS BEEN BASIC IN Chinese society. In old China children of the rich looked down on those of the poor, but after Liberation things turned topsy-turvy. The children of workers, poor peasants, and revolutionaries now had a strong sense of superiority. This was especially so in the children of high-ranking army leaders and cadres. They tended to take their parents' exploits as their own, and were proud to be more "in the know" politically. During the Cultural Revolution their political talents came to full display. They led the way in opposing the school leaders and later the working groups, and both actions were given the party's blessing. Compared with them, what did others know? Their sense of superiority suddenly flared into arrogance. They appropriated an old saying, "Dragons bear dragons, phoenixes phoenixes, and moles sons accomplished in digging holes," made it their *duilian*, and gave it the name "Bedevilling Devils."

A *duilian* is a three-line stanza often posted on a door-frame. It includes two vertical lines of rhymed poetry, side by side, and a short horizontal line on top. These two lines comprise an antithetical couplet whose words are in some way opposite to each other, such as "He must expand and increase" and "I must shrink and decrease." The horizontal line somehow serves to summarize the couplet. In the past, *duilian* were very popular in China. Even today one often sees them in rural areas.

On July 29 a *duilian* appeared on the campus of the Middle School Attached to the Aeronautical Engineering Institute in Beijing (MSAAEIB), where there was a concentration of students from high-ranking cadre families. The two verticals read, "The old man a trueman, the son is a hero" and "The old man a reactionary, the son is an asshole." The horizontal read, "It is basically so."

Opposition to this *duilian* arose the minute it surfaced. Stormy wars of words took place, but the originators obstinately stuck to their views. On August 1 they went to several major universities in Beijing and pasted the *duilian* in prominent places. Wherever it appeared, noisy controversy followed.

The *duilian* and the debates about it came to my school just after the Red Guard election. I was again confused. "What has this *duilian* to do with the Cultural Revolution?" I wondered. "Heroes or assholes, how could they be connected with the revisionists or black gangs? Why should anyone propose such a *duilian*? Why do people go crazy over it?" And I felt more frustrated. "Why can I never keep pace with this revolution? Every time I barely catch up something else crops up and throws me back in the dark."

Yet I knew I couldn't afford to show my ignorance a second time. Failing to catch the significance of Yingqiu's poster had done me enough damage. I hid my qualms and tried to predict which way the cat was about to jump. Some Red Guards were on the pro-side of the *duilian*, and our headquarters probably was too; otherwise, during the election it would not have required all Red Guards to be from "good families." Such specifics about family background had never been a formal concern in student elections in the past. I quickly made up my mind and joined those shouting support below the stage. Listening to the arguments, I some-times vaguely realized that the speakers on our side weren't very cogent. But it didn't seem to bother them, so I tried not to let it bother me.

"The *duilian* is right! Take our school. Yingqiu is from a good family and she's the most revolutionary. Do any of you know someone from a bad family who has done so well in this revolution?"

"What you said is right. Yingqiu is in the vanguard of revolution in our school. I agree: family plays an important role in forming one's political views. But society, schools, and the media also have an influence. In fact, it can be so great as to make a person betray his family. We all know that many famous revolutionaries came from exploiting families. Our beloved Premier Zhou for one. How do you explain this?"

"How dare you use Premier Zhou to bolster your position! Don't smear Premier Zhou!"

"All right, forget Premier Zhou. Let's talk about a person, a Red Guard for example, whose father is a revolutionary cadre today. What if the father gets convicted as one of a black gang tomorrow? What would this Red Guard become? Would he be changed from a hero to an asshole overnight?"

"What are you talking about?" The supporter almost lost control. She couldn't answer immediately, and when she did speak again she evaded the question: "It depends on the person, her father, the situation! We can't comment without a concrete case!" Indeed, they didn't want to worry themselves with subtleties like that. It was still early in the revolution. Not too many cadres had yet been labelled "capitalist roaders," those who walk the capitalist road. And so long as *they* were on the side of the angels, why should they care?

"Chairman Mao teaches us: unite all that can be united. This couplet hurts people and pushes them apart!"

"Our revolution doesn't need assholes. If they don't behave themselves, they will become the target of our revolution! Anyway, why are you fighting this couplet so hard? Are you an asshole?"

"You don't have to attack me personally. That won't help you get me on your side. I believe nobody is born red and nobody born black. . . ."

Before she finished, another supporter appeared beside her and yelled: "We are *born red*! The red comes with us from our mothers' wombs. And I say right here you are born black! What can you do about us?" They were no longer debating, they were acting shamelessly. But nobody could stop them. With each passing day the supporters became more pugnacious and the opposition more timid.

Taking inspiration from the *duilian*, some Red Guards wrote and composed a song:

> *The old man a true man, the son is a hero,*
> *The old man a reactionary, the son is an asshole.*
> *If you are revolutionary, then step forward and come along,*
> *If you are not, damn you to hell.*
>
> *Be faithful to the revolution and the party,*
> *The party is our mother and father.*
> *Whoever dares say one bad word about the party,*
> *We'll send him to Yama* immediately.*
>
> *Damn you to hell!*
> *Depose you from your fucking post!*
> *Kill! Kill! Kill!*

The tune of this song was anything but melodious, and its words far from beautiful. Nevertheless, it soon became the Red Guard anthem. All the Red Guards in my school learned it, and I did too.

*The King of Hell

The first few times I sang the anthem, I didn't sing it loudly. Manners had not been emphasized much before the revolution, but my generation was not completely uncouth. But I soon grew accustomed to the dirty words. Together with other Red Guards, I sang it marching on the streets, riding in trucks, and at every available opportunity.

CHAIRMAN MAO RECEIVES
THE RED GUARDS

ON THE AFTERNOON OF AUGUST 17 OUR HEADQUARTERS instructed all students to arrive at school by five the next morning. It was not revealed why, but the headquarters did promise a very important event. Buses didn't run before five. If I had gone home for the night I wouldn't have been able to get to school before a quarter to six, so I stayed. Like other students who couldn't go home, I made myself a bed on a table in one of the classrooms.

Night came but nobody went to bed. We all wondered excitedly what tomorrow's "very important event" could be. Several times I visited headquarters, formerly the school leaders' office, hoping to find out more. On my last trip I met Yibing, one of Yingqiu's pals. "So you are Zhai Zhanhua!" She measured me up and down, head tilted. Yibing had a short bob slightly below her ears, with one handful of hair tied on the top at the right rear. She took an instant liking to me. "Come with me; we'll have some fun," she said, putting her arm around my shoulder, and took me to their quarters.

There I met Xiaomin, Sutao, Yalin, and others, all prominent figures in the Red Guard. On the table stood a basket full of crunchy Chinese pears. "Help yourself," someone said. We ate, chatted, made jokes, and laughed heartily. Nobody seemed to care about tomorrow's big event. The revolution was forgotten, life was joyous and peaceful.

Suddenly one of them noticed my clothes. By then the Red Guards had started to wear army uniforms. "Don't you have an army uniform?" she asked. I shook my head. My father didn't work in the army, so I couldn't get one. Literally, "Red Guard" is "Red Defending Soldier" in Chinese, and a soldier must have a uniform. "Wait a second," Yibing said. She thought for a moment, then hurried out of the room. Ten minutes later she came back with a full uniform, except for shoes. I tried it on. It was beautiful. The colour was the most fashionable green and the style was elegant, with a pleated waist. It fitted me so well that it looked as if it had been specially made for me. After I buckled the belt and put on the hat, I clicked my heels together and saluted, feeling like a real soldier. "Gee! It looks good on you!" Yibing exclaimed. I was ecstatic. From then on I wore the uniform day in and day out.

Chairman Mao's decision to receive the Red Guards in Tiananmen Square was made on August 17. The CPGLCR immediately began to arrange the Great Assembly to Celebrate the Cultural Revolution for the next day. Starting at one o'clock in the morning, one million people were led into Tiananmen Square. At five o'clock Mao Zedong, in an army uniform, came down from the Tiananmen rostrum, crossed one of the Golden Water Bridges over the moat that surrounds the Forbidden City, and walked among the masses shaking hands.

Several minutes after five the crowds in Tiananmen Square learned that Chairman Mao was walking among them and started to seethe with excitement. At the same time we were lining up in the yard in front of our Red Guard headquarters. Orders were given for all Red Guards and students from good families to step out from each class to form a team. What this was all about still hadn't been revealed, but it was clear that whatever awaited us would be wonderful. Those left out were envious.

My classmate, Guomei, the daughter of the famous painter A Lao, approached me. "I'm also from a revolutionary family. My father has rank fourteen. Can't I please get on the team?" she asked anxiously. Aha! I thought she never wanted to talk about her father with us! None of the Red Guards in my class knew that A Lao was a revolutionary cadre as well as a painter. Since all artists were deemed suspect during the Cultural Revolution, we didn't count her as coming from a good family. Now that I had learned her father was of rank fourteen, the highest in the middle level, I thought it best to reconsider. "Let me go and ask at headquarters. I'll meet you back at the class," I told her.

Yingqiu was standing on the steps leading to the patio in front of the headquarters' office. I walked up to her and said, "A student in my class, whose father is A Lao, wants to join us. She said her father's rank is fourteen. Should we let her?" Without hesitation Yingqiu said, "Who does A Lao think he is?" Her voice was cold and her nose turned up. I knew there was no room for argument. I went back to tell Guomei the bad news. "Sorry, it's orders," I reported, but I wasn't really sorry for her. By then the *duilian* had already begun to take root in me. My sympathy towards students from non-revolutionary families was rapidly disappearing.

Fifteen minutes later, after overcoming this and that difficulty, the selection was completed. When the contingent was ready to go, the rest of the students were told to return to their classrooms to study Chairman Mao. The loudspeaker in school would keep them posted. Later they heard a live radio relay of the Great Assembly.

On the way to Tiananmen we kept in step and sang revolutionary songs eulogizing Chairman Mao and the party. One of them was a peasants' song we called "The Heavens Are Great, the Earth Is Great."

The heavens are great, the Earth is great,
The party's kindness is greater still;
Father is dear, Mother is dear,
Chairman Mao is dearer still;
A thousand goods, ten thousand goods,
The socialist system is better still;
The river is deep, the ocean is deep,
The feelings of class brotherhood are deeper still.

Mao Zedong's thought is our revolutionary treasure;
He will be our enemy who dares oppose it.

We also sang our crude Red Guard anthem several times. The girl who started the song set it in such a low key that at times we couldn't continue singing. She must have been trying to make our team of teenage girls sound like Amazons.

Before six o'clock we arrived at the foot of the Tiananmen rostrum. One of the organizers took us and led us to our places on the east stand, one of the two where national representatives review the National Day parade. When I had marched in last October's parade, little did I dream I would be on the reviewing stand this August!

The real thrill was still to come. At eight o'clock one of the Red Guard leaders took out a list and called the names of twenty students who were to step forward. Most were senior Red Guards; I was the only one in my grade. We were issued five-inch-wide red silk armbands to replace our crude three-inch cotton ones. With no explanation, we were led off towards the central Tiananmen rostrum.

Flanked by two armed soldiers, a small side door in the wall of the east arched entrance to the rostrum opened when we arrived. I had at times been in the Forbidden City, but I had never noticed this door. We ascended a long stairway and on the side of the stairs at the end stood

Premier Zhou Enlai to greet us on behalf of Chairman Mao! He shook hands with each passing Red Guard and said, "Welcome! Welcome!" As he talked, he gestured vigorously and laughed. When it was my turn, he held my hand in his while his eyes, bright and kind, looked directly into mine. Somehow I felt he was waiting for me to tell him something, but I couldn't find anything suitable to say. I was ecstatic just to see him up close and shake his hand. After standing before him a second or two, I moved on.

Passing the stairs and turning right, we entered a big patio which was several thousand feet square. We were shepherded through it and then through the central hall, where Chairman Mao and the other leaders took rests when reviewing parades, and finally reached the west side. There were already hundreds of Red Guards from different schools clustering in groups. Only now did I realize we might have the biggest honour — seeing Chairman Mao in person. One of my heroes, Liu Hulan, died a heroic death at the age of fifteen, now at fifteen *I* was going to see Chairman Mao! Not as glorious, but not bad either. I was proud.

It was still early. We were allowed to move around on condition we would return quickly when called. Of the twenty Red Guards from my school, I couldn't find a single familiar face. None of Yingqiu's group had come with us. They were true leaders to cede such a chance to others. To pass some time I walked around the patio, but except for the brick floor, there wasn't much to see. In the end I went to the parapet facing Tiananmen Square and looked over it.

The horizontal scrolls of Beijing and Qinghua universities, the earliest to become involved in the Cultural Revolution, were at the right front of the square. The Beijing University group even held a model of the first revolutionary big-character poster to indicate its special status. Looking farther, I saw the vast square of forty acres filled with colourful banners, streamers, scrolls, balloons, and masses and masses of people. How grand and magnificent all this was when viewed from the rostrum! The organizers, whoever they were, did a good job to please Chairman Mao's eyes.

When the meeting had started and how a million Red Guards would parade through Tiananmen Square didn't concern us. We could read everything in tomorrow's newspapers. What filled our minds was whether Chairman Mao would receive us. If he was too tired, he might well send someone else to represent him. At ten o'clock we were called to gather into two lines, each with four rows, on the two sides of a pathway leading to an entrance at the back of the patio. There, ten minutes later, Chairman Mao and a group of leaders walked towards us.

I was standing in the second row, fairly close to the entrance, so I saw them clearly. Naturally my eyes were on Chairman Mao. Much had been written in the newspapers about Chairman Mao's great health and his "ruddy-coloured face," so when I actually saw him in person I was a little disappointed. He looked older than I had imagined and more than half his hair was white. His face showed the marks of old age and did not glow either, as it was supposed to. His movements were sluggish. He was a senile old man. I then shifted my eyes to the other leaders, all of whom were smiling, but I could only recognize a few. Lin Biao was there, waving his "precious red book" as usual. He was a small, thin, weak man, his face as white as paper.

From the entrance Mao and his retinue walked slowly between our lines, waving to us and turning to increase their exposure. Suddenly I saw a Red Guard shake hands with a leader. With my left hand holding the precious red book, which by then we carried everywhere, I stretched out my right to fish for whatever I could get. By chance I grabbed the small hand of Comrade Jiang Qing! We were told not to shake hands with Comrade Jiang Qing, since her health was not good, but I wasn't about to lose the opportunity. I mercilessly held her soft hand in mine as long as I could, all the while trying to catch her eye. But she did not look at me. She leaned her head back and smiled shyly like a young girl, as if uncomfortable with the attention.

After the handshaking started, the lines collapsed. The Red Guards at the outside pushed forward with their hands out, hoping to reach the leaders, while the eager ones at the ends also closed in. Before Chairman Mao and his party reached the centre of the patio, they were mobbed by young people and couldn't move. Seeing this, the security guards pushed through and led the leaders away. The whole event lasted no more than five minutes.

The Red Guards who did not get a chance to see Chairman Mao close up were disappointed. The representatives of CPGLCR proposed that if the Red Guards promised to maintain order, they would try to persuade Chairman Mao to come out again. The Red Guards promised, and this time we were formed into a square of four lines on a side. The inside two lines sat down on the ground and promised to stay seated even if the sky fell. Absolutely no handshaking! When all was ready, the representatives went to invite Chairman Mao out again, while the rest prayed he would agree.

At 10:40 Mao and his party came onto the patio for a second time. I sat in the second line, waved my little red book and chanted, "Long live Chairman Mao!" But the excitement I felt was not as strong as earlier. I tried to cry, but couldn't. I did love Chairman Mao, but I couldn't make myself cry over seeing him. Reporters circled around, and photographers' cameras flashed frequently. Mao's second visit was more orderly, but less fun.

Mao spent more than ten minutes with us and made two leisurely rounds inside our square. Then he went to the parapet where I had been standing a little earlier. To give him prominence, the other leaders stayed at his back, away from the parapet. Mao took his hat in his right hand and waved at the masses in the square. Once his hand stopped high on the right, a pose we saw in movies and newspapers from that time on. Muffled exclamations reached us from the square below. Then one of Mao's guards went up to take him away. The two of them walked unhurriedly towards the front centre of the rostrum, the rest following behind.

On my way home after the reception people on the street and buses recognized me as a Red Guard from my armband and uniform. They greeted me with a smile, calling "Red Guards" — one even raised his thumb. In high spirits I walked into the big compound where my family lived. But the yard was empty. There were no neighbours to see my triumphant homecoming as one of the first Red Guards. I had dashed home to share my joy, only to find no one. It was early afternoon, and the members of my family were busy in their own revolutionary units.

In my family, for a long, long time, we did not share our thoughts in a meaningful way. I told my parents little about what took place in school and almost never sought their advice in the confusion of the Cultural Revolution. We really did not see each other that often. Besides, what did they know about my school? Why should I worry them with my frustrations? It seemed to be the same for them, and I did not learn how the revolution touched them until years later. However, when a spectacularly good thing like being received by Chairman Mao happened to me, I wanted them to know all about it.

The next day the *People's Daily* reported the event in full, omitting only the chaos of Mao's first visit to us on the rostrum. We read that during the reception a Red Guard named Song Binbin asked the CPGLCR whether she could present Mao with a red armband printed in his own calligraphy with the words "Red Guard." She was said to be the daughter of a famous leader. The CPGLCR granted her wish and arranged for her to come to Mao.

"What's your name?" Mao had asked, while letting her put the armband on his left arm.

"Song Binbin," she answered.

"Is it the 'bin' that means suave?"

"Yes."

He smiled and said, "You should be martial."

Binbin was known as Yaowu (Be Martial) from then on, and by accepting the Red Guard armband Mao tacitly accepted the title of Red Guard General.

Mao's short conversation with Binbin made many Red Guards, including me, ask themselves what he meant. Did he think that the Red Guards were too refined, despite the hints of savagery they had already displayed? The Chinese newspapers and the party's instructions didn't make a practice of spelling things out clearly, so we had learned to guess what lay unsaid behind the words.

When I showed up outside my classroom again after the reception, a group of my classmates rushed out to meet me and asked eagerly about the details of my experience. What did the rostrum look like? Who did I see? Did I see Chairman Mao clearly? They wanted to know everything. So I sat down on the edge of the patio outside our classroom and held court. I described how I had shaken hands with Premier Zhou and Comrade Jiang Qing and how near I had been to Chairman Mao, but I didn't mention how old Mao looked. As we sat there and talked, I felt I had almost regained the affection I had lost after becoming the Revolutionary Committee member. I had valued that affection before, but now it didn't matter very much. Why should I want to be liked by "assholes"?

For days after August 18 the *People's Daily* printed photographs of Chairman Mao and the Red Guards at the so-called 8/18 Reception. Some of our twenty Red Guards spotted photos of themselves and Chairman Mao. They went to the New China Agency and came back with free reprints. I also went, but I could only find one photograph in which I appeared clearly. I was sitting on the ground and waving the precious red book at Mao and his party. My expression was sour. It must have been the result of trying to cry. At the corner of my mouth there was a black scab from a cold sore. I looked disgusting, so I decided not to ask for a copy. It seemed easy enough to get to see Chairman Mao. In my fifteen years I had already seen him once. Later I might get another chance, or even more, to see him again.

Indeed I did see him again. It was more than a decade later when he lay in the crystal coffin in his memorial hall, no longer able to receive or fight anybody.

Despite my opinion of it, the photograph appeared in the *People's Daily* on August 23. That evening, while glancing through the paper at home, I saw it right away. "Look! That's me," I called out to my family. "How stupid and ugly I look!" They all came over. Some thought it looked like me, some didn't. "No matter; it's your history. Keep it as an sovenir," my mother advised. Obediently, I cut out that page and put it away.

DESTROYING THE OLD FOUR
AND RAIDING HOMES

THE 8/18 RECEPTION GAVE THE RED GUARDS THE IMPETUS to continue the Cultural Revolution, which had reached a low point in schools. Writing big-character posters had become a bore, but besides that there didn't seem to be anything else we could do. At the meeting of the 8/18 Reception, Lin Biao, in the name of the party, called on the Red Guards "resolutely to destroy old ideas, old culture, old customs, and old habits of the exploiting class." These came to be known as "the old four." He appealed to people all over the country to support the "rebellious proletarian revolutionary spirit of the Red Guards who dare to charge, dare to do, and dare to rebel." According to Mao's strategy, this was the time to enlarge the battlefield of the Cultural Revolution from art and education to the entire society. Thus the Destroy the Old Four campaign started.

We all poured out of school to put big-character posters on walls throughout the city. We stood at busy intersections reading Chairman Mao's quotations and party documents about the Cultural Revolution through a megaphone. Others found more innovative ways to destroy the old four. They rushed into stores, tore off the traditional lanterns and old paintings, and put up Chairman Mao's portraits or quotations instead. They covered every poster on the streets with Chairman Mao's quotations or slogans in red ink to create a "red sea." They changed the names of schools, restaurants, and streets to reflect the revolutionary spirit. The Middle School Attached to Qinghua University was renamed the Red Guard Fighting School, Chang'an Street became Red in the East Street, Dongjiaomingxiang, where many western embassies were located, became Anti-Imperialist Street, and Xijiaomingxiang, where the Soviet Embassy was, became Anti-Revisionist Street. Some people even started to change their names to Red Rock, Defending the East, Continuing the Red, Forever Revolutionary, and so on.

Dress also changed. For the next ten years the Chinese wore monotonous dark clothing. The leaders in this were the Red Guards in the Second

Middle School, who put up a big-character poster in the centre of Beijing proposing that hair stylists not cut hair in the Hong Kong style, that dressmakers not make dresses in the Hong Kong style, that photographers not take obscene photographs, and that booksellers not sell erotic books. For existing clothes their suggestion was, "Narrow-legged pants can be cut into shorts, and the left-over fabric used as patches; 'rocket'-shaped shoes can be cut at the top to become sandals; high-heeled shoes can be changed to no-heeled ones."

Some Red Guards acted immediately. They stood on streets and stopped passersby to cut their narrow-legged pants and destroy their sharp-toed or high-heeled shoes. Girls' long braids were deemed feudal remnants and cut by force. Before Liberation women in China were not allowed to cut their hair short; now the Red Guards didn't allow them to wear it long.

I never cut anybody's pants or braids. Our headquarters hadn't instructed us to do so, and I myself thought it silly and embarrassing. But I did worry about how I could contribute more to destroying the old four to repay Chairman Mao's trust in me. Then the home raids started.

A few days after the 8/18 Reception the Public Security Minister, Xie Fuzhi, said at a meeting that earlier rules — meaning the existing laws of the People's Republic — should not be binding. Although he didn't support beating people to death, he suggested that the police not use force to stop revolutionaries from beating bad people. "Police should stand with the Red Guards," he also said, "establish connections with them, foster mutual feelings, supply them with information, and let them know who the members of the 'five categories' are and how they are behaving." The five categories Xie mentioned were landlord, upper-class peasant, counter-revolutionary, bad element, and rightist.

Xie's speech was immediately relayed to the police, who then contacted the Red Guard leaders and supplied them with information about who in their district were in the five categories and how they were behaving. The Red Guards quickly grasped the point: the five categories were "dregs from the old society" and the embodiment of the old four. And the old four were to be destroyed.

Early one morning in late August I was told to go with five other Red Guards to search a "five-category" home. At 8:30 in the morning we arrived by bus at a huge compound with several courtyards and many households. Our leader, who was from the senior school, had a piece of paper giving the name and address of the object of our foray, but when we inquired as to his whereabouts, nobody seemed to know who he was. Meanwhile, many children and even adults came out of their homes to watch these young people in their army uniforms and red armbands. Ignoring their stares, we walked deeper and deeper into the complex and kept asking about the man, until a woman in the neighbourhood committee came forward. She led us to the entrance of a dark passage, asked us to wait, and went in to get our man.

He was a stout yet fit-looking man in his early fifties. His face was full, round, and glowing with health, with little wrinkles and no beard. Although he was in a short-sleeve shirt and a normal pair of pants, he reminded me of the landlords we had seen in movies, who wore long satin gowns and old-fashioned skullcaps. Our unsolicited visit seemed to unsettle him. As he approached, I saw fine beads of sweat on his shining scalp, although it wasn't hot that late summer morning. To avoid the eyes of his neighbours, he took us through the long, dark passage to his door before asking what we wanted.

"We come to search your home. You are under suspicion of engaging in conspiratorial activities!" our leader told him.

"I'm not guilty of anything. Why should you say that? What evidence do you have against me?" he responded, but his tone was neither bold nor convincing.

"We don't have enough evidence yet. That is why we've come to search your place."

"You're not the police! By what law do you come and search my place just like that?"

For a moment we were stumped. Indeed, we had no official papers or warrant. But we were sent here by our headquarters, and they must have received orders from above. Suddenly I had a brainwave: "If you have nothing to hide, why are you afraid to let us in?"

Another Red Guard added: "Chairman Mao and the party centre called on everybody to support the Red Guards and their revolutionary actions. Why aren't you supporting us?"

He didn't answer, but neither did he let us enter. In the gloomy corridor we stood in a deadlock for a long time. We didn't press too hard because we weren't very sure of the legality of what we were doing. Yet we didn't want to come all the way here and be rebuffed so easily. So we waited, and watched the agitated man walking up and down before his door. He must have been thinking hard: What would I lose if I do let them in? What will the consequences be if I don't and offend the Red Guards, whose star is in ascendance now? In the end he made a clever choice: he opened the door for us and then disappeared. We guessed he went to ask the local police for help.

"Fine. If he brings the police back and they tell us to stop, we'll stop," I thought. We divided into two groups to rummage through his two rooms. He had some antique dark wood furniture and six heavy wooden trunks stacked in two piles. We looked under the chairs, the tables, the beds, and opened all the drawers and trunks except two locked ones. One hour later he came back alone, and his attitude had improved. He was less hostile to us, and when we asked him to unlock the two trunks he did so right away. Had he been instructed to cooperate?

Our persistence paid off. At the bottom of one trunk we found an official certificate of appointment by the Kuomintang government; in another, four hundred yuan hidden inside a sock and a lot of satin, which may have been very good quality, but we didn't know about those things then.

The certificate was certainly evidence of counter-revolutionary thought. There were many stories about how landlords kept restoration records. They were preparing for the return of the Kuomintang so that they could take back their property and land from the poor peasants. This man was also dreaming that the Kuomintang would recover China. He could then show his certificate, tell the reactionaries how faithful he was, and get his good job back. As for the four hundred yuan, since he couldn't explain how he got it, we concluded it must be dirty money he made illegally. Triumphantly, we headed back to school and handed the certificate and the money over to our headquarters.

Our task was complete. How the headquarters dealt with the booty we didn't know, nor did we know how our victims were later treated by the government. I learned afterwards that many were exiled from Beijing to the countryside where they had been born.

We were a lot bolder when we invaded a painter's home. We strutted into his tastefully furnished residence and loudly exclaimed, "Today is the day we search your home!" He was a handsome and dignified man, about forty-five. His face was clean-shaven, with thick eyebrows, and sparkling eyes. Dark-framed eyeglasses on his straight nose gave him a refined, well-educated mien. Unperturbed, he told us to go ahead. We quickly scattered to rummage through his possessions, but didn't find anything of importance. He must have heard about home raids and prepared himself, we thought.

"Where have you hidden your stuff? At your relatives' or friends'?"

"I didn't hide anything; this is all I have," he said blandly.

"Nonsense! You must have counter-revolutionary writings or paintings. We advise you to hand over all your certificates from the Kuomintang, your weapons, or other evil belongings. Otherwise you'll face the consequences!"

"I don't have any counter-revolutionary material. I'm not a reactionary. Had I been one, I would have fled the country to Taiwan, Hong Kong, or America before 1949, like most rich people."

"Who believes you?! How could a man like you like the Communist Party and the people's government? How could you be happy when your property is forfeited to the people's government? It is only natural for you to fight to get it back. That's what we believe. Besides, our source suspects you are against our socialist country!"

"Your source could be wrong, couldn't it?" He shrugged his shoulders.

"Are you attacking our source? Do you take us Red Guards for simpletons who can't tell who's right and who's wrong? We can see you're not afraid of us. You look down on us because we're young. We must teach you a lesson for underestimating us!"

We put our heads together to discuss what to do. I remembered how the Red Guards in my school had shaved and painted the president's head and suggested that we do the same to the artist. The others couldn't think of anything better, so they agreed. He had a thick, black head of hair. I found two scissors and gave one to another Red Guard, and the two of us stood on stools to cut his hair. We were impatient and not interested in doing a good job, so we left tufts and scratches here and there. When his scalp showed clearly, two other Red Guards took brushes soaked in some black ink the painter had and painted his head and face. Having transformed this dignified man into a clown, we were satisfied. We then ordered him to butt his head against the wall and went to make a more thorough search.

The maltreatment of the painter was our first act of violence in our home raids. In comparison with the treatment meted out by others, though, our methods were neither creative nor terribly cruel. On August 23 a group of Beijing Red Guards burnt a pile of things they had confiscated. While it was burning they caught about thirty famous writers and artists, hung signs saying Member of the Black Gang, Reactionary Academic Authority, and Cow Devil and Serpent Spirit around their necks, forced them to kneel down, and beat them with belts and other items destined for the fire. The famous writer Lao She, who wrote *The Tea House* as well as many other popular stories, was beaten so badly that he collapsed in a faint on the ground. The following night he jumped into Superior Peace Lake and ended his life.

Three days later Xie Fuzhi's speech about the five categories was relayed to the public security system in Daxing County in a rural suburb of Beijing. The police immediately provided the Red Guards with information about members of the first four of the five categories: landlords, upper-class peasants, counter-revolutionaries, and bad elements. To further inflame the Red Guards, the police explained how "lawless" some of these people were. The next day the Red Guards put the "badly behaved" ones to trial and torture. They wanted their victims to produce their "restoration records" and confess their "crimes." When they couldn't get what they wanted, they beat them to death and transferred their anger to the families of the dead and to the others that remained. From September 1–27, in the thirteen communes of Daxing County, 325 such "criminals" and their relatives were killed. The oldest was eighty and the youngest thirty-eight days. Twenty-two families were entirely exterminated.

Towards the end of August beating people became a popular Red Guard tactic in Beijing. When I first saw a Red Guard remove her canvas belt to beat her victim and saw his clothes tear and blood appear on his skin, I was afraid. I was not the most bloodthirsty person in the world; I was even afraid to watch wars or fighting in movies. However, I was a Red Guard leader and a member of my school's Revolutionary Committee. In this Great Proletarian Cultural Revolution not only had I not been among those who led, I always seemed to fall behind. I felt unworthy. If by beating these people from the five categories I could prove my political consciousness and my valour in the class struggle, I would do it. Thus, when that Red Guard left off, I removed my belt and learned to beat like her.

In the beginning I dared not look at the person under my feet. I had to stiffen myself mentally to continue. I kept thinking, "These are class enemies, bad people. Before Liberation they lived a decadent life, sucking the blood of the working people and treating our revolutionary martyrs brutally. Even today, to regain their lost wealth and status, they seek the return of the evil old society. They're only getting what they deserve. I shouldn't feel sorry for them. In class struggle, either you die or I do."

For people to change for the better is not easy, but for them to change for the worse is not hard. There is an evil, barbaric side in every person. Under normal circumstances it remains dormant, but in the proper environment it will wake up and dominate, as it did in my case. After a few beatings, I no longer needed to rehearse the rationale behind them. My heart hardened and I became used to the blood. I waved my belt like an automaton and whipped with an empty mind. Once I was out of their homes, I wiped off the buckle of my belt and fastened it outside my army jacket again as if nothing had happened. The Cultural Revolution had transformed me into a devil.

Of all the home raids in which I participated, I was in charge just once. That afternoon before leaving school the headquarters passed me a piece of paper that told me everything I needed to know. It included my victim's name (Xiuying), her age (late forties), and her status. She had no job at the time, but before Liberation she had been a landlord in the countryside. The paper said she didn't love Chairman Mao and the party, didn't support socialism, was insolent to revolutionary masses, didn't reform herself well, and so on. My team was composed of two Red Guards from the first grade of senior middle school, one from my grade, and five from the first grade of junior middle school. So off I went, fifteen years old, to lead a group of girls, thirteen to seventeen years, to invade the home of a former countryside landlord.

I had high hopes for this mission. Let me at least find something like a Kuomintang certificate! But fate wasn't with me. We searched high and low, everywhere except under the bricks on the floor, but we didn't find money or anything worthwhile, let alone a gun or counter-revolutionary leaflet. And the woman was arrogant! She wouldn't even talk to us or answer our questions. I was annoyed. Everything about her — her loose, large body, her flaccid face, and her fishy eyes — was hateful. "You don't want to talk with us? All the better, save me some saliva. Beat her!" I ordered my soldiers.

As soon as they started to strap her with their belts, she slid down onto the floor with her back against the wall and from then on hardly moved. Her eyes never looked up. Before we left, we grabbed some of her belongings at random to turn over to our headquarters.

The next morning, as I walked towards the headquarters' office, Xiaoli, a Red Guard from the third grade of junior school, was leaving. We exchanged hellos as we passed each other. After a few steps, she suddenly stopped, turned, and asked me, "Did you raid Xiuying's home yesterday?"

"Yes, I was in charge."

"She's dead," Xiaoli said casually.

"Dead?" I repeated.

She nodded several times and went on her way.

My heart jumped. Dead? She was alive yesterday when we left. Or was she? It wasn't our habit to check whether our victims were dead or alive when we left them. But I didn't mean to kill her! I didn't! Although I had no problem beating people hard to make them suffer, I never wanted to kill anybody and I never beat people on their heads. Perhaps Xiuying committed suicide after we left or had a heart attack during our beating. No! It was impossible. Why should she die on the only home raid I was in charge of? Xiaoli must have made a mistake. Or maybe she was kidding with me. I wanted to go after her to find out, but I didn't have the courage. It was too frightening. I wasn't about to ask the headquarters either — let them come to me. If Xiuying was dead and I had to pay the price, I would do so.

Nervously I entered the headquarters, but the leaders didn't say a thing about Xiuying. They simply ordered me to deliver a wheelbarrow full of forfeit goods to a compound in an adjacent lane. As the number of families being looted increased, the booty became too bulky to keep in school, so it was handed over to this compound for storage and management. I pushed the barrow in, talked to one staff member who worked there, and was instructed to dump everything in the yard, where there was a large pile out in the open — toys, books, ancient swords, Peking Opera costumes, fabric, everything. Absent-mindedly, I wondered whether anybody would come and move it if it happened to rain.

The headquarters never did talk to me about Xiuying. I never discovered whether she died or not, but I suspected that there were many victims of home raids who had died during or after the attacks. Xiuying's death would hardly have been news, but the thought that I might have killed her weighed heavily upon me for days. Still, eventually I managed to persuade myself it was all right. We were in a war and there are always casualties on battlefields. I shouldn't be intimidated by the death of one class enemy. The revolution had to succeed, and I had to continue to do my part. When I was assigned new tasks, I tried to be as brave as before.

Days later we raided an entire family. We arrived at their quadrangle at about ten o'clock in the evening when the middle-aged couple and their three daughters were all at home. The family seemed well off and occupied the whole quadrangle. "The richer, the worse," I thought.

My first job was hardly exciting. I was assigned, together with another Red Guard, the job of guarding the three girls. We were to keep them in one of the two side wings so that they couldn't interrupt the interrogation, which was taking place in the centre of the house. Their ages ranged from ten to eighteen. The middle one was about my age. She kept asking me, "What have they [her parents] done wrong?" I didn't have an answer. Our leader was a Red Guard in the second grade of senior middle school. She didn't show us the paper with the information on it, and I wasn't curious enough to ask. I had no idea what crimes they were accused of, but I couldn't tell the daughter that because it would make us, the Red Guards, look stupid. Nor could I rebuke her or tell her to shut up because she wasn't the object of our raid. That left me no choice but to resort to a formula that was widely used during the Cultural Revolution: "Ask your parents. They must know what evils they've done."

Finally, two other Red Guards came to relieve us. We were then ordered to rummage through the wing on the other side of the quadrangle. This family had more possessions than any of the others. There was even an upright piano at one end of the room. During the search I found some heavy gold rings hidden among the clothes in trunks. That was the first time in my life I had touched real gold. It didn't seem so great to me. What was all the fuss about? Such a dull golden metal. Why was it so desirable to wear gold rings? It was said that some Red Guards stole gold during the home raids. I don't know if that was true, but it never even crossed my mind to put one of them into my pocket. The rings didn't strike my fancy, and I was loyal to the Red Guard organization and trying my best to do my work faithfully. And what was I going to do with a ring even if I took it? I couldn't wear it. Nobody wore gold rings in China now. I couldn't hide it at home. There was no privacy; everything was under my parents' eagle eyes.

So, rings in hand, I went to the central living-room and presented them to our leader. She told me to put them in the pile of capitalist goods that were to be taken back to school. Besides the leader, there were two other Red Guards sitting at a table. One was busy writing. "How are things going? Getting anywhere?" I asked her. "Not really," she said.

Turning around I saw the couple on the floor of a large closet at the end of the long living-room. Their eyes were closed, their clothes torn and wet, and their skin scratched. They looked badly beaten. Now it was my turn to show some revolutionary spirit! I went closer to study them before I made up my mind what to do. The man's head drooped and he looked defeated, but the woman's head was turned up and rested against the wall. Somehow I thought I detected an unyielding expression on her lean face and this provoked me. I left the man alone and walked towards her.

There was nothing to ask her, other Red Guards had done that already. I took off my belt and beat her just to show my indignation and to change her "wrong attitude." On my first stroke she groaned, winced slightly, and opened her lustreless eyes to look at me once. Then she closed them again and showed no further reaction when my belt fell on her. After a few more strokes I stopped. She was like a wooden trunk. Why did she feel no pain? Could it be she was dead? I panicked: "Have I just killed another person?" I turned towards the table and asked the others, "Is she dead?" One of them looked at her wearily and said, "Just pretending." She stood up, fetched a bucket of cold water, and poured it over her. Now I knew why they were wet.

The poor woman stirred, and her eyes opened again for a couple of seconds. "You fooled me, bitch!" Delirious with anger, I resumed beating with all my strength. "Stop your insolence! Change your nauseating expression!" I shouted. But no matter how hard I beat her, the jeering expression on her face remained. When I became exhausted, I lost interest and made excuses for myself: "Maybe her face is naturally that way." I spat on the floor, walked to the side of the room, and rested on a chair. A little later another Red Guard took over.

The searching, rummaging, and torture lasted until three o'clock the next morning. It was too late to go home, so we slept in their living-room for a few hours, some on the table, some on the floor. Tired as we were, we didn't lose our "class vigilance." A Red Guard had been killed during a home raid by a "class enemy" with a cleaver, so one of us stood sentry duty to forestall any attack as we slept.

The Red Guards called the period from the end of August to the end of September, when the home raids took place, the Red Terror, in contrast to the White Terror when Chiang Kaishek's Kuomintang had killed many Communist Party members. The Kuomintang had a famous slogan: "It is better to kill one thousand innocents than to let one Communist get away." No matter how ruthless we were, we couldn't be worse than that, the Red Guards reasoned. According to some sources, during the Red Terror, more than 1,700 people were killed in Beijing, more than 33,600 family homes were raided, and 84,000 people from the condemned five categories were driven out of town.

THE CAPITALISTS
AND THE PRIVILEGED

I WAS VERY, VERY BUSY FOR A MONTH. BESIDES FREQUENT HOME raids, there were many large meetings requiring a Red Guard presence. After the 8/18 Reception, all Beijing was on the move. One day there was a Ten-Thousand-Person Cultural Revolution Oath-Taking Rally for peasants, the next a Ten-Thousand-Person Assembly to Celebrate the Victory of the Cultural Revolution for workers. We had to run all over Beijing. Some of the meetings were in the far suburbs, hours from our school. On these occasions we would be picked up by buses and then transferred to army trucks. We became so busy that I had to spend some nights in the school.

In the beginning my parents asked for explanations when I came home late. I told them briefly what I was doing: destroying the old four, searching the homes of the class enemy, and attending important meetings. Soon they stopped inquiring, even after I spent a night away. They knew I was a Red Guard leader and a member of the school's Revolutionary Committee. I could not have been doing anything wrong.

Once, leaving school at 11:00 p.m., I met Weiwei, a Red Guard in the second grade of our senior middle school, who was also leaving. That night she was wearing an army uniform and, incompatibly, a pink silk scarf around her neck and shoulders. We discovered that we took the same bus home. When she learned that I lived much farther away than she did, she became concerned about my safety:

"It's late. You shouldn't go home alone at this hour."

"Don't worry! Who dares to attack a Red Guard? If some desperado really does attack me, I can fight him with my belt."

"But you're too young! My home is much closer. Come home with me and stay over for the night."

"I haven't been home for two days. My parents are probably worried. This isn't the first time I've gone home late. Where I live is quite safe. We never have crime in our neighbourhood."

"You were just lucky. The class struggle is complex. Anything could happen. Go home and see your family tomorrow. You are coming with me tonight," she persisted. When the bus came to her stop, she half-dragged me with her.

We made two turns, entered a small alley, and stopped in front of an old-style Chinese gate guarded by two stone lions. The two large door panels looked very heavy. She pushed one open and we went in. There was no light inside. Out of the street light I had difficulties seeing, so I stood still. Weiwei knew her way in the dark, however. Closing the door behind us, she turned to my right and headed towards a row of houses hidden among groves.

I looked carefully at the ground behind her and was finally able to see a path paved with small pebbles. As I walked rapidly to catch up with her, I looked around in curiosity. On one side of the path was the wall, on the other was a darkened courtyard thick with bamboo clusters and bushes. In the wind their leaves rustled pleasantly, reminding me of the noble heroine's residence in *The Dream of a Red Mansion,* a famous Chinese novel about the decline of a very large aristocratic family at the end of the Ming Dynasty. The heroine was fond of bamboo and the yard of her compound was lavishly planted with bamboo groves.

Weiwei had quite a home. I wondered who her father was. Later I learned he was the first associate minister of the metallurgy ministry.

"Is this compound all yours?" I asked when I finally caught up to her.

"Yes."

"Do you have guards at the door too?"

"Yes. They weren't on duty because we told them not to wait when it's so late."

"Don't you think this place is too big for one family? Isn't this a waste?" I continued, boorishly unappreciative of the fact that she had invited me into her home. It was in the middle of the Cultural Revolution and the campaign to destroy the old four. I was a Red Guard and truly believed anything capitalist should be fought against and eliminated.

"Yes, I do. In fact, my father told them we don't want to live here. It's too big and too good. But they wouldn't let us have our way."

"Then tell them again!"

"I will," she said readily, seemingly unoffended by my officiousness.

When we arrived at her living quarters, she took me to the guest-room next to her bedroom. There was a bathtub and a single bed with snow-white bedding. It was like a hotel, ready for guests at any time. I figured they must have servants too, to take care of these things. She turned on the water tap and said, "You take a bath, then go to bed. Don't wait for me."

"Where are you going? Aren't you going to bed soon?"

"I'm going to see my father. I have a few questions about the revolution to ask him if he's still up."

Ah, a close father-daughter relationship, I thought with a little jealousy.

While the water was running, I noticed the door that connected my room and her bedroom was open, so I strolled into her room to look around. It was simple and unadorned: a single bed, a desk, a chair, and a book-shelf, filled with books I would love to read, such as the works of the brothers Grimm.

When the tub was ready, I slipped in. Only then did I realize I had gone a long time without a bath or shower. We didn't have a bath at home, and I was too busy in the revolution to go to the public bathhouse. Who cared about such trivial things, anyway? Now I was learning how nice it could be to sit in a bath after a long day.

Relaxing in the tub, I remembered Sheng Qiang's home in Jinan and my classmate Xiaonan's home, which was one floor of a large, two-storey building in a compound guarded by sentries. Neither was luxurious inside, but they were spacious, with beautiful gardens surrounding them. Both families had cooks and servants too. By Chinese standards their living conditions were extravagant. Of all the homes of "capitalists" and people from other "exploiting classes" I had searched, there were no better residences than those of the "proletarian" revolutionary cadres and army leaders.

The rationale for this was that revolutionary cadres, and especially army leaders, had wounds or had ruined their health in the long fight for the people before Liberation, so they deserved a better life now. Cars and servants were to save them time so that they could work more efficiently for the people. Besides, there was the socialist distribution principle: "from each according to his ability, to each according to his contribution." High-ranking cadres were considered to contribute more, so they received more. I had accepted this reasoning before, but I became less convinced as I grew up. Now, during the Cultural Revolution, I was even more skeptical. Even if the Chinese people were willing to offer privileges to revolutionary cadres, how could the cadres accept them while claiming to seek nothing but a better life for the people and the liberation of humanity? And what about their spouses and children who had contributed little or nothing before Liberation? Why should they live a life of privilege?

Nevertheless, privilege wasn't as hateful to me as it would become two years later. I thought about it and quickly forgot it. The next day when I returned to the battlefield, to my busy revolutionary life, all my questions about equality were left behind.

FIGHTING THE
"SONS OF BITCHES"

A S THE RED GUARDS WERE ASCENDING, THE STUDENTS from "bad families" were descending. Before the 8/18 Reception, the latter could still say a few words for themselves during the debates about the *duilian* "Bedevilling Devils." After the reception, they had to remain silent. How could they oppose those whom Chairman Mao so obviously supported? Unfortunately, by that time their silence wasn't enough to placate the Red Guards. They were openly called "Sons of Bitches" by the Red Guards and were put under their dictatorship.

Following Chairman Mao's analysis of all the classes in Chinese society, the Red Guards divided students into three groups: Red Five, whose families were worker, poor and lower-middle-class peasant, revolutionary martyr, revolutionary cadre, or revolutionary army leaders; Black Five (formally called Sons of Bitches), whose families were of the five categories defined earlier, plus the capitalists, intellectuals, artists, and office staff; and Red Periphery, whose families were in neither the Red Five nor the five categories — for example, the urban poor.

By the end of August the Red Guard team in my class had grown from three to eight members. Among the forty students in class, fourteen were Red Five, three or four Red Periphery, and about twenty Black Five. While we Red Guards carried out important revolutionary tasks outside school, the other six Red Five students were given the job of running the class. With the assistance of the Red Periphery, they supervised the majority of their fellow students in studying Chairman Mao's books and party documents.

Every morning the Black Five students came to school with school bags filled with Chairman Mao's works, volumes I to IV, as well as the ubiquitous little red book. In fear and mortification they headed directly to classrooms, where they were forced to use Mao Zedong Thought to reform their own. They were born bearing the stigma of the exploiting class, we told them. Whether they conceded it or not, capitalist and feudalist thought was rooted deeply in their minds. To save themselves, they must first learn to be ashamed of and hate their evil family backgrounds and their parents.

When off duty, we Red Guards would monitor how they were doing. We would walk cockily in front of them and at times stop before a student. She would be directed to recite a quotation from Chairman Mao's books or to report her progress in her own personal reform. Whenever we felt like it, we would mount the platform and give them lectures. In my most memorable lecture, I stood on top of the three-foot high lectern on the platform. Scowling down at the class, with my belt hanging down from my right hand, I bawled:

This is called the "proletarian dictatorship!" It is the opposite of the "capitalist dictatorship" your parents imposed on the working people before Liberation. You probably think that we are too hard on you, but let me tell you, compared with what your parents did to our parents, we're gentle! What have we done? We only push you a bit so that you become better people. Let's imagine how it would have been if we were still in the evil old society. How would you have treated us? You wouldn't have allowed us to sit in the same classroom with you! No, you would never even have allowed us in school! You would ride roughshod over us, starve us, and make us child labourers!

My imagination carried me away and aroused a strong indignation in me. I liked that because I really wanted to prove that our actions were justified. "Yes, you would have made us toil in the field, work in factories, or crawl in the pits! Yes, taught by your parents, you would have brandished your whips over our backs!" I yelled out at the top of my voice, lifting my belt, and swinging it down ferociously towards my audience. I was making myself distraught. My face contorted, and my jaw opened so wide that I had difficulty closing it. Oh, how I hated my classmates at that moment — only because of my own flights of fancy.

After a brief pause, I continued, "Listen carefully! The days of you and your parents are gone forever! Your world is finished! The power is in our hands today, and it will always be! Don't you ever nurse resentment towards us! It will only rebound and harm you!"

My classmates sat below me and listened, eyes downcast. Some might have been thinking that they indeed needed to reform themselves, some might have been arguing in their minds that they wouldn't have whipped me, and some might have been nursing a hatred for me like mine for them. A month earlier they had elected a modest girl they liked and respected to be a Red Guard. To their delight, she even promised to make more friends and unite all students. A month later she had become their fierce enemy, vilifying them and trampling their dignity.

We believed that by intensified study of Chairman Mao's works most of the Black Five could be refashioned, but this wasn't good enough for the worst Sons of Bitches. For them severer measures had to be taken. When other affairs were less pressing, we held a meeting to identify the worst of the class' Black Five.

Before the Cultural Revolution our Old Bear, Yixie, was probably the most unpopular student. She was disliked for various reasons. As soon as I mentioned her name at the meeting, everyone agreed that she was one of the worst without even discussing why. Then somebody mentioned Ying, another girl from an intellectual family, claiming that she was unbending and headstrong, and hence dangerous. Another mentioned was Geping, from a capitalist's family. The complaint was that she paid too much attention to her dress and looks and that her thoughts were "too sophisticated" (a bad thing in a student). I didn't know much about Ying and Geping, but if some Red Guards said they were bad, that was good enough for me. After this "democratic" discussion, it was decided that these three would be our major targets.

We had two meetings against Yixie. The first was a four-hour session in the afternoon. We began by making her stand in the centre of the room and read her confession, while we sat in a half-circle around her. It was not a formal meeting like the one we had had with our teacher-in-charge, Yuying. That was early in the revolution, and things were different now. Every few minutes I chided Yixie for some reason or another, most often to give her the order "Lower your head!" She lowered it so often that finally we couldn't even see her face.

"Why do you hang your head so low? Are you trying to hide your face so that you can sneer without our seeing it? Go and stand on the desks!" I pointed at the desks piled together against a wall. She went there and clumsily climbed up; we followed and stood below her. In this position we could see her face clearly except that we had to raise our heads high to look up.

With all the interruptions, her confession went slowly. One hour passed and we didn't hear anything we wanted to. I decided it was enough, "Cut it out! You call this a confession? According to what you say, you didn't even make a tiny error in your life. Preposterous! How dare you do this in front of revolutionary students! If you are thinking that not admitting is not doing, you're dead wrong! As your classmates, we know who and what you are and we remember everything!" I then waved to the students to launch the offensive. Red Guards, Red Five, Red Periphery, and even some Black Five murmured words of accusation at Yixie:

"Old Bear! You are a lazybones who doesn't do housework or anything physical. If you had, you wouldn't have two left feet! Laziness is typical of your exploiting class!"

"You are a typical 'white' student! What else do you care about beside studying? The revolution? No! The working people? No!"

"You think yourself the best of all of us. You are so conceited. Did you foresee yourself having a moment like this?"

"Ass licker! Confess how you licked Yuying's ass! Why else did you find so many excuses to visit her? What is the sinister purpose behind those visits?"

"You are a hypocrite, too! Why do you always wear pants you've grown out of? They barely cover your calves. Everyone knows your professor parents make tons of money. You don't have to pretend to be thrifty or poor by dressing so badly!"

Yixie would not accede. Whenever she had a chance, she would argue. Once she argued so vehemently her face turned crimson. To me her resistance was incorrigible. By then the home raids had made me so used to beating people that several times I had the urge to beat her, and my hand went unconsciously to my belt. But in the end I didn't take it off. Yixie wasn't counter-revolutionary, at least not yet. I knew that much, and I knew I had to be more discreet in class. If anything went wrong on the home raids the headquarters would always take ultimate responsibility, but in class no one stood behind me. To vent my wrath, I yelled fiercely and banged the desk beside her. Some students copied my example.

At the end of the afternoon we decided to stop and continue the next day. "Go home and write a better confession! Don't dream you can get away with such a bad attitude! If you don't bend, we'll fight you to the end!" I warned her.

The next day Yixie's attitude changed. Her parents must have counselled her. After reading her confession, she stood still and played dumb. She didn't accept our censure, but she didn't resist it either. For two hours she struggled to endure our screaming, kicking, and desk banging. The battle was entirely one-sided. Finally, we lost interest. "We won!" we concluded and called it off.

After the meeting against Yixie, we held one against Ying and one against Geping. I was not as active in these. While all the students stood close around them, I stayed at the periphery most of the time. Let everybody have a chance to contribute to the revolution! However, I was ready to support the Red Guards any time it became necessary. Once during the session against Geping I heard the accusations stop, so I pushed my way in to see what had happened. In the centre I heard a student with a thin voice saying, "You told people that you would return good to whoever was good to you. What if a counter-revolutionary is good to you? Will you help her oppose the revolution?" I smiled in approval and made my way out again.

Honed by all these skirmishes, my fighting spirit had now reached its peak. One day I talked with Wang Xiaonan, one of the three original Red Guards in my class, about making our Red Guards more revolutionary. Xiao Ping, another of the original three, had a lot more clothes than others, I thought, and I told Xiaonan. Some of them seemed to be made of very good fabric, too good for a student. This was a capitalist phenomenon, wasn't it? Xiaonan agreed. So I had a talk with Ping.

"Xiao Ping, you know we are in the Cultural Revolution. Its purpose is to destroy all capitalist and revisionist thought and behaviour. As Red Guards, we should set good examples for others, don't you think?"

"Yes, of course," she said innocently. "That's what I try to do."

"All right, then. We think you should re-examine your lifestyle. For example, don't you think you have too many clothes?"

"No, I don't. Most of my clothes are hand-me-downs from my mother," she said anxiously, her voice rising.

I didn't expect such an answer, but I was quick: "Your mother has too many clothes then!"

"No! No! That isn't true!" She looked hurt. Tears shone in her large eyes and were about to run down her face.

I dared not look at her again. Perhaps I had misjudged her. Giving it more thought, I had to allow that her family wasn't decadent. Her father was an associate minister, but they lived like commoners in three rooms in a big compound surrounded by all kinds of people. Their home had some upholstered chairs, but that was about it. Ping was her parents' only child. When her mother's clothes didn't fit, they would naturally be passed to her. Some of her clothes did look too loose. Her narrow shoulders couldn't prop up the sleeves, so they tended to hang down and cover part of her hands. But even knowing I might have criticized her wrongly, I didn't have to admit it. "Don't be offended. Chairman Mao teaches that you should say all you know and say it without reserve, blame not the speaker but be warned by his words, correct mistakes if you have made any, and if you haven't, guard against making them, OK?" Reluctantly she nodded. I hurriedly left and never mentioned anything about clothing in front of her again.

During that period our operations were appreciated and praised by the party centre. On September 15, in the heat of the Red Terror and Fighting the Sons of Bitches, Chairman Mao received a third batch of Red Guards. It was at this meeting that Lin Biao proclaimed, "Red Guard warriors . . . the major direction of your fighting has been correct all along. Chairman Mao and the party centre support you! . . . Your revolutionary actions have shaken the whole society and stirred the dregs of the old society. You acquired brilliant achievements in the battles of the 'Destroy the Old Four' and 'Establish the New Four' campaigns. The people in power who walk the capitalist road, the capitalist reactionary 'authorities,' the blood suckers and parasites, are in a sorry plight because of you. You did right; you did well!"

THE GREAT CONTACT

THE GREAT CONTACT WAS ANOTHER PRODUCT OF THE Cultural Revolution. Since June 1966 Beijing had moved rapidly in the direction Mao had hoped, but the major leaders in the provinces, cities, and units resolutely opposed this "student commotion." Students who rebelled in response to the calls of the party newspapers were attributed with all kinds of crimes, but they nonetheless believed they were right. They met and discussed their dilemma and how to let the central party and Chairman Mao know their revolutionary spirit. The only solution seemed to be to go to Beijing.

Some "wronged" students and teachers in Tianjing University were the first to walk to Beijing. Tianjing is about eighty miles from Beijing. They marched side by side, hand in hand, sang revolutionary songs, and read Chairman Mao's quotations aloud as they went. Rain didn't stop them, nor did the blisters on their feet. When the news reached Beijing, the CPGLCR sent a special train to pick them up. They were shouting, "Long live Chairman Mao!" as they stepped on the train.

More and more students followed the lead of those from Tianjing University, and the CPGLCR saw it as a way of spreading the revolution to the whole country. On August 16 the CPGLCR held a meeting for such visitors. At the meeting, the leader of the CPGLCR, Chen Boda, gave them support in the name of Chairman Mao, and demanded that they propel the Cultural Revolution forward in their home regions.

Arrangements were made for those who came to Beijing from the country to live in universities and colleges. They circulated actively, told their stories, and tearfully asked for help. In response, groups of Beijing Red Guards rushed out of the city, "up north, down south, into the west, around the east," to help light and fan the flames of the Cultural Revolution.

On August 31, when the second batch of a million Red Guards and revolutionary masses from around the country were received by Chairman Mao, the Great Contact was publicly confirmed. On September 5 the State Council sent out a circular "to organize a visit to Beijing by revolutionary teachers and students from the country," thus legitimizing the Great Contact. Red Guards outside Beijing, still only a limited number, started to take free trains to Beijing.

I was indifferent when I first heard of the Great Contact. The Red Guards in the country came to Beijing to see the capital and Chairman Mao, but what was I to see in the rest of the country? I didn't know anyone outside Beijing who needed our help, and we had too much to do in Beijing. By the end of September, though, the wind and storm of the Red Terror was over. No more home raids, no more meetings of ten thousands that needed a Red Guard presence, and no more fighting the Sons of Bitches. When we went to see the Red Guard leaders for instructions about what to do next, we would sometimes find one or two on duty who had no instructions to give; sometimes we found nobody. Leaving their followers behind, our leaders had gone for the Great Contact.

It was time for me to go out and have a look. From all the Red Guards in my class, I chose Xiaonan and Ping to go with me. We three were the original members, and I considered them my right and left hands. I especially appreciated Xiaonan. She had a sharp tongue and could talk very fast. Like me, she could also make good speeches vilifying the Black Five. I talked with her more than anybody else about the revolution and class struggle.

As we were making plans, Danan from the second class in our grade happened to visit and asked to join us. We hardly knew each other, so Xiaonan and Ping were not enthusiastic. They left it to me to decide. I wondered why Danan didn't want to go out to the country with the Red Guards in her own class. Didn't she get along with them? Then I remembered the meeting at which she was the only one who could answer Yingqiu's question. It would be nice to have a politically sensitive person along, so I agreed.

Indeed, Danan did turn out to be much better informed than us. When we were discussing where to go, she suggested Shanghai. She had heard the revolution there was intense. Some Red Guards in Beijing had already been sent to help paralyze its stubborn municipal government. We might see big events again, she said. Shanghai was the biggest city in China. None of us had ever been there, and no one objected to going, so it became our first stop. On September 30 we brought our student cards and a recommendation letter from Red Guard headquarters and went to an appointed place in Beijing, where we received four free train tickets to Shanghai for October 4.

When I told my parents about the trip, I was prepared for a veto. A group of fifteen-year-olds leaving home to run around the country? Unexpectedly, they agreed without a word and gave me thirty yuan in spending money. It was the largest sum I had ever had. Our financial situation had improved by then: my two half-sisters were working, and my older sister, Aihua, had gone to live on her own in Xinjiang at the end of 1965. My parents' salaries were also somewhat higher now.

Once Danan was in the group, my life as a Red Guard went downhill. She was full of rebellious spirit and had no respect for anyone, including me, especially when she discovered that despite all my titles I wasn't as well informed and politically advanced as she was. She tried to thwart me at every opportunity. At her instigation, Xiaonan, who used to think highly of me, demanded that I change uniforms with her before we left school for the train station. Mine was beautiful, while hers was an ugly yellowish-green, called shit yellow by the Chinese. I was totally against the exchange and didn't understand why she insisted. She could easily have arranged to get a better uniform from her father in the army, whereas this was my only one. Ignoring my protests, she forced the trade. If I hadn't given in, we would have never gotten away to Shanghai.

Although I was unhappy about this incident, and about having to wear a shit-yellow uniform (which, on return from the Great Contact, I put away for good), I was their leader and supposed to show model behaviour. I controlled my sulking. October 4 was before the peak of the Great Contact, and it was still possible to find a seat on a train. The trip from Beijing to Shanghai took a day and a night. During the night we slept sitting on the seats or lying down on the filthy floor underneath.

In Shanghai we contacted the local government and were billeted at a school. Our beds were desks pulled together, our quilts and pillows had been brought from home by the school's students, and our food came from the school kitchen. The school organized our activities as well. It didn't introduce us to any rebels in Shanghai, but arranged for us to read big-character posters in various places — the Shanghai Film Studio, Fudan University, and Tongji University. In the end, far from willingly, we spent three days in front of posters. We were veterans from Beijing and they were still in the preliminary stage of writing big-character posters. On the fourth day we visited the Ten-Thousand-Ton Hydraulic Press and watched how the huge machine compressed large chunks of red-hot iron like dough. At the time the press was the pride of Chinese industry, and everyone visiting Shanghai had to see it.

Four days passed, but we didn't see any sensational events or even any signs of one, as Danan had predicted we would. As advanced as she was, she didn't know where we could find any rebels to help. We decided to move on. It was then we heard that some students had branched out from their revolutionary activities and were starting to visit scenic spots and enjoy the "beautiful motherland." This was also permitted by the party. Premier Zhou said it was a good thing for "revolutionary little generals" (Red Guards) to see their beautiful motherland and to deepen their love of their great country. Why shouldn't we?

Near Shanghai were Suzhou and Hangzhou, two beautiful cities known as paradise on earth by the Chinese. But Danan thought that these two exquisite garden cities were too artificial and refined: "They're for feudalist and capitalist ladies, not for Red Guards like us." She proposed we see the Three Gorges at the upper reaches of the Yangtze River instead. We had all heard that the scenery there was spectacular. The clear Yangtze torrent zigzagged between high stone mountains, which were sometimes so close together that one could see only a narrow band of sky from a boat. Danan's proposal was again accepted.

Two days later we boarded a huge boat, which carried hundreds of passengers. Unfortunately, our tickets were fifth class. We each were assigned a narrow place on a straw mat, barely wide enough to lie down sandwiched between others, in the lowest bowels of the ship. Sitting on the mat without anything to lean against was uncomfortable, and lying down in public in broad daylight was embarrassing. We got out of there quickly.

The Yangtze is China's largest river, about 3,500 miles long. Its distant upper reaches are beautiful and rightly famous, but in its lower channel the river runs muddy and thick. Bearing all the soil it washed away from its banks, the Yangtze flowed heavily to the sea. The shore was far away, and the country houses surrounded by few trees looked tiny. The land was mainly flat, with an occasional low, rounded hill.

Our boat slowly moved against the current. It took three days to go from Shanghai to Wuhan, the central city of China, and it would take four more for us to reach the Three Gorges. Later during the trip we were elevated to third-class bunk-beds on the upper deck. Sitting on our beds, we could see out through a small porthole. But what was there to see? Muddy water or the unchanging shoreline scenery. By the third day I was homesick. We had been away for eleven days, I missed home and was worried about the situation in school. Perhaps we had already missed something very important! "Forget about the Three

Gorges, I'm going home!" I said. This time, Danan agreed with me. We went ashore at Wuhan and headed directly to the train station to obtain tickets home.

Back in school I found nothing new. Indeed, it was hard to find anyone on campus. Everyone — Red Guard, Red Five, and even Black Five — whoever could get away was away on the Great Contact. Those who didn't want to go simply stayed home. There was now complete anarchy.

Ten days later Ping appeared and said the three of them wanted to go out again. "Do you feel like coming?" she asked. "Not me!" I had heard that the trains were now so crowded that passengers sat on the small tea tables, the backs of seats, and the luggage racks, and in the aisles. To go to the toilet one had to walk over people's shoulders, and to get in and out of the cars one had to go through the windows. There were often fights at stops when people tried to break windows with stones to enter. The revolution needed me, but not that much! Free travel wasn't worth the discomfort and hassle.

Off they went. Two weeks later they came back and reported that they had walked sixty miles on small mountain paths to visit Chairman Mao's hometown of Shaoshan in Hunan Province. The rail line to Shaoshan wasn't finished then. Ping showed me photographs they took on the way, clutching precious red books to their bosoms. I wasn't envious. I thought it was crazy to climb over the mountains just to see the few rooms where Chairman Mao was born. It must have been one of Danan's rotten ideas again.

Still, to make the Great Contact by foot was the fashion. Taking inspiration from the students and teachers of Tianjing University who walked to Beijing, on August 25 fifteen students from the Sea Transportation Institute in Dalian walked over six hundred miles to reach Beijing, holding up a pennant that said, "Red Guard Dalian-Beijing Long March Team." To reduce the pressure on various transportation systems, the *People's Daily* of October 22 published an editorial calling on students to carry out the Great Contact on foot if possible. Soon various Long March teams had walked to all parts of China, some even following the route of the original Long March.

Shaoshan was one of the hot spots of the Great Contact. Other popular destinations were Jinggangshan (the first base area of the Red Army), Yan'an (the base area of the Red Army after the Long March), and Dazhai (a model village in agriculture). These were the ones the young people had heard of and read about most. Unfortunately, these famous places were all located in isolated areas with undeveloped transportation facilities. The supply chain was tight even without the extra burden of Red Guards. With that many "guests of Chairman Mao," supplies became so short that military planes had to air lift food and medicine.

The most overloaded city was Beijing, the capital of the country and centre of the revolution. After Mao received three batches of Red Guards and revolutionary youth in August and September, more and more hopeful young people poured into Beijing. To see Chairman Mao in person was considered life's greatest happiness. It was doubtful that Mao was equally happy to see them, but this was his wish since his revolution needed them. In October and November he received five more batches of Red Guards, each time more than a million. Those receptions were made the subject of documentaries that were shown in cinemas before the main features. The screen was filled with Red Guards laughing and crying as they saw Mao high up and far away on the rostrum. Recalling that seeing Mao from a distance of five feet couldn't reduce me to tears, I couldn't understand how their feelings towards Mao could be so deep.

PUNISHING THE PICKETS
AND JOINT ACTION

AT THE END OF NOVEMBER THE PARTY ISSUED CALLS TO
end the Great Contact, which was causing numerous problems in the
country. By then most students in my class had already returned. At about
the same time our Red Guard headquarters circulated two documents con-
demning the atrocities in Beijing's Sixth Middle School and First Middle
School. That was the last time the headquarters exercised its power.

The Sixth School was home to many members of the Pickets of West
District of Beijing, an organization that appeared after the 8/18 Reception. It was composed of Red Guards from the west district whose
parents were, for the most part, high-ranking cadres and army leaders.
The Pickets were radicals who pushed violence in the home raids to the
limit. Instead of warning and stopping them, on National Day, October
1, 1966, the CPGLCR assigned them the important task of guarding the
Golden Water Bridges, which connect Tiananmen Square to the Tiananmen-
men Rostrum. After that National Day most Beijing Red Guards ended
their violence, but the Pickets kept on until they were publicly rebuked
by the party.

In the Sixth Middle School they established a reform institute for the
Sons of Bitches and other people who held views that were different from
their own. The "reform" consisted of smearing their victims' faces with
paint, hanging them by the arms, giving showers of boiling water,
burning their hair, making them kneel on coal cinders, and other forms of
torture. A student in the third grade of their senior middle school dared to
disagree with the lineage theory of the *duilian*. He was put in the "institute" and beaten to death. No fewer than twenty people received bone
fractures or cerebral concussions or were disabled in that institute. I saw
photographs of the instruments they used and the slogan "Long Live the
Red Terror!" written with the blood of their victims on a wall of the interrogation room.

In the "prison" set up in the First Middle School of Beijing, similar
things occurred. About three hundred "dissidents" and students from

"bad families" were imprisoned and subjected to cruel tortures learned from the prisons of the Kuomintang and Tibetan slave owners, as well as those used by ancient Chinese.

Two months after we had raided homes and fought the Sons of Bitches, I read these documents. After a period of peaceful living, my revolution-swollen head had almost shrunk to normal. When I looked back at what we had done two months earlier, I thought we had gone crazy. Now I found that others were even crazier. They beat those who *weren't* class enemies, merely Sons of Bitches and dissidents. I felt scared too. Had I been in a school with a maniacal group like that and been told to do what they had done, would I have carried out orders and become as notorious as they were?

The Pickets of the West District were in trouble. On December 5 a union of certain factions of the Beijing Red Guards, the Joint Action, was established by Red Guard leaders in ten middle schools of the Haidian District of Beijing. Their views were similar to those of the West District Pickets. The two organizations were soon in contact, and most Pickets members shifted into Joint Action.

The main purpose of Joint Action was to oppose the CPGLCR. As the Cultural Revolution evolved, more and more cadres and army leaders were identified as being in the Black Gang, and the attitude of those Red Guards who were their children changed. At its inception, members of Joint Action put up slogans in the centre of Beijing to make their position known.

On December 16 the CPGLCR held a "Rally against the Capitalist Reactionary Line in Middle Schools" at which both the Pickets of the West District and "Bedevilling Devils" were officially criticized. It was decided that the Pickets had been used by bad elements to attack the revolutionary rebels. Following that, the police attacked the stronghold of the Pickets and arrested the "chief criminals," who were also the key figures of the newly established Joint Action. That evening some Joint Action members gathered and charged the Public Security Ministry, demanding the release of their comrades. In the first two weeks of January they charged the ministry three more times.

I didn't know much about Joint Action at the time. I did hear they attacked the ministry three times and rode their bicycles all around shouting "reactionary slogans" (much later I learned they were shouting, "Long live Liu Shaoqi!" and "Deep-fry Jiang Qing!"), but that was all. I was curious about them but not really concerned. What worried me was the rally on December 16. The authorities were again targeting the "capitalist reactionary line." The capitalist reactionary line of the working groups had already been repudiated in August. At the same rally "Bedeviling Devils" was officially censured. How could that *duilian* possibly be related to the capitalist reactionary line?

At the time of the rally we Red Five weren't fighting the Black Five, although we still thought ourselves superior to them. We still walked with our heads high and knew the Black Five were still a little afraid of us. After the rally, they changed. Their humility disappeared, and sparks of defiance and challenge occasionally shone in their eyes. What was this? Had they forgotten so quickly how to behave?

On January 17, 1967 the Public Security Minister, Xie Fuzhi, announced that Joint Action was a counter-revolutionary organization. On January 21 about a hundred of its leaders were arrested. Joint Action was no more.

PURGING THE
RED GUARDS

NEXT ON THE BLACKLIST OF THE CPGLCR WERE THE RED Guards. At the end of February teams from the People's Liberation Army (PLA) were sent to schools to take control temporarily. With the help of the army, the CPGLCR was to purge the Red Guards, wipe out any remaining influence of Joint Action, and force the middle schools to start criticizing the capitalist reactionary line again.

When the PLA team entered our school in early March they didn't hold any meetings with the Revolutionary Committee or the Red Guards, as I had expected they would. They simply gathered all students in the school together and announced that the Red Guards were accomplices of the working groups in pushing a new capitalist reactionary line. They said that after the working group left, the Red Guards didn't direct their fire at the capitalist reactionary line but at students from bad families. The PLA urged the students to rise up against them. All Red Guards were to make self-criticisms in class and stand again for election.

It was a head-on blow. Like the members of the working groups, I was changed from a leader of the revolution to its target overnight! I never dreamed this could happen to me.

Scene after scene of the Cultural Revolution replayed itself in my mind: puzzling over the meaning of Yingqiu's big-character poster, criticizing the school leaders and teachers, joining the Red Guards and being received by Mao, and raiding homes and fighting the students from bad families. How foolish I had been! I didn't understand the revolution, but strained to catch up and be in its vanguard. Time and again my ability in proletarian politics had been proved wanting, but I never lost heart or gave up trying to improve myself. All because I had such blind faith in Chairman Mao and the party.

Suddenly my faith in Mao and the party centre fell away. I saw all the flaws of the Cultural Revolution: there were no revisionists or capitalist roaders in school, the working group didn't push a capitalist reactionary line, the home raids were nonsense, and fighting the Sons of Bitches was totally insane. If anyone had made a mistake, it was Mao and the party by starting this damnable revolution in the first place. If they hadn't done so, I would still be studying peacefully with my classmates. Instead of bullying them I would be friends with them. Before punishing *us*, why didn't Mao and CPGLCR admit their mistakes and apologize to the Chinese people!

For the first time in my life I wanted to rebel, rebel against the PLA and against this campaign. But I knew it would be useless. Standing on the stage and being denounced by all the students in school was worse than reading a self-criticism in class. Indeed, if worst came to worst, I might even be locked up, like the members of Joint Action. Since the Cultural Revolution started our eardrums had been inundated with rebellious slogans, but when one really wanted to rebel one dared not. "To rebel is right!" said Mao. What a load of crap! Only a rebellion he officially endorsed was right!

The campaign went ahead. We spent the first few days studying documents; after that the Red Guards were isolated. The class held meetings without us to cheer our fall and selected five students who would lead the new movement. Two were in my Young Pioneer group before the Cultural Revolution: Guomei, A Lao's daughter, and Jiamei, the class beauty. The other three I knew little about. They were from families of common office staff: Yunyan, Liping, and Xiaohui.

Then the self-criticism started. To keep us in suspense the group of five didn't make a timetable. They took us one at a time. Two Red Guards went before me. It took three days to complete the process for each of them. They were given time to prepare, and then they read what they had written to the class. In the end they were told that their self-criticisms weren't acceptable.

It was now my turn to write a confession. "When the *duilian* came out I didn't use my brains to think it over, but followed the current and embraced and preached it. After Chairman Mao had received us, I lost even more of my sense and started assailing students from 'bad families.' Chairman Mao asks, 'Who are our enemies? Who are our friends? This is a question of the first importance for the revolution.' I was politically immature, and in the heat of the complicated class struggle of the Cultural Revolution failed to distinguish who were the friends and the enemies."

These were the main points of my self-criticism. Adding a bit of editorializing here and a snippet of Chairman Mao's quotations there, I dragged it out to one and a half pages. I could easily have made it work better to please my classmates had I said things like "You trusted me and elected me a Red Guard, but I failed to live up to your expectations" and "I deeply regret what I did to you during the Red Terror"; but I didn't. I knew I was wrong, but I had been victimized by Chairman Mao and CPGLCR myself. Besides, I had sunk so deeply into the mire of the lineage theory that I couldn't turn 180 degrees and kowtow to those former "third-class citizens" in just a few days. I needed time.

At the meeting the class was set up exactly as it had been before the Cultural Revolution started. I sat in my old seat and read my insipid self-criticism in a low, flat voice. When I finished, the group of five asked me to leave the room and told the rest of the Red Guards to go home. I wandered in the yard but didn't go far in case they wanted me back. My proximity must have been a distraction. Half an hour later they came out and sent me back in alone. The classroom set-up was different. All the desks and chairs had been pushed to the rear, and the front two-thirds of the room was now empty. Looking out of the windows I saw no one in the yard. "Where are they now? Have they left school?" I wondered, but I dared not go outside to look.

After a long time the five leaders came back. I was standing in the centre of the room and they marched towards me until six feet separated us. Yunyan, a girl with full lips, deep eyes, and thin eyebrows, stepped closer and delivered their verdict:

"Your criticism is not satisfactory."

"Why?" I was shocked, although, knowing the result of the previous two cases, I shouldn't have been.

"Because your attitude is not sincere."

They had me there. I wasn't sincere. How could I be when I felt so wronged? Why didn't they try to see things from my viewpoint?

"We want you to write another criticism and read it to the class," Yunyan continued. Her eyes radiated hostility. Behind her the other four stood like a wall. Until then my spite had been mainly towards the policy makers. I now became mad at my classmates as well. In a huff I whirled about and stormed out through the door.

Back home, the more I thought about it, the madder I got. I never bullied Yunyan! I never singled her out or even stopped in front of her during my class inspections! And Guomei! I had even tried to save her feelings! If I had told her in front of our classmates what Yingqiu had said about her father — "Who does A Lao think he is!" — she would have cried in humiliation.

They wanted me to write another criticism and be sincere, but I would not humiliate myself further. Never. On an impulse the next morning I went to see Jiaquan, a platoon leader and the PLA representative assigned to my class, although I realized he would hardly side with me. But I had to give it a try. He was the only one who might be able to put a stop to the Group of Five.

Jiaquan was a small young man with the face of a child, dull eyes, and a flat nose, not good-looking. Nonetheless, he was cool and urbane. As we talked, I sat on the banister against a pillar outside the classroom. He stood upright by another, six feet away, during the whole conversation.

"I cannot do a second self-criticism as required by the Group of Five. I've owned up to all the mistakes I made and have nothing else to say."

"Are you so sure about that? In your self-criticism you didn't even mention the capitalist reactionary line, let alone admit that you had helped to support it."

"I didn't! I'm not a capitalist or a reactionary! And I have nothing to do with their line! I blundered! That's it: I blundered. They don't have to put such a scary label on me," I pouted.

"To say you put forward the capitalist reactionary line doesn't mean you are a capitalist or a reactionary. Don't be confused. You are still a good comrade if you correct your mistake and come back to Chairman Mao's side."

"That is if I knew what Chairman Mao's side is! How can I know if nobody bothers to spell it out? Last September, when we were supposedly pushing the capitalist reactionary line, why didn't anyone tell us what we were doing was wrong? One little article in the *People's Daily* would have stopped me, or any of us. As it was, we were exalted to the sky and supported by Chairman Mao himself. Naturally I thought we were on Chairman Mao's side!"

"Perhaps you had reasons. Perhaps there were special conditions when you committed your error. Nevertheless, you did unduly fight your classmates, baffle their initiatives, and cause damage to the Cultural Revolution. I presume you have realized that? Yesterday you recanted to the class. It's a good start. But in your classmates' opinion, for what you did in the past, what you acknowledged is far from enough."

"My classmates now have opinions! What were they doing last September? They were as quiet as mice! Now that the tide has changed, they all become heroines and jump out to get even with us!"

"Don't hold a grudge against them. They're only trying to carry out Chairman Mao's instructions."

"Indeed, isn't that what we all try to do? It was only because I tried too fervently that I made such an ass of myself!" I felt like crying.

"One can never try too hard to follow Chairman Mao and the party. I know it's not easy for you to go through this, but this capitalist reactionary line must be thoroughly criticized. Otherwise, the Cultural Revolution in schools cannot continue."

"I don't understand. The working group and the capitalist reactionary line were criticized long ago in July and August, and our fight against students from bad families stopped five months earlier. Since then we haven't done anything, bad or good. Why, all of a sudden, should we become obstacles to the revolution now? And why should there be this campaign against us Red Guards? For God's sake, after all we've done for the Cultural Revolution!"

"You seem to be full of grievances."

"You bet I am! If fighting fellow students is a crime, which we Red Guards are accused of, what are our fellow students up to now? Don't you think they are fighting us, and hard? Not only did they fail me, they also failed the two before me. I don't think they'll let any of us pass! Aren't they afraid they'll become followers of the capitalist reactionary line themselves? Then they'll be criticized in the next campaign! You fight me, I fight you back. When will it all end?"

Jiaquan was short of words. How could he know the answers to all these questions? He turned towards the yard and mused, while I stood up from the banister to warm up. It was cold and damp that day, with an early spring rain coming down. Even in my cotton-padded coat I felt chilly. The large stone curb under my feet was wet; so was the brick ground in the yard. Water trickled along the eaves. When the wind passed, fine drops of water were blown on my hands and face. In the patter of rain, I became more worried. So far Jiaquan hadn't given me any sign of encouragement. Would he help? If he didn't, what would I do? Write a second criticism, then a third? No! I must try harder! Maybe I should cry?

It wasn't too difficult to squeeze out a few teardrops. Ostentatiously, I wiped them off and talked with more emotion, voice quivering. "What is over is over. They can't hate me forever! If I have done wrong in the past, it wasn't intentional. I'm from a revolutionary family, and I'm still of the revolutionary masses, not a counter-revolutionary. They don't have a right to treat me like this. I will not do another self-criticism!"

Jiaquan gave in. "All right. Don't be so upset. I'll have a word with them and see if they won't change their minds. But you should try harder to make up with your classmates. All you students should unite. After all, you have one common task, to fight the revisionists who are still in power."

I nodded through his words. "Whatever you say," I thought, "so long as I don't have to write another criticism."

Jiaquan's efforts worked. The Group of Five withdrew their request for a second criticism from the three Red Guards they had already interviewed and didn't pose it to any of the ones who followed, but that didn't mean we were pardoned. In the next election I failed, with only fifteen votes out of forty. Clearly no one other than the Red Five and the Red Periphery students voted in my favour. Of the eight Red Guards, five were re-elected with a bare majority. Xiaonan wrote a better self-criticism and was re-elected with twenty-one votes, and Ping got the most, twenty-two.

Being ejected from the Red Guards and officially criticized at the age of sixteen had cut me to the heart. So much for my revolutionary aspirations and enthusiasm. In a fit of pique I damned politics, proletarian and capitalist alike, and decided never to get caught up in it again.

From then on I hated the Cultural Revolution. It was nothing but a poorly contrived social experiment Mao Zedong was carrying on, in which all Chinese were his specimens. Improvising as he went, Mao did not mind scratching, bending, or even breaking millions of people. He really cared nothing about human values and dignity.

I hated the revolution for what it had done to me, but I had not yet come to feel a pang of conscience for the harm I had done to others. Like almost all the events of the revolution, in my eyes the home raids were now foolish exercises, and I wished they had never happened. However, the idea of class struggle still held me fast. I still believed that most of the victims of the home raids were bad people, and I had little sympathy for them. I was brought up hating my class enemies and had never heard another side.

Years later, the confiscated goods that survived were returned to their owners, and in 1976, when the Cultural Revolution was over and repudiated, the home raids were cited as examples of human rights violations. I felt nervous, but the many who had taken part in them were not individually denounced or prosecuted.

More years passed. I grew older and was exposed to different ideas. My remorse grew. Despite telling myself that I was only fifteen years old at the time, that I had been pulled into these excesses unwittingly, that it was not my fault, and that I should not have to take responsibility, I realized I had done some very bad things. The victims of the home raids may all have been innocent.

WATCHING THE REVOLUTION
FROM THE SIDELINES

I
N APRIL THE PLA LEFT. ITS TEMPORARY GOVERNANCE OF the school was meant to put all the students back onto the correct road of the Cultural Revolution again, but instead even more were driven off it. All Red Guards, ousted or not, were in disgrace and started to view the revolution as a nightmare. They only wished for it to end right away. Those from bad families, the winners of the recent campaign, also saw the capriciousness of the revolution and thought it better to withdraw. Before this campaign, the revolution in my school had stagnated; afterwards, it died.

The same month two major factions of Beijing middle school students emerged to oppose each other. One was the 4/3 Faction; the other, the 4/4 Faction. On April 3 (4/3) a leader delivered a speech, and the next day (4/4) another leader gave another speech that contradicted the previous one. Each had its own supporters among the students — hence the two factions. We thought both were ridiculous: "Haven't they had enough?" To declare our stand, we professed to belong to a third faction, the Unfettered Faction. Standing aloof, we chanted, "All people in the world are drunk, only I am sober," and we watched the others with pity as they continued to struggle against one another in the revolution. In due time all would learn their lessons.

And they did learn their lesson, but not just yet. Many still enjoyed the excitement of the revolution. While we, the "young" Red Guards from middle schools, were rectified and purged, the "old" Red Guards from universities went unscathed. Their spirits were as high as when the Cultural Revolution first started, and they were as active as ever.

The most famous old Red Guard was Kuai Dafu from Qinghua University, a third-year chemistry student. During the anti-working-group movement of June 1966, he was dauntless and used all means, including fasting, to achieve his ends. He then became the right hand of the CPGLCR. Whenever the CPGLCR needed its rebels to make a new move, it merely had to leak some information to Kuai. In Beijing he gathered tens of thousands of university Red Guards under his flag, and in the country many rebel leaders followed his commands.

On April 10 Kuai Dafu and his Red Guards fought against Wang Guangmei, Liu Shaoqi's wife, in Qinghua University at a meeting attended by 300,000 people. The next day I saw big-character posters reporting the meeting all over town. Accompanying them were caricatures vilifying Wang by depicting her in high-heel shoes, a *qipao*, or close-fitting Chinese dress with a high neck and slit skirt, and a necklace made of ping-pong balls.

That latter was a reminder of a pearl necklace Wang wore during a visit she and Liu Shaoqi made to several Southeast Asian countries in 1963. Jiang Qing had advised Wang not to wear expensive jewellery. Later Jiang saw pictures of Wang dressed up in many different outfits and even wearing a pearl necklace at a party in Burma. Jiang was not pleased. She was first lady, but Wang had the limelight and was obviously paying no heed to her instructions. In July 1966 Jiang Qing revealed to the Beijing University Red Guards that she had "suggested to Wang Guangmei not to wear a necklace, but she didn't listen," reminding those who had seen the news documentary about that trip of how Wang looked. Before the meeting at Qinghua University Wang was forced to put on one of her outfits from 1963 and a ping-pong-ball necklace.

The public denunciation and criticism of Wang Guangmei was the preamble to that of Liu Shaoqi. This was not altogether unexpected by Beijingers. As early as November 1966 slogans reading, "Down with the black headquarters led by Liu Shaoqi and Deng Xiaoping" had begun to appear on the streets. Slowly the idea was planted in the public mind that Liu and Deng would be toppled sooner or later.

Liu Shaoqi's official fall from power came a year and a half later, on November 2, 1968. All newspapers carried the red-ink bulletin of the Eighth Plenary Session of the Twelfth Central Committee, which said,

The Central Committee has approved 'The Investigative Report on the Crimes of the Traitor, Collaborator, and Scab Liu Shaoqi' of the Central Committee's special case investigatory group. It has been established with ample evidence that the leading capitalist-roader Liu Shaoqi is a traitor, a collaborator, and a scab hidden within the party. He is guilty of many crimes and is a running dog of imperialism, modern revisionism, and the Kuomintang Reactionaries. The committee holds it a great victory of Mao Zedong Thought and the

Proletarian Cultural Revolution to have the counter-revolutionary side of Liu Shaoqi revealed by the party and the revolutionary masses during the Proletarian Cultural Revolution. The committee showed extreme indignation at the counter-revolutionary crimes of Liu Shaoqi and passed a resolution to expel him from the party, dismiss him from all his posts in and out of the party, and continue to expose and criticize his crimes and accomplices. . . .

I didn't believe one word of it. Liu Shaoqi now the worst villain? What a lie! He had been chairman of China for years. How could the party have let him climb so high without looking carefully into his background? If Mao disliked Liu, he should just fire him. It was totally unnecessary to slander him like that. Must a power struggle be so dirty? Must all losers in it be painted as evil inside out from birth? Must our party, which I once truly loved, make a fool of itself and lead all Chinese to despise it?

The year 1967 was one of armed fighting. In 1966 the Cultural Revolution had started in Beijing universities and schools. By 1967 the Chinese working class rose and became its main force. Unlike the students, the workers didn't all become rebels, as Mao and the CPGLCR had wanted. Although some tried to overthrow provincial or municipal leaders, others, led by model workers and party members, tried to protect them.

The Shanghai Worker Rebel General Headquarters (WGH) was established to overthrow the leadership of the Shanghai Municipality. Later loyalists formed a Defend Mao Zedong Thought Red Guard Team (RGT). In the beginning the RGT was more popular, but with the support of the CPGLCR from Beijing, the leftist WGH quickly gained an upper hand.

In January 1967 the WGH launched an all-out offensive to crush the RGT, taking control of the media and many important organizations in Shanghai. Whenever there was resistance, the WGH applied force to clear the way. This offensive was named the January Storm. On February 4 the Revolution Committee of Shanghai was born. Its leaders were Zhang Chunqiao of the CPGLCR and several members of the WGH. Mao suggested that all newspapers report these events favourably.

Through the CPGLCR-controlled media the January Storm was noisily advertised all over China. "At last, the sensational event predicted by Danan in our Great Contact has come, although a bit late," I thought when I read the news in the *People's Daily*. The January Storm had a powerful impact on the country. All factions in the country claimed they were leftists and threw themselves into a struggle for power. Imitating the Shanghai workers, they fought with their hands, feet, and clubs. Conflict became acute.

For years Lin Biao had wanted to purge those army leaders whose loyalty to him was in doubt, whereas Jiang Qing wanted to grab military power for her leftists. On July 25 Lin and Jiang "exchanged" ideas with Kuai Dafu, the rebel commander. Several days later Kuai met with a hundred rebel leaders from the country and told them to seize arms, saying, "Liu and Deng have guns. They can't be fought without them. 'Power grows out of the barrel of the gun,' right?" These hundred or so leaders hastily returned to their home provinces and cities and immediately organized fighting teams. They barged into military areas and broke into armouries to get weapons. Guns in hand, they could now shoot the loyalists who refused to surrender. The opposition soon learned to fight back the same way. Like lifelong enemies, former fellow workers now shot at each other.

In comparison with the country Beijing was peaceful, almost free from armed fighting. Yet we heard a lot: shooting bursting out in such-and-such a place with so many people dead; so-and-so going away on a business trip and being killed by a stray bullet. "What has our country come to? How obsessed people now are!" Beijingers all sighed. Still, the armed fighting continued on a large scale until 1970. Even in 1973 I heard occasional discreet mention of it.

THE UNFETTERED LIFE

WHILE OTHER PEOPLE WERE ENGAGED IN LIFE-AND-DEATH struggles with automatic weapons, I did nothing but play. My unfettered life actually started in October 1966, and with occasional interruptions it lasted more than two years. Every day, my classmates and I gathered at the school as usual, but there were no lectures and no teachers. Instead, we taught each other how to bicycle, swim, and play cards and Chinese chess. In spring we bicycled to the Summer Palace to view the flowers and in autumn to Fragrant Mountain, which was then clothed in red maples. When winter came, we played cards in the unheated classrooms, and in summertime we soaked in crowded swimming pools.

In the summer of 1967 a former Red Guard told me she knew a way to slip into our barred school library and asked whether I wanted to go. I went along. The library was in a remote courtyard of the school. It was unrecognizable because many of its windows had been broken and were covered with a jumble of wooden boards. My companion walked to one of them, which, it turned out, was nailed at the top but not the bottom, pushed the lower part aside, and climbed in. I followed her through and rotated the wood panel back to its original position.

Before the Cultural Revolution the teacher in charge of the library, Cao Sha, never allowed us in. Book representatives handed him little pieces of paper through a small window with the names of the books students wanted written on them, and he then passed the books back out through it. I was a bit afraid of Cao Sha because he had a bluish face and never smiled. From other students I learned that long ago he had been a writer of odd books — one was entitled *The Story of the Big Crotch*. In 1957 he was labelled a rightist and demoted to working in our library. Today, standing among the dusty bookshelves, I wondered how Cao Sha had survived the revolution. As a rule, all those who had once been convicted were attacked again each time a new political campaign came along.

That day I picked out a few books and carried them home. When I finished, I put them back and took some more. One day I found Yibing, the senior Red Guard who had given me the army uniform, in the library. I asked her to recommend a book, and she said, "*Madame Curie* is good. We all liked it." I took *Madame Curie* home. As I read, I endured with her the hardships she went through in her scientific research, as well as the excitement after each of her discoveries. Closing the book, I recalled that many girls in my school dreamt of becoming a second Madame Curie. To succeed in science like her, to bring honour to our country, and to benefit humankind had been our inspiration; but we were now caught up in the middle of the Great Cultural Revolution, unable to do the things we wanted or to pursue our dreams.

August 18, 1967 was the first anniversary of the 8/18 Reception. Despite my "unfettered' status, I couldn't help but remember past glories with some feeling. I took out and unfolded the newspaper with the photograph of me sitting in front of Mao on the Tiananmen rostrum. It was already turning yellow. "How do others remember this event? Is anyone going to commemorate it in Tiananmen Square?" I suddenly had a desire to visit the square.

By then, all the arrested members of Joint Action had been released. Before letting them go, the CPGLCR called them together and repeated that Joint Action was a counter-revolutionary organization and its purpose must be criticized. Later they did stop shouting slogans like "Deep-fry Jiang Qing" in public and shifted their anger to the Sons of Bitches: "Wipe out all Sons of Bitches! Let their corpses be a mountain and their blood run rivers!" and "Sons of Bitches fall aside; the Red Five want to be back in power!"

But these days slogans were just slogans. Joint Action couldn't take any action towards the now-awakened students from bad families. What they actually did was to beat thieves and hooligans on the streets. I arrived in Tiananmen Square to find no official gatherings, but there were several hundred people in a dozen or so clusters. My instincts told me that inside those clusters Joint Action members were beating people. I wasn't interested in watching people being beaten, but thus far I had never seen a Joint Action member, so I edged my way into one crowd.

In the centre was a ring of about eight hundred square feet. Inside it, two ordinary-looking youngsters in army uniforms were chasing a middle-aged man and striking him with belts. "Oh! Oh!" the running man cried out. His hands sometimes protected the back of his head, sometimes his hips. He wore an untidy tunic, grey khaki trousers, and a pair of running shoes. He hadn't shaved in days, and the stubble on his face was half an inch long. After a few rounds, one youngster tired of the game, "Stop! If you don't, we'll beat you to death!" The man stopped. "Stop howling, too! I hate that," the other one added. They then walked close to the man and whipped him as we all had during the home raids. After a while they had a new idea to entertain the audience. "Take off your pants now!" I decided that was enough and started to push out, but I couldn't get free right away. When I did, I stole a glance over my shoulder to see if the man had indeed dropped his pants in public. He hadn't. Half-lying on the ground, he had his pants pulled down just enough to expose his white buttocks for the youngsters to slash at.

These two must have been members of Joint Action. They wore no Red Guard armbands, because like me they had also been kicked out. To celebrate the anniversary of the 8/18 Reception they beat people in Tiananmen Square. Did they know what they were doing? I suddenly felt bad. Before coming I had looked forward to sober people and heartening orators who could arouse me once again. Instead, I found mobs. Was this all that was left of the Red Guard movement?

On October 23, 1967 the party centre issued a document announcing that students should return to classes while continuing the revolution. In November some teachers, excluding teachers-in-charge, came back, and selected courses resumed.

To pick up from where we had left off after a year and a half was not easy. Sitting in class, I didn't know what the teacher was talking about. Opening the textbooks, I couldn't understand the text. The atmosphere just wasn't right. The revolution wasn't over yet. Teachers lacked enthusiasm, fearing they might at any time be denounced and criticized. They didn't care whether we understood their lectures and gave no tests or homework. On our side, we took our classes no more seriously than the teachers did. None of us believed it would last, and few worried about not being able to catch up. Once, we were asked to do a biology experiment. I went to the lab but saw no teacher. I didn't know what I was supposed to do, so I just went home.

The situation in the country was grim. Workers stopped producing, peasants treated their crops perfunctorily, and there was armed fighting in one place after another. The country's leaders must have had bad headaches. We heard that Premier Zhou often put in twenty-hour days. Besides his ordinary routine, he was called upon to receive batch upon batch of squabbling faction leaders in the Great Hall and mediate between them. Compared with all the much more urgent events, the question of whether and when students could return to their studies could be neglected. Two months later the campaign to resume classes and continue the revolution was aborted. We were again at large.

THE IMPACT OF
THE REVOLUTION

HAD WE BEEN WITHOUT SUPERVISION FOR A FEW MONTHS IT might have been different, but we were neglected for a year and a half. In school, no teachers watched over us. At home our parents' once-sharp eyes had shifted elsewhere; they were either too occupied by the revolution or in trouble themselves. The character of my generation began to change.

Yang Yanping was the girl I had invited to spend life with me Nemo-like under the sea and away from the rest of humanity. She had been one of the Red Guards and, until now, a friend. Her home was close to school. I visited her often and had met her father, a section chief in the ministry of public security. He was gracious, with big eyes like Yanping's. I also met two of her younger brothers. In my memory, they were dark, thin, and glum-faced.

In 1967 Yanping's father was put in detention and isolated from his family. It was a long detention, too, not just a couple of months. That was the source of the family tragedy. When a cadre was under detention his salary was considerably reduced, I learned later. Yanping and her four younger brothers might have been in a bad way because of their father's misfortune, but at the time I didn't know that. Yanping never told us about her plight or asked for help.

On an early summer morning of 1968 a group of my classmates and I met together in Yanping's home. On returning to school I noticed I had forgotten my school bag. It contained a few trinkets and a new blouse of artificial silk, which I had only worn twice. This was my first silk-like piece of clothing. I didn't want to lose it, but I didn't make a special trip to get it back. I took it for granted that Yanping would bring it to school and ask whose it was.

A couple of days passed, Yanping didn't bring the bag. Not only that, one morning I saw her wearing my blouse inside her army uniform! The design on the blouse was distinctive — light green rings in different sizes — so I knew I couldn't possibly be mistaken. I wasn't too happy

133

about it, but I decided to wait a little longer. Let her wear my gorgeous blouse a while — I wasn't rich, but I wasn't chintzy.

After two weeks, I was no longer so blasé. "Yang Yanping, two weeks ago I left my school bag at your place. There was a short-sleeve silk blouse and some other little things in it. Would you please bring it back next time?" She was ill at ease. After some thought she said: "All right, I'll bring it back if I find it." The next day I stopped her at the school gate.

"Where is my bag?"

"It's lost!"

"Have you searched everywhere?"

"Yes, I did," she said firmly. Then, ignoring me, she pushed her bicycle on into the schoolyard.

I was flabbergasted! Never did I expect to be robbed by my own classmate, especially Yanping! I once picked her from all the humans to be my life-long companion under the sea, got her admitted into the Red Guard, and treated her as a friend. How could she do this? I stomped to and fro inside the school gate and schemed how to settle the score.

The first thing that crossed my mind was to tell a teacher. Two years ago that would certainly have brought me justice. Now it was useless — the teachers had no more authority than I or anyone else. The next choice was to see her parents but I didn't know where to find them, or whether I should exacerbate their situation by informing them of their child's misconduct. In the end I concluded there was nothing I could do, furious as I was.

From then on I avoided Yanping. Half a year later we led completely different lives and never saw each other again. I didn't care to hear anything about her the rest of my life, but in the summer of 1969 my classmates told me that one of Yanping's younger brothers had been killed. By coincidence, he was in the same school and class as my younger brother, Weihua, and I learned the gruesome details from him. Yanjie had been killed in broad daylight in their living-room, despite the proximity of two neighbouring families in the compound. He was found kneeling on the floor with his arms bound against his sides and a knife in his back, the position in which criminals were executed in ancient times. Rumour had it, according to Weihua, that Yanjie had joined a street gang and the killing resulted from internal dissension. Perhaps he had owed other gangsters money and refused to pay. By the way he died, the killers seemed to be asserting that Yanjie died guilty.

Many families were bruised during the Cultural Revolution, but Yanping's was one of the most unfortunate. In comparison, my family had not really fared too badly. Luckily, my father was neither a writer nor artist. Changing his job six months before the revolution also helped. The people in his new unit did not know enough about him to vilify him, and the people in his old unit did not hate him enough to take the trouble to chase him to his new unit. Some big-character posters were directed at him, but not many.

The alleged aim of the Cultural Revolution was to clear away all Black Gangs under the "Black Headquarters" run by Liu Shaoqi and Deng Ziaoping. But as far as the vast majority of the people knew, there was no clear demarcation between Liu and Mao. Thus, whether a cadre would be labelled a "capitalist roader" was really quite arbitrary. Except the most famous ones whom CPGLCR itself organized attacks against, the majority of cadres who were singled out were those who had offended people, were involved in corruption, misused privileges, or had a "living style problem," that is, carried on an affair outside marriage.

My father was always cautious. People might think him old-fashioned, rigid, or even timid, but he didn't make big mistakes. Even in daily life he was careful. He never revealed party secrets to his family and never misused privileges — for example, by getting a free car to drive us around. My family always lived simply. Our financial situation hadn't allowed us to live otherwise.

However, Father did have one trait that had the potential of making him enemies — he was sometimes harsh to those who worked with him. In 1973, when Father's unit, like many others, was under the control of army officers, he had a close call. One of his subordinates, whose name never came out, alleged that he had contacts with the so-called "5/16 Counter-Revolutionary Corps," a cabal that was eventually proven never to have existed. The officers suspended Father and prepared to denounce him. Two months later, after failing to find a shred of evidence, they allowed him back to work and acted as if nothing had happened. In exasperation Father demanded an explanation, but he never got one.

My mother wasn't as lucky. In June 1966 she was appointed a member of a working group and sent to a college. Later, she was criticized for carrying out the capitalist reactionary line and was put in custody in her own unit. For two months she had to write self-criticisms and clean the yards and toilets as punishment.

She didn't tell us anything while this was going on. Years later, Mother and I were talking about our family friend, Auntie Zhao, when she mentioned those two months for the first time and confided how she had felt. "I didn't mind the physical labour. You know me. I'm a compulsive worker. What was hard for me was the isolation. When I met acquaintances and even friends, none said hello. Only your Auntie Zhao exchanged greetings with me. Once, when I was washing the toilet floor, I slipped and fell. My lower-back problem was at its worst then [an operation later cured it]. I struggled on the floor but couldn't stand up. One 'comrade' after another passed by, but nobody stopped to give me a hand. In the end your Auntie Zhao came and hurriedly helped me to my feet."

"Why didn't you tell us when this happened?" I asked her gently.

"What good would that have done? It would only have made you unhappy as well."

"We could at least have comforted you."

She just shook her head and sighed.

THE OTHER HALF
OF THE FAMILY

I HAD ALWAYS BEEN CURIOUS ABOUT MY FATHER'S FIRST wife, Shuxian, and my two half-sisters, Fuxiang and Fuzhen. In the summer of 1968 I paid a visit to Shuxian and Fuxiang, who were living together in Tianjing, and went twice to the airbase where Fuzhen lived and worked. I had no earlier opportunities to get to know them. My mother was always upset and reacted bitterly when I even mentioned their names. I argued with her a lot in my mind, that she was wrong to be so miserable about a fact she couldn't change, that with a correct attitude we could all co-exist in peace, but I never dared to open up in front of her.

Perhaps the revolution did accomplish one thing: it educated cadres to treat all people, old or young, with more respect. After almost two years of the revolution, my mother had become more tolerant. She was less autocratic at home, and I became less afraid of her. I could finally open a discussion about Father's "other" family and express my wish to visit Fuxiang and Fuzhen. After all, they were my half-sisters. This was the perfect time to go, since schools weren't operating. I might never get another chance. Mother gave her permission.

In Tianjing, Shuxian, Fuxiang, her husband, and their son lived in two rooms with no kitchen or toilet. This was a common arrangement in large cities. In winter the coal-burning stove was put inside the rooms to cook and generate heat; in summer it was moved into the corridor outside. It mattered to no one that the corridor walls turned black from smoke and fumes.

Fuxiang tried to be a good hostess, but she was too busy. Both she and her husband were low-level party functionaries in the factory where they worked and couldn't even take one day off. More than once Fuxiang voiced her regret at not being able to take me out. "Never mind," I would say, "I came here mainly to see you. Tianjing doesn't have much to offer anyway." "Well, that isn't entirely true. There are some nice places, like the People's Park and a couple of historical spots. It's too bad we're so busy. Maybe next time," she smiled genially. She was short and a bit chubby. Her round face was like my father's, especially her raised eyebrows and bright, piercing eyes.

Shuxian was fair-skinned, fine-featured, tall, and slim. She must have been a very good-looking young woman, a lot better looking, I think, than my mother. However, I couldn't help but notice her yellow teeth. "Has she ever used a toothbrush?" I wondered. "Doesn't she know she should?"

She wore her hair in a bun at the nape of her neck like my grandmother. Her feet were bound, too, though they were not as small as Grandmother's. Perhaps she wasn't as faithful about binding them tightly every morning.

I tried to be as kind to Shuxian as she was to me. During my three days' stay she made noodles and steamed buns by hand and cooked all my meals, save for one dumpling dinner we prepared together for the whole family. That day she rolled out the wraps and I put fillings in and sealed them up. As we were doing this, I asked her to tell me what happened between my father and her long ago.

"Go to the village and ask about me. Everyone will say I am a good person!" She started her story this way, with a heavy Shandong accent. "After your father ran away from home, my life was never easy. I had to serve your grandmother and bring up Fuxiang and Fuzhen under the Japanese occupation. In all those many years I never complained and never gave up waiting for him, even though communication between us was impossible. Then came Liberation. Not long afterwards your grandma and I found your father's address. We went to visit him and found he was remarried! God Almighty! How could he be so conscienceless?

"Your grandma was angry, only she knew what I had gone through for him. But neither my sorrow nor your grandmother's wrath could make your father come to his senses. He proposed a divorce. At first I didn't want to give it to him. I could have put him in deep trouble by not agreeing to a divorce — the Communist Party didn't allow bigamy, and he'd broken the law. Let him eat his own bitter fruit! But when I saw him crying, beating his head against the wall and with his hands, I became tenderhearted. I let him off lightly!"

Even after so many years, she still held a grudge against my father. I had sympathy for her, but at the same time I thought it was bad she had carried the grievance for so long. Instead of living a life of regret, she could have found someone else, got remarried, and lived happily. It was at the tip of my tongue to tell her so, but I didn't let it slip out. She wouldn't understand. She was an old-fashioned countrywoman, and in her the countryside feudalist tradition of "following one husband to the end" was very strong. It was unthinkable that I should broach the subject of her marrying another man.

Soon Shuxian finished rolling the wraps and sat down to help me finish making the dumplings. "How do you get along with them [my parents]? Do they treat you well?" she asked me.

"Yes, they treat me well. Sometimes we bicker, but every family does. They are strict with us. I'd prefer them to be less strict, but I think they do care about us."

"Do they give you enough pocket money to spend?"

"No. They don't give us pocket money. They buy all our clothes. When we need money to buy little things like pencils or notebooks, we ask them and usually they give us what we need."

"They should give you money. Ask them for money. They have lots of money, don't they?"

"No. I don't think so," I said honestly.

"Yes, they have lots of money. You don't see it because they hide it away. Ask them for money. Why not?"

I felt disappointed. Was this the way she brought up her children? As I was shaking my head and telling her no, no, she put her hand into her loose Chinese jacket and took out one yuan, and then another, and handed them to me. I refused, "I can't take it. I've no need for it. As you know, I can always get money from them. It's not easy for you to save. Keep it yourself." But she insisted. As an older person she felt obliged to give me something on our first meeting. In the end I had to take it.

"Where did you live before you moved to Tianjing?"

"In the countryside of Qufu, in your father's household with your grandmother. She didn't want me to move out."

I now understood why my grandmother didn't come to live with us in the city and enjoy a better life. My parents had always invited her, but she always turned them down. She didn't want to leave Shuxian home alone in the countryside. I also better understood my mother's bitterness. Not only were Shuxian and her daughters against her, but so was my grandmother. Grandmother had never forgiven father for deserting Shuxian.

Back in Beijing I decided to talk to my father and get the other half of the story. If he didn't want to talk, I would try again later. But he did talk. In a somewhat uncomfortable tone he told me his version: "I didn't know Shuxian was still alive after I had to run away from home in 1940. One day the Japanese devils came to arrest me. My family told them I hadn't been home for a long time and no one knew where I was, but they searched the house and found my pen. They knew I was nearby and decided to wait for me. A boy ran out of the village to warn me. I then ran away and never went back. Later I heard that Shuxian and your grandmother had both been arrested by the devils. Until Liberation my movements were uncertain and I changed my name many times, so I never received a letter from home. I thought she had been killed."

When he stopped, I didn't carry on. What right did I have to question his morals? He had risked his life to fight the Japanese. But some doubts did linger in my mind. Hadn't he ever asked himself whether by chance Shuxian was still alive? Wasn't it more due to the fact that, when he met my mother, his feelings towards Shuxian had died? He didn't realize I wouldn't have blamed him even if it had been like that. After visiting Shuxian herself, I couldn't imagine him living with her. He was a revolutionary, and she was backward and illiterate. If they had been forced to live together, neither would have been happy.

Remarriages of revolutionary cadres were heard of now and again after Liberation. They were not without public comment. The cadres were accused of being dissolutes who loved the new, young, and pretty girls from the city. But my father didn't pick a beautiful city girl: my mother was also a countrywoman, and she was not even as good looking as Shuxian. He chose my mother because they had the same ideals and a similar enterprising spirit. When Father married Shuxian in the 1930s, he was only a teenager, and their marriage was arranged. I believed he deserved a second chance.

My other half-sister, Fuzhen, inherited Shuxian's beauty. She was five-foot-six, slim, and fair-skinned, with large, soft eyes. She wore glasses for near-sightedness, the only one in my family who did.

My two visits to Fuzhen were two months apart; the second one was for her wedding. When I first saw Qiuyuan, her fiancé, I was disappointed. He was about the same height as Fuzhen, tawny, and pedestrian-looking. Fuzhen deserved someone much more handsome than that, I thought, but Fuzhen was very happy. Qiuyuan was a squadron leader in the air force. In her eyes, he was a bright man with a very bright future.

Their marriage hadn't come easy. One morning on my earlier visit I saw Fuzhen's eyes were swollen, obviously from crying the night before, but she offered no explanation. She now told me it was because their marriage application had just been turned down. My father's oldest brother had committed suicide, and in China that was considered a betrayal of the party and people. The family background of a pilot had to be spotless for three generations, as did his wife's. But they were both very persistent, and the leaders subsequently changed their minds.

The wedding was simple. On a long table were candies and tea, and around it sat a few leaders and twenty-some pilots. There was no wedding cake or special dress. All wore their newest air force uniforms, army green jacket and blue pants, and I wore my daily clothes. After Qiuyuan's leader and comrades-in-arms gave short speeches, the performances began. Customarily the bride and groom had to offer something. Fuzhen couldn't dance and her singing was poor, so she decided to get me to sing with her. "Don't you dare sing alone if they ask you!" she warned me. She didn't want the pilots to know who the poor singer was.

When our turn came, we stood up and Fuzhen positioned us so our backs were to the audience. The pilots protested but Fuzhen wouldn't budge. She poked me and told me to start. While I sang, she followed along as best she could. The song she chose was "A Lamp in Front of Chairman Mao's Window":

A lamp in front of Chairman Mao's window,
Shines through nights in spring, summer, autumn and winter.
Beside it sits our great leader,
Who spreads out our motherland's glorious future.

Chairman Mao wields the brush to rivers,
Over rivers rainbows fly.
Chairman Mao wields the brush to mountains,
In mountains rain dragons stalk.
Chairman Mao wields the brush to sand,
On sand green grows.
Chairman Mao's magic brush waves the east wind,
The wind blows and the sky turns red throughout.

The morning after the wedding, Qiuyuan brought home his breakfast to share with us as a special treat. Milk, eggs, dumplings, spare ribs, cookies, chocolate, and everything one can think of, all freshly made. The cooking was excellent. Long before my visits to Fuzhen I heard that pilots were entitled to special food, now I knew what that meant. They ate in a separate dining-room while their relatives, including wives, ate in the common ones.

I stayed with the newlyweds for ten days. During this period Qiuyuan took practically no time off. He worked every day and one afternoon even insisted I come along. We went to his barracks and climbed onto a truck together with the other pilots, and twenty minutes later we were in a field picking beans.

When Qiuyuan was away Fuzhen and I often went swimming or strolled to the airbase PX to buy candies, but there was still time to kill. To entertain us Qiuyuan sent his pilots to our hostel. They chatted with us and played the harmonica and *huqin*, a two-stringed bowed instrument.

Fuzhen once asked me what I thought of the pilots. "They're nice. Some are very handsome!" I made a funny face. "But too shy."

"That's because they don't know you. How about marrying a pilot? Later if you decide to, just tell me. I can help you find a good one."

After my return from the base, the unfettered life became unbearable. In childhood, when I could never play enough, I dreamt of playing all the time. Now I was fed up. I missed my studies, I missed the old times when life was more meaningful and substantial. Every day we went to school and left having learned something new. Every day we were one step closer to university. Now the Cultural Revolution had cost us two precious years. What was done could not be undone. I was not asking Mao and the party centre to pay for our losses, but they could at least end the revolution and return things to normal. They owed us that much, and it was still not too late. If they did so, I would give them my forgiveness, my gratitude, and even my love again, I promised to myself.

PART THREE:

LIFE AS A PEASANT AND WORKER

WALKING THE 5/7 ROAD AND
JOINING THE BRIGADE

THE GAP BETWEEN CITY AND COUNTRYSIDE, CENTRAL and remote outlying areas, is huge in China. To eliminate this gap was one unchanging policy of the Communist government. Since the 1950s, it urged graduates and demobilized young soldiers to go to poor rural areas to aid in development. Before the Cultural Revolution, some young people did volunteer to leave their homes and go to undeveloped mountain and country places.

On graduation from junior middle school in 1964, my older sister, Aihua, signed up to go to the Great Northern Wilderness in the northeast. Her motives were not idealistic. She wanted mainly to escape from school and my parents and thought that in the wilderness she could meet people on an equal footing and live a happier life. She abandoned this plan only at the last minute when her friends convinced her that life there would be too hard.

Under pressure from my parents, she then reluctantly took the entrance exam for senior middle school and was accepted by one of a middle rank. "See, she isn't dumb. If she works at it, she can study as well as anyone." My mother kept telling me this even years afterwards, but Aihua's heart just wasn't in school. After a year she again resolved to "support the border areas," this time in Xinjiang, to the northwest. My parents argued and argued with her, but her determination didn't waver. Grudgingly, they gave in and let her go.

In Urumqi, the capital of Xinjiang Autonomous Region, Aihua got a job in a mica factory belonging to the Xingjiang Production and Construction Corps. At first she was a worker, sitting at a table and separating mica sheets all day long. Later she became an accountant. The new life agreed with her. Every year she was allowed one visit home, and each time I saw her she had changed even more. In three years she had become a different person. Formerly bitchy and bitter, she was now happy and calm. When my mother criticized her for not being "progressive," she just giggled. When Mother asked her to do some housework, she did it without a word.

"Why are you so relaxed?" I asked, thoroughly amazed at the extent of her transformation.

"I finally figured it all out. Being angry doesn't solve anything. Parents are parents. They mean no harm. If they like to pick at me, let them. It can't hurt me."

On May 7, 1966 Chairman Mao wrote Lin Biao a letter in which he said that all people should be required to learn alternate skills. This was named the 5/7 Instruction. Before anything could be done, however, the Cultural Revolution erupted and overwhelmed all else. On May 7, 1968, when the revolution was ebbing, the Revolutionary Committee of Heilongjiang Province established the first 5/7 Cadres' School in the countryside. Together with so-called capitalist roaders, many cadres were sent there, to work, live, and transform and improve themselves. The 5/7 Instruction later came to mean that the city people should learn farming skills.

The 5/7 Instruction affected many lives but fell hardest on my generation. In the summer of 1968 the dispersal of middle school students began. The first to go were "the 1966 graduates," those from the third grades in both senior and junior middle schools who should have graduated in 1966. The ones from my school were told to join the Production and Construction Corps in the Great Northern Wilderness. Unlike my sister, who worked in a factory, these students were to be pioneers, to open up wasteland and till it. And unlike the cadres who went to the 5/7 Cadres' School for a year, or at most two years, and whose official residence was still Beijing, the 1966 graduates would become permanent residents of the places to which they were sent.

It was unthinkable to me that the government would transform a whole year's worth of graduates permanently into peasant farmers. However, I did not feel too threatened. I refused to believe that this would be our lot as well, and kept deceiving myself that the party leaders would change their minds when it came our turn. But others knew better. In the summer of 1968 some parents started a rescue movement to save their children from being sent to the countryside. Those who had wits used their wits, and those who had power used their power.

The most powerful of all turned out to be the army leaders. "Power grows out of the barrel of the gun," Mao had said. During the Cultural Revolution many local leaders suffered badly, but army leaders didn't. Mao had a special feeling towards those who held the guns — maybe he was afraid of them. Every time the CPGLCR assaulted the army leaders,

Mao would come out and speak on their behalf. He would not do this for civilians. The PLA was called "the great wall of iron and steel that never collapses." Whenever the party lost control in an area, the army would be sent in to take charge.

To provide a safe haven, the Military Committee of the Central Party made a new regulation that allowed army leaders above a certain rank to send their children into the army through "inside recruitment." Indeed, during this special time when all schools and universities were closed, there could not have been a better place than the army for city youth. Careers in the army could bring prestige, easy entrance into the party, and rapid bureaucratic advancement. Outside the army, bureaucratic advancement stagnated, whereas the army, with its constant circulation of personnel in and out, offered a much better chance for promotion. Upon demobilization, officers could then transfer to civilian life and keep their rank. Above all, army recruits were guaranteed jobs in their home cities after demobilization because their official residences remained unchanged. Little wonder that inside recruitment came to be widely used. The army leaders used it for their own and their relatives' children. Local cadres used it too, if their contacts in the army were powerful enough. These contacts could always allow one more "niece" or "nephew" into the ranks, and nobody would say a thing.

In August my former comrade-in-arms, Wang Xiaonan, joined the army through inside recruitment. She became a nurse in a hospital for the air force in the northeast. In October my other comrade-in-arms, Xiao Ping, left Beijing for Guangzhou. She had an aunt in that military district who later made her a nurse in an army hospital in the suburbs. Neither met the conditions for official recruitment. The age requirement was eighteen and Xiaonan was only sixteen, Ping seventeen. Ping also had a chronic kidney condition. I didn't know how she managed to pass the physical, or whether she even had to take one.

Now the old Chinese saying about dragons, phoenixes, and moles really applied. Xiaonan and Ping turned out to be phoenixes, I turned out to be a mole. My father was not an army officer, and my parents were not willing to try to get me into the army by the back door as they thought that violated party discipline. They trusted the party and Chairman Mao to arrange my future properly.

Standing on the ground where I belonged, I watched the two phoenixes fly away and sneered at my past gullibility. Why had I been so fanatical about the *duilian*? Why had I felt so proud to be a heroine and stirred up such hatred towards students from "bad" families? After all, we were all in the same boat. I couldn't believe how stupid I had been.

Inside recruitment made an abrupt change in my attitude towards the privileged. I could tolerate the fact that they occupied big houses and had servants, but I could not condone their abuse of power in favour of their children. They did not even bother to do this covertly — they cooked up a regulation and used it blatantly. What impudence! I was so exasperated that I have felt contempt for all army leaders ever since.

My indignation, however, was directed towards the corrupt individuals, not the system. Until I got my chance to see the West, no matter how frustrated I became, I never questioned whether Communism was right for China. What else could China hope for? Certainly not a return to colonialism and feudalism, nor to Chiang Kaishek's rotten dictatorship. Capitalism, as an alternative, represented to me just one more evil ideal: the hands of capitalists were stained with the blood of working people. Only Communism cared for working people, I firmly believed, and I kept dreaming that one day everything would work out.

In September the remaining students were encouraged to go live with the herders on the grasslands of Inner Mongolia. It wasn't compulsory so I paid no attention, but three of my classmates, Yishu, Xiangzhen, and Rongxi, decided to respond to the call. They had been very progressive in the past, so progressive that in our "unfettered" years, when everybody else was only playing, they formed a secret group to study Chairman Mao's writings. All three were good friends of mine, and they wanted me to go with them. Xiangzhen, a dark, dumpy girl with short braids, begged me to join them but I hardened my heart and refused. So long as there remained any hope that I could continue my studies, I would stick it out.

They left without me. In the fall I received light-hearted letters from Xiangzhen and Yishu, in which they described how blue the sky was and how beautiful the grasslands: "Vast is the sky, boundless the wilds, flocks and herds show when the tall grass bends to the winds." They relished learning to ride horses, tend herds, and eat mutton with their hands. In the photographs they sent me I saw them astride horses, dressed in Mongolian robes, their cheeks glowing like herdsmen's. They looked completely different.

On October 4, in a report about the 5/7 Cadres' School in Heilongjiang Province, the *People's Daily* published Mao's instruction: "Working in the countryside provides masses of cadres an excellent second chance to study. Except for the old, weak, sick, and disabled, all should do so. Cadres on the job* should go in batches as well." After this, all ministries established their own 5/7 Cadres' Schools in the countryside, and all cadres except the sick and aged took turns working there. That was called walking the 5/7 road.

My father did not walk the 5/7 road because of his age, but in 1973 my mother spent a year in the 5/7 Cadres' School in Henan Province established by the First Machinery Ministry, for which she worked. We all worried about her. She was then fifty-five and had gone through a major operation on her lower back. But she was very positive. None of her adversities had ever shaken her faith in the party, and she accepted all its new policies without reservation. "Don't worry! I come from the countryside," she assured us. "A little farm work doesn't frighten me. We've had a good life in the city for a long time now. We should refresh our memories of the peasants' hard lives. One should not forget one's roots."

After Mao's new instruction, more people sensed the danger. Parents who couldn't send their children to the army tried other ruses. Some sent their children to their home villages in the countryside, where they could live among relatives and friends. Then, once the storm passed, they could shift them back to Beijing again with relative ease. Towards the end of November Guomei, the painter's daughter, went off to her father's home village in the countryside of Shunde County in Canton Province. By then Guomei and I were friendly again, and I went to see her off at the train station.

A group of our classmates, including Yunyan and Liping, who had been the most active in criticizing me, were there too. My relations with them were passable at best. At the time they were not talking to me and kept a good distance. Guomei's parents, a distinguished couple in overcoats and scarves, stood apart. In the fluorescent lights of the station, everyone's face had a bluish tinge. Guomei moved from one group to another saying her goodbyes. When she came to me, I saw her weeping. "Zhai Zhenhua, are we ever going to see each other again?" She hugged me and buried her face in my coat. I was depressed too. If only somebody could tell me what awaited me!

In just a few months, most of my friends had gone. I became more and more anxious. Let the end come soon, I thought, for better or for worse.

*During the Cultural Revolution many cadres were suspended from their jobs. Here Mao means to include both those who are suspended and those still on the job.

But in my heart, I never really prepared for a bad ending. I kept dreaming that a miracle would happen. The school would reopen, and I would be allowed to study again.

On December 22, 1968 the *People's Daily* published Chairman Mao's new Supreme Instruction at the top of the front page: "It is necessary that school graduates go to the countryside and accept re-education from the poor and lower-middle-class peasants. Cadres and other people in the cities should be persuaded to send their children who are graduating from universities and junior and senior middle schools to the countryside. Let us mobilize. Comrades in the countryside everywhere should welcome them."

Was he saying that we were all going to become peasants? That was impossible! Mao couldn't be that heartless! Not after all we did for him in his Cultural Revolution! I sprang up and rushed to school to confirm that I was right. Indeed, that day nothing happened.

The next day, however, the 1967 graduating classes of both junior and senior middle schools were organized to study Mao's Supreme Instruction, and the school announced our graduation assignment: all of us, with very few exceptions, were to go to Yan'an region to "Join the Brigade" in the countryside. Yan'an, a small town on the Loess Plateau, was where Mao and the Red Army were based from 1936 to 1947 after the Long March. In China it is known as the sacred shrine and cradle of the Chinese revolution. There we were to take root, live, and accept re-education. The teachers would do "ideological work" on those who didn't want to go until their attitudes had been "corrected."

We weren't even as lucky as the 1966 graduates. They were now farm workers. They enjoyed a state salary, worked eight hours a day, and had Sundays off. We were to earn the same as the peasants and work from sunrise to sunset year round. Worst of all, Yan'an was one of the most impoverished regions of China. Mao and other party leaders might have strong attachments to it, but to us Yan'an was only slightly better than hell.

Without one word being asked about what we wished, our fate was settled. From childhood we had been imbued with the idea that our lives did not belong to ourselves, they belonged to the country and the people. Once I had liked this idea, but only now did I know what it really meant. No schooling, no university, no future. My hopes were shattered, my dreams perished. It felt like the end of the world.

Ignoring students' reactions, the school pushed forward quickly. That afternoon the few exceptions were made clear. A position in a military factory in a suburb of Beijing was to be allocated to one of the thirty-some students in my class. Quite a few students went to see our teacher-in-charge, Yuying, to try to get it. Two years ago she had undergone our criticism and her life had been put in limbo. Today she was back, in charge of our banishment.

Even though my fate was now in her hands, I did not go to plead with her for forgiveness and help. I didn't feel like apologizing. What I had done was not my fault. Anybody in my position would have done the same, if not worse. Yuying should hate the Cultural Revolution, which had brought about everybody's ruin. My prospects were far worse than hers. Hated by my classmates, I was facing exile in the countryside, maybe forever. If she happened to take pity on me and assign me the factory job, fine, and if she didn't, that was life.

In the end she gave the job to Jiuhong, on the grounds that Jiuhong's family had financial problems and she most needed the work. Whether or not this was true, we all knew Jiuhong was her favourite.

On the morning of December 26 I stepped through the school gate and saw a piece of paper the size of a big-character poster on the wall facing the gate. "Those Students Who Respond to Chairman Mao's Call to Join the Brigade in Yan'an Sign Here," it read. I moved closer to have a look. A few names were already on it, but none I knew. If I signed now, I would be the first in my class. The last thing I wanted to do was to show my "progressiveness" by taking the lead in this damned campaign, but I had decided to go soon after the factory job was filled. What else could I do? As the Chinese say, "In twisting, thin arms will not win over thick legs." If I were going away, I might as well sign up and get it over with. I put my name down.

A friend in need is a friend indeed, they say. At this difficult time of my life, however, the one friend I had who remained in Beijing, Su'e, added to my disillusionment. Su'e came from a worker's family and had been one of Yuying's favourites. On the same day in March 1966 she and I joined the Communist League. In August 1966 she became a Red Guard, and in the re-election in 1967, like me, she failed to get enough votes. Since then we had been best friends.

Her parents and three brothers were all in Shanghai but, at her grandmother's insistence, she lived in Beijing with her grandmother and her uncle's family. Their home was right on my way to school. Every so often when my bus passed it, I would jump off and stop in unannounced. There I would gossip with Su'e and her grandmother and even spend the night if Su'e urged me to.

They had just two rooms. The small one was for her uncle and aunt, and the large one for the remaining five family members. Su'e, her grandmother, and a three-year-old cousin slept on a huge bed, and her two older cousins, thirteen-year-old Guangbin and seventeen-year-old Guangtao, occupied two single beds. There was no separation in the room, not even a screen.

When I stayed, I would share the big bed with Su'e, Grandma, and the toddler. It felt strange to sleep in the same room with Guangtao, a big boy of my age. Going to bed was OK — with the light turned off, no one could see anyway — but when I got up in the light of day, I couldn't help feeling Guangtao's presence. "How does Su'e feel about it?" I wondered. "She's lived like this for years."

I wanted to get Su'e to come to Yan'an with me so that we could keep each other company in the hard times ahead, but I never got a chance to talk with her about it. Whenever I even mentioned the word "Yan'an," Su'e's grandmother would break in and cut me short. In her hoarse man's voice she attacked Yan'an and the whole idea of sending us there. "What is this Yan'an? It isn't a place for humans! How can they ask you young girls to go and live there?" I certainly agreed with her there, but she didn't even care to hear that. "Whoever of you wants to go can go. Just don't try to talk our Su'e into it. She isn't going, and that's that!"

Su'e grew up on her grandmother's knee and was her darling. There was no way Grandma would let Su'e go to Yan'an. The old woman was uneducated and had never worked. She didn't care what anyone thought of her and was determined to play the heavy for Su'e. No matter who came to see her from the school, they would hear the same threat: "If you force Su'e onto a train, I'm going to lie on the rail and let it roll over me!"

While this went on, Su'e sat on a stool, hands in the side pockets of her cotton padded coat (households heated by a stove never got comfortably warm, and people had to wear the same outfits inside as they did outside), and bit her tongue. She didn't try to stop her grandma, nor did she indicate to the school that she was going anyway despite her grandmother's threats. Su'e was still a league member. I never expected her to be so backward but she did remain in Beijing. After several unsuccessful attempts, the school stopped bothering them with "ideological work" and counted Su'e out.

Su'e's cousin Guangtao was in the same grade as I was. While his grandmother fought for Su'e, he was vexed by another problem. His teacher-in-charge, whose favourite he was, gave him a choice: take the only factory job allotted to his class or join the brigade in the countryside. Had the factory been in Beijing, things would have been perfect. Unfortunately it was in Dalian, a large, industrialized city to the northeast. Guangtao was torn.

I didn't understand his problem and had a big mouth. "What's the matter?" I asked Su'e. "Why doesn't he take the factory job? Dalian isn't a bad city. It's on the sea and I hear it's beautiful. The life of a worker certainly beats that of a peasant!"

"Shifting jobs is very difficult for a worker. He may never be able to get back to Beijing."

"Who says those who join the brigade are going to be allowed to return to Beijing? If it were me, I'd take the job. Don't be too greedy!"

Days later Guangtao did choose Dalian. I hope my "wise" advice wasn't the decisive factor. It later turned out that the factory, a military one, was not in Dalian. According to Su'e, they intentionally misled Guangtao's school during the recruitment period. He was only to be trained in Dalian. Three months later he was sent to where the factory was really located, an isolated and backward gully in Ningxia Province. When those who joined the brigade later had a chance to go to university or return to Beijing, Guangtao had nothing. The factory would not let him move anywhere.

I felt great pity for Guangtao. He was a smart boy who deserved much better than he got from life. His school was the Beijing Fourth Middle School for Boys, a well-known key school. Li Na, the daughter of Chairman Mao and Jiang Qing, attended my school; Liu Yuanyuan, the son of Liu Shaoqi and Wang Guangmei, attended Guangtao's school. I happened to know this because Yuanyuan was in Guangtao's class. From Su'e I learned that Guangtao was the best student in his class. He had promise, until the Cultural Revolution interfered.

The entire quadrangle Su'e lived in actually belonged to a "democratic personage," a phrase used in China to describe distinguished non-Communists, either patriotic capitalists or reformed Kuomintang officials. Several years after Liberation the Communist government confiscated two wings and rented one to Su'e's family and another to a couple and their young son. At times this personage visited Su'e's home when I was there, so we became acquainted. Occasionally, I even went to his quarters to play cards with his family, which was a large one. I didn't know his name. Behind his back Su'e called him Cripple, because one of his legs was lame.

One day when I was chatting with Su'e, Cripple dropped in. "Su'e is staying in Beijing and Guangtao is going to Dalian to be a factory worker, but I have to go Yan'an to become a peasant. Everybody is better off than me," I told him dejectedly.

"No, no! You may be quite wrong!" He limped about the room, his hands behind his back and his round, tonsured head lowered. His voice was annoyingly cheerful. "Let's see how things are after ten years! Yes, we'll know the outcome in ten years!" he boomed confidently. At the same time he raised his head and moved his hands to the front to make a cross with his two forefingers, the Chinese character for ten.

Nobody in the room chimed in to agree with him. In silence Grandma did her needlework, Su'e knitted a sweater, and I watched him gloomily. At the moment I didn't think much of his prediction. I was completely down on life and didn't want to think what the world would be like in ten years. But for some reason I remembered what he had said. Ten years later things did turn out well. I then thought he was a seer.

FAREWELL, BEIJING

THE DEPARTURE DATE WAS JANUARY 7, 1969, SIXTEEN DAYS after Mao's Supreme Instruction was published.

The New Year's holiday didn't bring me any joy. There was no laughter or celebration. Instead, I went with my parents to the Great Department Store in the centre of Beijing to do some final shopping. With the extra cotton-product coupons issued us, they bought me a cotton-padded hat and navy blue overcoat to keep me warm on the cold plateau. They also bought me an enamel washbasin. As we shopped, they showed great patience, which they never had before, helping me try clothes on and allowing me to waste time picking a basin with a design I liked. The clerk in the store also served us attentively rather than leaving us to fend for ourselves, as did most shop assistants at the time. I felt as if everyone were trying to please me.

On January 3 I went to hand in my residence registration card at the police substation. Once this was done, I could no longer legally reside in Beijing. Walking carefully on the icy sidewalk, I felt as if I were in a dream. Why was I suddenly leaving Beijing? Maybe I would wake up soon and find everything back the way it was.

In fifteen minutes I reached the substation. There I took out my registration card and the recommendation letter from the school and handed them to a clerk. While he sat at his desk and read, I prayed for the impossible, that he would say, "Your card has a special mark, so I cannot take it and let you leave Beijing," or, "You aren't allowed to leave so soon; you'll have to wait for two months more." But he said nothing. In less than two minutes he had finished. "Good. That's all we need. Now you may go."

January 7 came. Mother didn't go to the station with me, but she went to work on the same bus I had to take. During the forty-minute ride we sat close to the door and talked little. Most of the time I stared out at the passing scene, the familiar wide streets, the hordes of buses of all colours,

155

the stone North Sea Bridge with its carved marble balustrades, the mirror-like ice surface of the North Sea Lake, and the uniquely shaped corner towers at the back of the Forbidden City. This bus line was the one I took to school, so this was what I had seen every day for the past four years, but I had hardly noticed it. Now everything looked so beautiful.

When the bus neared the stop closest to my mother's unit, she said goodbye to me and stood up to line up with those getting off. The bus stopped. She moved along with the others towards the door and kept her face away. At the last moment, when she was already on the lowest step of the bus, she suddenly turned to me and clasped my hand on the rail. Her face was covered by a gauze mask (we wore masks in the winter to keep warm and to ensure that the air we breathed was clean), so all I could see were her eyes. They were red and drowned in tears. Before I could react, she let go of my hand and stepped off the bus. On the sidewalk she half-ran a few steps and turned back for one last look. By then she was really crying.

Oh, my strong-willed revolutionary mother, I didn't know you had this sentimental side! I had thought she wasn't coming to the station because she didn't want to take a few hours off from work. Suddenly I realized that she couldn't stand the sadness of seeing me off. This thought brought me to the verge of tears, but I held them back. The bus was crowded, and people were watching. I turned my head towards the window again and tried to think of nothing. I had resolved not to cry during my leave-taking.

The station was full of students, parents, and friends, some stepping onto the train with handbags and washbasins, others holding onto windowsills to talk to those inside. In the background, loudspeakers broadcast revolutionary songs and songs composed for Chairman Mao's and Lin Biao's quotations. The organizers were trying to create a lofty, heroic atmosphere — the right kind of atmosphere for revolutionary youth going to Yan'an.

One of the songs had lyrics set from Mao's quotations: "The world is yours, and also ours. But it is, in the final analysis, yours. You young people are full of vigour and vitality like the eight or nine o'clock sun in the morning. You are our hope." I had heard this quotation hundreds of times before, each time with patriotism and pride. Today it sounded cynical. "The world is ours?" I asked myself. "Bullshit!"

After wandering around the platform for a while, I found my father. He was in his full winter attire, black wool hat, long black herringbone overcoat, and black fur-lined leather shoes. A long scarf of grey wool tartan was wrapped around his neck. Father was only five-foot-six, but I always thought he was very handsome and dignified.

We walked to my coach and stood by the door. "Your mother and I won't be beside you any more. From now on you'll have to look after yourself," he said to me. "Stay close to the party. If you have any problem, go to the local party organization and ask for help." He also told me to try to get into university one day. "Fat chance!" I thought, but dared not answer back.

There was only so much to say in farewell. When the words ran out I asked him to go home, but he insisted on waiting. Standing face to face with him in silence, I saw things I hadn't noticed before. His back was bending, his face had begun to sag, and his hair was greying at the temples. Even his bright, piercing eyes were losing their lustre. He was getting old, and I was leaving.

The warning bell rang. "You and Mother take care of yourselves. Don't worry about me," I said as I stepped onto the train. Turning back, I saw him lift his hat and hold it in his hand, ready to salute me with it like an honoured guest. For the first time, he was treating me as an adult. His well-kept hair, combed to the back, was ruffled by the freezing wind. "Put your hat on, it's cold," I admonished him. "I'm all right," he said gently. The train jerked. The last moment arrived. I raised my hand to wave good-bye and looked into father's eyes. Unexpectedly, I saw they were moist.

Suddenly I felt wretched. "Are you sad to see your daughter off to Yan'an? Do you regret not being able to save her?" I wondered bitterly. "I'm going to a backward place I don't want to go to, to live a hard life I don't want to live. I didn't steal, rob, or commit any crime. Why do I deserve this?" Tears welled up and blurred everything.

Feeling the train move, I wiped my eyes with my sleeve to see my father again, but more and more tears came. My resolve fell to pieces and I started to cry. All the anger, indignation, bitterness, and sorrow that had accumulated inside me since the publication of Mao's Supreme Instruction now came gushing out. The train gained speed, Father and the people running alongside were left behind.

Finally I was all cried out. Through my tears I saw that the train was passing through the Beijing suburbs. "Goodbye, Beijing. Goodbye, my family. It's all over." Until then I hadn't really thought about living in Yan'an, but now it was time to turn my back on the past and face the future. Despite my deep resentment towards Mao and the party, I still loved my country and people. I was not a pampered girl from a rich family. I could put up with a hard life if I had to.

YAN'AN — "THE SACRED SHRINE
OF THE REVOLUTION"

STOOD AT THE DOOR OF THE RAILWAY CARRIAGE A LITTLE
longer, and then, having regained my composure, I entered. It was
occupied by a special group of thirty students from six schools in the
east district of Beijing. They were all from my grade save for three from
the first grade of senior middle school. The three had not been required
to come, but they had insisted and finally gained approval. "Lunatics!"
I thought. "After everything we've been through, you still want to be the
most progressive!"

We thirty were to settle in the Dates Garden Brigade, named for its
famous garden. From 1942 to 1946 Chairman Mao and other party leaders
had lived in the garden itself, which was located on the lowlands by the
Yan River.

On the train someone told me we might not have to do hard labour
because we were to act as tour guides for Chairman Mao's and other
leaders' former residences in the garden. I was skeptical, but I did thank
Yuying in my heart for sending me to Dates Garden Brigade, not to the
commune where the rest of my classmates were headed. It didn't have a
famous name like Dates Garden, and it was even more isolated and less
developed. Besides, some of my classmates still hated me. Living with them
for the rest of my life was dreadful even to think about.

The journey from Beijing to Yan'an was arduous. We sat on hard seats in
the train for a day and a night until we reached Tongchuan, a small city north
of Xi'an, the capital of Shanxi Province and the home of terracotta. We
then spent nine hours in the back of an army truck, sitting on two benches
along the sides. The truck tossed and swivelled wildly on the narrow mountain dirt road, and the ride was jarring and scary. When a vehicle passed
from the opposite direction, it seemed to just miss us by inches. Our driver
drove at white-knuckled speed even around the hairpin turns. At each one I
thought we were going to career off into the abyss. Goodbye, world!

All the way from Tongchuan to Yan'an we were shrouded in the dry
dust stirred up by our truck and the vehicles ahead. Talking in that noise

was next to impossible. At first, I kept busy looking out the back of the truck at the mountain slopes and terraced fields. Later I rested my eyes mainly on my fellow travellers' hats, coats, and gauze masks, amazed at the speed with which the dust accumulated on them. In the end, I just closed my eyes and prayed for the journey to end.

We were exhausted when we arrived but the welcoming ceremony awaited us. Reporters and filmmakers who had come all the way from Beijing with us followed us through the streets. They were to report back to the party and Chairman Mao on how Mao's Supreme Instruction had been successfully carried out. People stood on the sidewalk and waved, and a big parade was held with singing, dancing, and a "waist drum dance." The drum dancers had tied "sheep tripe towels" (white towels that had the appearance of sheep tripe) on their heads and wore white cotton suits with red sashes at the waist. In unison they beat the drums on their waists from all different angles constantly changing their formations.

We saw the Pagoda Mountain and the Yan River, emblems of the "sacred shrine," Yan'an, mentioned often in the revolutionary stories on which we had been brought up. Many of the young people who came to Yan'an in the thirties and forties cried when they first saw the Pagoda Mountain.

In my textbook there was a poem, "Back to Yan'an," written by a revolutionary poet, He Jingzhi. It describes how excited he was in 1956 when he revisited Yan'an after ten years' absence. I first heard it from my older brother, Xinhua, who used to recite the poem beautifully.

My heart, don't beat so fast;
My eyes, don't be blinded by dust.

Grabbing the loess I don't let go,
Close to my heart I hold it.

In dreams I returned to Yan'an at times,
Locking Pagoda Mountain tight in my arms.

Red girdle and "sheep tripe towel,"
Across the Yan River come my folk.

The present scene fit the poem well, but it failed to move me. Thirty years ago the revolutionary youth willingly poured into Yan'an, eager to join in the liberation and betterment of their country. Today we were driven here to "repair the earth," as Beijing youth mockingly referred to our cultivating the land, and to be re-educated by peasants. Thirty years earlier they came here because this was the place where Chairman Mao, the Communist Party centre, and the hope of China were. Today Mao and the party centre were in Beijing, from which we had been expelled. How could I feel the same? To me the Pagoda Mountain was only a small hill with an inconspicuous pagoda on top and the Yan River, in its deep bed, was down to a trickle.

The ceremonies ended before dark. A tractor approached. It was the only motor vehicle the Dates Garden Brigade had, and that was because of the brigade's special status. Many other brigades had none. We were told to get in and stand on the open trailer behind it. In the bitter cold plateau wind, with noisy chugs from the tractor, we were towed to the brigade three miles from town.

There weren't any further ceremonies, thank God, but some commune members were waiting in the brigade centre to take us to their homes and feed us. A short, chubby woman with a round nose, round mouth, and round eyes in her round face was led up to me and introduced as Heitu's wife. "Heitu's wife — doesn't she have a name of her own? What is her name?" I asked, but nobody bothered to answer. That was the local custom. Once a woman married, she would be called so-and-so's wife from then on, and her own name would be forgotten.

I was too exhausted to be hungry and told the commune members so. But they persuaded me to follow Heitu's wife to her home half a mile away. There I had a little millet rice and a dish of potato and pickled Chinese cabbage.

Afterward she took me back to the brigade centre. It was dark, and as we walked on the narrow, winding trail along the former bed of a valley river, I found it hard to see my way with no light but that of the stars. I followed Heitu's wife closely and was just able to keep to the narrow path, which was a bit lighter in colour than the bare loess beside it.

At the centre I sat down on the ground and waited for further instructions. Gradually all the students returned, and the peasants who had spare cave dwellings came to take us to their places. The brigade planned to build us new ones with the money the government allocated as our settling-in allowance, but they were not completed until over a year later. Until then, we were to live in different peasants' homes.

Cool in the summer and warm in the winter, cave dwellings are unique to that area. They are arch-shaped all the way to the rear and have doors and windows at the front. There are two kinds, earthen and stone. The earthen ones are simply big, deep holes into hillsides, and the stone ones are constructed out of large stones against the hillside. Most of the natives lived in earthen cave dwellings. Only the well-off families could afford the money and labour to build long-lasting stone ones.

The five girls from my school were given a cave dwelling halfway up the mountain. Fortunately, the peasants had carried our luggage up while we were eating our supper. With just washbasins in our hands and schoolbags on our shoulders, we followed our guide, Dejin, and puffed slowly upwards to the cave dwelling he owned.

Dejin was a middle-aged man with high cheekbones, dark, rough skin, and rosy cheeks. The plateau sun and wind had burned and marked his face. His eyes were a blurred yellow from constant exposure to the smoke of the wood fire in his home. He had the lean, weathered look of a peasant. "Are we going to look like that too, someday?" I asked myself.

When we arrived at the dwelling, he unlocked the door and turned on the dim five-watt light. I glanced in and saw a big *kang* occupying more than half of the eighteen-square-yard floor area of the cave dwelling. The *kang* is a northern peasant's everything. Made of stone and covered with a thick layer of mud, it is bed, chair, sofa, table, and closet, and all belongings are piled on it. The *kang* is built against the wall, and the chimney of the kitchen stove passes through a tunnel inside it. Smoke from cooking is vented outside, heating the *kang* on the way. Nothing is wasted; the burning wood cooks the food and warms the *kang* and, thus, the room at the same time.

Besides the *kang*, there was a large water vat in one corner of the cave and a simple wooden basin stand against the wall. That was it. "The toilet is that way." Dejin pointed upwards and left while we were still peeping inside the dwelling.

We had to go to the washroom before going to bed, but who wanted to look for a toilet in a state of near exhaustion, in the dark, without a flashlight? All we could think of was to get into bed as soon as possible, so we all went out into the darkness and used any convenient place. Then we perfunctorily washed our dusty faces and stinky feet in the washbasins, made five sleeping bags by folding our quilts side by side on the big *kang*, and slipped in.

That night I slept like a log and when I opened my eyes, it was daylight. Seated on the *kang* I dressed carefully so as not to wake those sleeping around me. Unbolting and opening the wooden doors, I stepped out and looked for the toilet. Too bad one can't do it just anywhere in the daytime. About twenty yards up from the cave dwelling I located an enclosure made from sorghum stalks that were a bit shorter than a person. That's it, I thought, but I couldn't tell if anybody was in it. I cleared my throat loudly as I approached so that any occupant could hear me. Good, no response. Close up, I easily saw the sorghum-stalk door and opened it.

On a dirt floor of about twenty square feet, there were two slabs of stone with a seam between them about four inches wide. Two wooden sticks about an inch and a half in diameter stuck up from the seam and tilted to the rear. I guessed one was supposed to aim for the sticks and let the subject matter slide down them into the liquid in the huge jar below, instead of letting it drop like a bomb and risking a reciprocal splash. Not so dumb, these peasants! As I squatted down and did my job, trying to make sure my aim was true, I was in a state of anxiety lest someone, especially a man, come to use the toilet. Although a person outside couldn't see in, from inside one could peek out through the seams between the stalks. I kept careful watch and had a shout at the ready, but no one came.

Going to the toilet in Yan'an was always a problem. There was a constant feeling of being watched, a worry of bumping into some man at the toilet, and a fear of being invaded by maggots. In winter there were hardly any, but in summer they thrived. All one saw, if one happened to glance down, was a mass of wriggling maggots in a thick, foul half-liquid, each one an inch or two long. Indiana Jones never stumbled into anything so disgusting! A few of the more adventurous ones would occasionally manage to climb out of the jar and wiggle around aggressively on the slabs. I was petrified one would climb into my trousers. As revolting as it was, I found myself perversely watching them twisting and roiling and wondered how the peasants could ever use this stuff as manure for the vegetables they ate.

When I finished, my bottom was frozen. I hurriedly cleaned myself with the toilet paper in my pocket. Later I heard that the peasants never used toilet paper. They just picked up anything handy on the ground, such as a piece of rock or brick, and used it as a scraper.

The next procedure should be to wash one's hands but I didn't feel like it. Some of my roommates were still sleeping and I didn't want to go back inside to wash and take a chance of disturbing them. Besides, water was too precious, and hot water even more so. There and then I decided that from now on, this prescribed hygienic measure would have to be forgone. The mountain slopes were covered with clean white snow. I just grabbed some and rubbed my hands with it.

Feeling fresh now, I looked around in curiosity. Everything was exotic: the big ravine below me, the scattered cave dwellings here and there, and the sharply contoured, terraced fields, their tops covered with snow. It was, despite my bitter feelings against this place, beautiful in its own way. How would it look from the top of this mountain, I wondered. On impulse I set off to find out.

I climbed and climbed until I found myself standing on top of the world and taking in the whole great loess plateau. I had imagined a jumble of undulating mountains, but what I saw was an awesome, vast, flat land stretching to the horizon. The lowlands and ravines where the plateau people lived and farmed were now deep, wide cracks cutting the surface into many jigsaw pieces. No sound, no villages, no traces of life. How insignificant human beings were in this tableau!

It had been snowing when I started and now it came harder. From near to far, snowflakes flew in the air, softening the panorama and turning the land white. I felt purified and touched, and my mind widened. Chairman Mao's poem "The Snow" came to me. It was a *ci*, a type of Chinese poem requiring a certain rhyme and a certain number of characters. I blamed Mao for wasting my life but I still liked his poems. "The Snow" was always my favourite. It was written in 1936 while Mao was in Yan'an, probably in similar weather. Today, standing before the snowy scene on the plateau, I came to appreciate Mao's words in a way I never had before.

The north country view,
A thousand li bound in ice,
Ten thousand li in whirling snow.
Both sides of the Great Wall
Are left in a white stillness,
And the big river
Has lost its billow;
Silver snakes dance among gorges,
Wax elephants gallop across the plateau,
Making the sky look low.
Wait till it clears up,
The beauty dressed in white
Will be ever enchantingly beautiful.

This land is so full of beauty and charm,
It made countless heroes bow in homage.
It's a pity that Qin Huang* and Han Wu
Lacked perfect literary grace,
Tang Zong and Song Zu
Were slightly inferior in excellence,
And the gods' favourite, Ghengis Khan,
Only knew bending a bow to shoot eagles.
So much for the past,
To look for truly great figures,
Try the present!

For the first three days we weren't required to work. Twice a day we went to the peasants' homes to have our meals, and in between we learned some basic skills of plateau living. We learned how to make a fire to heat our *kang*, to draw water from the nearest well, which was five hundred feet uphill, and to carry the two water buckets balanced on a pole without disastrous spills.

The second afternoon we received the first lesson of our re-education by visiting the cave dwelling where Mao had lived in the Dates Garden. (Liu Shaoqi's was there too, but it was now concealed.) In the yard a narrator talked in idiosyncratic Mandarin about how Mao commanded his forces in battle, what important articles he wrote, and how kind he was to the peasants when he lived there. Often Mao would walk out of the garden to talk to the peasants working in the fields, and every year he held a New Year's party for the peasants from adjacent villages.

When the narrator finally finished, we were allowed a look at Mao's cave dwelling. It was simple. A big *kang* at the back occupied a third of the dwelling. In the front was a table, a chair, and a long display case against the wall. Behind its glass were some booklets and manuscripts in Mao's own handwriting.

The lesson did not restore my love for Mao. We knew all these old stories by heart and did not have to come all the way to Yan'an to hear them again. Besides, his great past was over. In his present old age, he was paranoid. In the fall of 1968 I read his remarks about the educated on one of the big-character posters in the street: "According to me, intellectuals, inside the party or out, including the young ones who are now in schools, have basically a capitalist ideology because, in the

*Qin Huang, Han Wu, Tang Zong, Song Zu, and Ghengis Khan were the most famous emperors of the Qin, Han, Tang, Song, and Yuan dynasties, respectively.

seventeen years since Liberation, art and education circles have been controlled by revisionists. Capitalist thoughts are dissolved in their blood." At the time I read it, I didn't believe that was Mao talking. One never knew how reliable posters were. But now, after he had exiled us to Yan'an, I did. He really thought that all of us, students in universities, middle schools, and even primary schools, were capitalists. He was mad. By then, I firmly believed that China, and hence my own life, would be better only after he was dead.

IN THE STONE QUARRY

THE RUMOUR ABOUT OUR BECOMING GUIDES FOR MAO'S residence turned out to be just that. There weren't many visitors, and the Dates Garden certainly had no need of thirty guides. When the short period of rest, readjustment, and "revolutionary tradition education" ended, real life began. We found ourselves in the same position as the peasants who worked for the brigade to make a living.

On the fourth morning, when the sun was high in the sky, we were taken to a ravine full of stones. Some commune members were already there working. We formed two lines and listened to an address by the party secretary of the brigade, Zhifu. He was about forty-five, broad-faced, and heavy-featured. Like most other peasants, he wore a pair of homemade padded cotton shoes and a Chinese-style padded cotton coat and pants in black, and a white towel was wrapped around the top of his head.

"Today your workday begins. Shortly our commune members will show you what to do. I just want to remind you of two things: One, the most important is safety. Be very careful. Don't let the stones fall on your feet or any accidents like that happen. Chairman Mao put you in our hands, and we have to be responsible for you. Two, watch out for overexertion. You are from the city and are not used to hard physical work. Don't be too hard on yourselves in the beginning. The capacity for physical labour has to be built up step by step. Be sure to keep my words in mind. Especially you girls. Excessive strain will cause prolapse of the uterus!"

Some girls lowered their heads and giggled at his last sentence. How could he be so crude as to mention the word "uterus" in front of all of these young boys? I also felt embarrassed, but other than that, I appreciated his speech. As a peasant he was doing very well.

Zhifu gave his talk and left for a meeting, but no peasants came forward to tell us what to do. We stood to the side and watched them work. Some were using hammers and chisels to break large stones into smaller ones. The rest were bringing the chunks to two-wheeled carts that stood at the mouth of the ravine. The younger ones worked alone taking small stones to the cart, while the men formed pairs to carry bigger pieces suspended by two ropes from a pole on their shoulders. A few of the female students, like Guoqing from my school and Ying from another, joined the youngsters in picking up small stones. I turned to Jinli, who was the leader of the five girls from my school, and asked her to pair up with me.

Zhifu's piece of advice did not have its desired effect. Instead, it made me want to show the peasants I wasn't the useless city girl they thought. I had inherited a lot of my mother's zeal. Like her, I liked to excel in whatever I did. Even the setback of undergoing public criticism, ejection from the Red Guards, and exile to Yan'an hadn't changed that. "It is easy to change dynasties, but hard to change a person's nature." I hadn't wanted to come to Yan'an, but now that I was there, I felt obligated to do my utmost.

My partner, Jinli, with big round eyes and heavy freckles around the bridge of her nose, was "progressive." Her attitude was similar to mine. We looked only for stone chunks near the limit we could lift, about 180 to 220 pounds. Following the peasants' examples, we bent down to secure the two rope loops on the bottom of the stone, stood up, and then walked unsteadily among the sharp stones. At the cart we put the stone down, took the ropes off, lifted it up, and threw it in. Then the hunt for another stone began.

After several trips, I was sweating profusely. When the break came and we were allowed to sit down, my T-shirt and blouse inside my sweater were drenched. The plateau wind was sharp as a knife and cut through my cotton-padded overcoat and sweater to my wet undergarments. In a few minutes I was freezing and needed to work again just to keep warm.

We worked until sunset, about 5:00 p.m., I guessed, because no one had a watch. There were two rest periods of about twenty minutes each and no break for lunch; in wintertime peasants didn't eat lunch, just breakfast and supper. In the thickening dusk we shuffled to the peasants' homes to be fed. When I arrived at Heitu's cave dwelling, his wife had prepared the dinner, some corn bread and the same dish of potato and pickled Chinese cabbage. With no appetite, I ate it, took out fifteen cents and a grain-product coupon, as we had been told to do, and put them down on the table.

After dinner I went directly home and climbed onto the *kang*. Using my pillow as a table, I wrote a letter to a friend describing my first hard day's work. Nothing on earth could have gotten me on my feet again. I skipped washing and went directly to sleep.

When we first arrived, the peasants didn't know us, so they seldom invited us home, and the five of us from my school didn't associate with the other students very much. We were a mountain away from them, and having carried stones all day I never felt like climbing over to have a chat. Only when a students' meeting or a brigade meeting was held in the evening did I drag myself out of my cave.

The next morning when I woke up, my muscles ached and my right shoulder was swollen and sore. Ignoring the pain, I forced myself up to face the challenge of another day. In freezing coldness on the mountain slope I brushed my teeth, and then returned to the cave and washed my face with a wet towel. At about 8:30 a.m., I went to Heitu's home to have breakfast, and found the same food awaited me — corn bread and a vegetable dish. It turned out that the millet rice I was offered in the first meal was a treat.

Around 9:30, the work force gathered in the same valley. Jinli and I resumed our partnership and continued carrying stones. When the loaded pole first pressed on my swollen right shoulder, a sharp pain forced me to call Jinli to halt. She was feeling the same. We decided to use our left shoulders. Soon we discovered that left shoulders were not as good as right ones, and they wore out much faster. Midday, we gritted our teeth and shifted the pole back to our right shoulders again.

For two whole months we toiled in the stone quarries with no weekends off, not even Sundays. Day after day, I worked for all I was worth. Once in a while Zhifu's words about not starting too strenuously came to mind, and I wondered whether I had exceeded my limits, but I didn't care. I hated my life, an unwanted, pointless existence. My country could not find any better use for us but dumped us all like dirt in the countryside. The peasants did not need us; we were their burden and only gave them trouble. Torturing my body gave me a way to vent my spleen. Let me help them to destroy myself! Besides, if I got really sick, I might be allowed to return to Beijing. There was nothing to lose — or so I thought.

I did get sick, but not in the way I had wanted. First I caught a cold and, when it was over, my voice had disappeared. Occasionally, after a good night's sleep, I could utter some low and ugly sounds in the morning — but once back in the quarry, and weighed down by stones, I was entirely mute.

Every morning the brigade leaders communicated with each other about the day's arrangements by shouting. They stood on a high point near their homes, cupped their hands around their mouths, and sent their words from the bottom to the top of the mountain and then the other way around. I cupped my hands, opened my mouth wide, and strained as hard as I could. Nothing.

The commune, which was very close to my brigade center, had a crude hospital. I once visited it and was received by a callow doctor, or perhaps he was a nurse. He looked at my vocal cords with the help of a flash-light, found nothing wrong, and sent me away with no treatment or medicine. Nobody knew, including myself, that the excessively hard work was to blame. After I left the stone works, my voice returned.

Losing my voice was but one problem. Throughout my stay in the Dates Garden I suffered menstrual disorders. The heavier the work, the shorter the time between my periods. In the stone quarry every thirteen or fourteen days I would have a period, each lasting a week. I was hardly ever clean. Visiting the local hospital again didn't help.

This malady disgusted me. Why not a decent one, such as a heart attack or liver infection that might take me back to Beijing? Now I couldn't even tell people about my sickness, or take sick leave!

The postmen in Yan'an usually delivered the mail to the fields where work was under way, if it wasn't too far into the mountains. On the tenth day, when the mail came to the quarry, I got a letter from my father. Anxious to know what he had to say, I took off a few minutes and moved to the side to read it.

Zhenhua, my daughter:

We received your letter on the 10th of January and felt relieved that you arrived safely in Yan'an.

That you responded to Chairman Mao's call to join the brigade in Yan'an was progressive. As senior revolutionaries and party members we support you. But as your parents we worry. You have never been away from us for more than a month. Suddenly you are far, far away and living an arduous life on your own. This fact is not easy for us to accept. It's especially hard on your mother. She can't get used to the idea that you are gone and misses you so much that she cried every night the first three days you were away. I am telling this not to make you worry, but to let you know we do care for you.

Make sure you take good care of yourself. You were never very strong. How are you coping with all the manual labour? Don't work full out all the time. "Health is the capital of revolution" [a saying often quoted in China]. Your life hasn't begun yet; you can't afford to ruin your health. And don't be discouraged about life. I believe the party won't forget those faithful to her.

As I read, my tears dropped onto the letter. To hide them I turned my face away from my workmates. I had not known my parents cared so much about me; they hadn't shown it before. My adversity brought them closer to me. My heart grew warm, yet bitter tears kept welling up. They wanted me to take good care of myself. How could I possibly do that here?

Having observed us for one month, the peasants decided they were ready to award our work points. Work points formed the basis of all commune members' earnings. All members were given an evaluation of work points based on their performance, and their rates of attendance were marked down by the point recorders. After a period of time, the point recorders passed their books to the accountant, who calculated everyone's total work points. Close to the year end, the accountant would figure out the brigade's total income and the commune members' earnings.

In my brigade the highest number of points female peasants earned was six, males ten. The women weren't a major force in production. In wintertime they didn't even work, I guessed; I never saw a woman in the stone quarry. In spring they did, but they weren't entrusted with very important farm work, and they worked three or four hours less than the men. From spring through fall, the working day was divided into three parts: early work, morning work, and afternoon work. The time for breakfast was between early work and morning work. Women did not attend early work periods. They stayed home to prepare breakfast and lunch for their families, and they left the fields one hour early in the afternoon to cook supper.

The evaluation was carried out in our absence at a peasant meeting. A couple of days later the result was approved by the brigade leaders and passed on to us. The upper limits granted us were seven points for female students and nine for male. Jinli, Wenyu, and I were given seven points. Some girls got six and a half, but most got six points. Ying was the only one who got five, the lowest of all, but she didn't seem to be upset about it. Three male students got nine points, and the rest got two points higher than the females, on the average.

I had always taken for granted the equality of men and women. Now I saw it fail in reality. We female students did the same work and had the same working hours as men but scored two points less. Yet I didn't complain. How could I when I knew that in some work, such as in carrying stones, we couldn't match the men? I felt disturbed, though. Women in the city weren't discriminated against so overtly. All university graduates earned the same salary, as far as I knew. To make a living in the countryside brains didn't really matter. What mattered was strength and sex.

We now had our work points. However, they were not money. Only after autumn harvest could we get a share of grain and cash proportionate to our work points. Curious as we were, none of us knew how much our work points would really be worth. We didn't know either how the pay differentials would affect our lives in the following year, when the government wasn't scheduled to pay us a penny. Right now, for the first year only, we lived on government funds, ten yuan a month apiece regardless of sex. That money never touched our hands, however; it all went to our kitchen for food.

After dining with the peasants for about a week, we got our own kitchen. It was a cave dwelling in the brigade centre with a big stove and a wok five feet in diameter. Two female students were selected as cooks, whose work points would be taken from the rest of us, and our collective life began.

Our brigade had no chairs, tables, or dining room to offer us. We sat on the ground or on stones in the yard outside of the kitchen even in January and held the bowls in our hands. As we shovelled soup noodles or corn-flour porridge into our mouths, some inevitably dripped down on our winter coats. In the beginning I wiped these dribbles off with a wet cloth; later I didn't bother. Let the white lines hang! Who cared in such a place? There was no one I wanted to impress.

I wasn't just sloppy outside. I was actually dirty throughout my whole stay in the stone quarry. In these months I didn't wash my body once. Unbelievably, it didn't bother me. Every night, the minute I lay down I fell asleep. In the past I had heard that the peasants didn't wash themselves and thought they were uncivilized. I now changed my mind.

SPRING IN THE FIELDS

BY SPRING THE FIVE GIRLS FROM MY SCHOOL WERE NO longer living together. Jinli went with others to a former rich peasant's home, while Tiancui, a girl with long slant eyes and rosy cheeks, and I moved in with three female university graduates.

In spring, as the days grew longer and longer, we got less and less sleep, because our working days were defined by sunrise and sunset. In winter, after a long night's sleep we could wake up by ourselves in the morning; now we had to be wakened by the alarm clock owned by our new roommates. Before daybreak, we got up, walked half-asleep to the brigade centre, grabbed a wide-headed pick, and followed the peasants towards the fields. At times we traversed two mountains, each easily more than fifteen hundred feet high, to reach the field where we were to work.

Upon arrival Tiancui and I supported ourselves with our picks to recover from the climb, while the peasants set right to work. We had no choice but to follow suit.

"Aren't you tired after this mountain climbing?" I once asked them.

"A little."

"Then why don't we take a breather before starting work?"

"It's not necessary. This isn't tiring." They kept digging at the ground. "We can catch our breath while we do it, can't we?"

What could I say?

My first two jobs were turning the soil with a wide-headed pick and breaking clods left by oxen-drawn ploughs. This was considered the most menial work, requiring little skill. It was done mainly by women and a few men who were the least able farmers.

We worked for two or three hours on empty stomachs. Then breakfast arrived, usually a porridge of millet rice or coarsely ground corn with pickles on top. The peasants' was kept warm in thick pottery jars and carried to the fields by a professional "meal carrier," a young lad who collected the jars from each household. Ours came in two buckets carried up by one of our cooks.

At the end of breakfast the women showed up. When they joined in, the cultivating team was suddenly much stronger. We lined up horizontally on the mountain slope with an even distance between us and moved upward. There was little talk as we bent our backs, swung the picks high, and plunged them into the soil to pry it open. No one loafed. Even when my back became very sore, I dared not straighten up. We only sat down for twenty minutes between breakfast and lunch.

Lunch was also brought to the field. It was always cornbread and a dish of potatoes and pickled cabbage. Meat was rare and oil added sparingly. Like the peasants, we weren't supplied with cooking oil or meat, which we had been accustomed to in Beijing. Only when some peasants slaughtered a pig could we buy pork and fat. Even then we didn't buy much. Our ten-yuan budget had to suffice for grain, vegetables, fire wood, everything, so we couldn't afford much. The pork was gone in a few days, and the fat rendered into lard and rationed carefully so we wouldn't run short of grease. Like the peasants, we lived mainly on grain and vegetables.

Most of the year the staple in Yan'an was cornflour. Traditionally the main grain on the plateau was millet but it is a low-yield grain. After Liberation, to solve the perennial problem of starvation, the government advocated growing corn, a high-yield crop. The government made city dwellers eat corn as well. Ever since I could remember there was grain rationing. For many years in Beijing twenty per cent of our grain coupons were for rice, fifty per cent for wheat flour, and thirty per cent for cornflour. Altogether an adult man would receive thirty-five pounds of grain, a woman thirty-two pounds.

People in the West may say they like corn, but they eat it only sporadically and not as flour. They don't know what it is like to have it every day, at every meal. Worse yet, we students never learned how to cook it well. The peasants often let us try their cornflour buns. They weren't bad — fluffy, soft, with a fermented taste and a natural sweetness. But our buns were hard and tasteless.

We were each given two buns. With the help of the vegetable dish I could swallow one and a half. Once that was gone I couldn't force myself to eat a single additional mouthful. I knew I needed it to sustain me through the afternoon, but I just couldn't. Fortunately there were always some male students who wanted more. I could generously offer them my leftover.

After lunch we had half an hour to relax. Some lay on the ground and napped, and others sat and chatted. If it was a beautiful sunny day, one or two peasants would walk away from the crowd, take off their cotton-padded coats, and busy themselves catching lice. With their coats off they would be stripped to the waist. Under the coat there was nothing else — no sweaters or T-shirts.

The villagers all had lice. In the beginning when visiting peasants' homes I hesitated to sit on their *kang*s and flinched when they put their babies in my arms. Nevertheless, I had to sit down and felt compelled to cuddle their babies. The longer I lived with the peasants, the more resigned I became to their bugs. Sooner or later I would be infested, I thought. Even if I was, the lice wouldn't suck me dry. With this adjustment in attitude, I became more at ease in their homes.

Of the three working sessions, the afternoon stint was the longest. We worked from one-thirty to sunset with only one twenty-minute break. In constantly swinging the pick, the energy I absorbed from my lean lunch was quickly gone, and there was no fat reserve on my body. The fat from the better life in Beijing had long ago burned off. Every afternoon, an hour and half before we were due to finish, I was starved. My body became debilitated and my limbs shook. The pick in my hands felt a hundred pounds heavier than earlier in the day. I had to concentrate all my will power to lift it up. At every stroke I thought I had used up all the remaining strength in me, yet another one followed.

Out of the corner of my eyes I observed the peasants beside me and wondered how they felt. Most were skinny, and I guessed they were probably in the same state I was. If they had shown signs of exhaustion or hunger and suggested to the leader that we should stop working, I would have supported them fully. But none did. Their motions were as fast and smooth as ever. Hungry or not, the work had to be done. Spring sowing didn't allow delay.

"Women are going!" At last a prolonged shout came from the brigade leader. The women immediately stopped working. They skilfully ground one foot along their picks to wipe off the dirt, swung them onto their shoulders, and took off.

Now there was only one more hour to go. During this last, hardest hour I raised my head frequently to look at the sun in the west as my hands struggled with the pick. In the late afternoon sun the mountain slopes and the hard-working people on them were bathed in a golden colour. Once in a while the ploughman waved his whip in the air and let it fall lazily on the back of his ox. It was a peaceful rural scene, but I was beyond seeing it. All I could think of was the sinking sun. Please, move faster!

I stayed at the lowest work level for about a month. Then I was promoted to the sowing group to learn to spread manure. With a shallow, oval-shaped basket half-filled with manure hanging from my neck, I ran behind the seeder. At each step he made, he dropped a pinch of seeds into the furrow left by the plough, and I grabbed a handful of manure to spread over them. As the plough made the next furrow, it covered the seeds with the soil. When the basket was empty I went to the manure pile, knelt down, and scooped in more with my hands.

The manure was black with half-dissolved straw in it. It smelt like horse shit but not quite as foul. At first I felt disgusted to have to touch it with my hands, but that soon passed. After all, I didn't have to eat with manure on my hands. When breakfast arrived, I asked another student to ladle some water over my hands and washed them the best I could without soap.

At lunchtime I noticed that the two peasant manure spreaders never came to the water buckets. They rubbed their hands on their clothes and then grabbed their buns and ate. "You didn't wash your hands!" I exclaimed. Their only reply was an impish smile. I felt challenged. There was nothing they could do that I couldn't! So the next day I ate with dirty hands like them. I tried not to look, think, or smell. Like every-thing else, once begun, it didn't feel too bad.

There were three jobs to sowing: ploughing, seeding, and manure spreading. I tried them all. Seeding was a light job and often assigned to a young boy. I was allowed a half day of practice, and then I graduated to the master job: ploughing.

To control the plough wasn't easy. I had to plough straight furrows, keeping a good distance between them, and at the same time lift the plough to maintain the right depth. Ploughing too deep would exhaust the ox, and ploughing too shallow was bad for the crops. After a few days I was able to plough straight lines with the correct distance between them, but I was never confident about depth. At the end of each furrow I would look back and wonder how I had done.

After my transfer to the sowing group, life in the Dates Garden became less painful. The skilled jobs were more interesting and lighter as well. (However, if the peasants had asked me to carry my forty-pound plough all the way up to the field, things would have been different.) Consequently, I seldom suffered starvation again and was able to enjoy myself a bit. I could feel the pleasure of walking barefoot on newly cultivated soft soil and bring myself into a romantic mood when the peasants sang their folk songs.

Shanbei (north of Shanxi Province) people were fond of singing. They said that singing made long days shorter and the hard life less so. Unfortunately, they rarely sang. The Cultural Revolution had banned most of their songs. Love songs were labeled "yellow" (erotic) and others "old four." After a while nothing was left but "Red in the East." The tune of "Red in the East" was a Shanbei folk song, and the words were created by a Shanbei peasant in the forties:

Red in the east rises the sun.
A man called Mao Zedong was born in China.
He seeks the happiness of the people;
He is people's great saviour.

Chairman Mao loves the people,
He is our guide.
To build a new China,
He leads us forward.

The Communist Party is like the sun,
Wherever it shines, the place becomes bright.
Wherever there is the Communist Party,
People are liberated.

It was a fine song if not sung too often. The peasants never sang it in the fields.

One day at ploughing, Dejin, my former landlord, could no longer restrain himself. Suddenly he launched into "Blue Flower," a famous love song. Knowing it was "yellow," he didn't sing the words but sang the tune loudly six times, enough for all the verses to run out.

Black thread, blue thread,
What a beautiful blue;
Blue Flower was born,
How lovely she grew.

Among the five kinds of crops,
Sorghum is the tallest;

Among the maids in thirteen provinces,
Blue Flower is the best.

In January the matchmaker came,
In February it was agreed;
In March with piping and drumming,
Blue Flower was married.

Blue Flower was bitter,
Blue Flower was crying;
The rich man she married
Was old and dry.

In April with the Spring
Blue Flower ran away;
She returned
To her lover of the old days.

Let the old man rot,
Let him die.
Blue Flower and her lover are now together
To live or to die.

That day, listening to his straightforward singing of this beautiful song and watching the spring sowing, I felt in good humour for the first time since I arrived in Yan'an. The moment reminded me of what my older brother, Xinhua, had said about Yan'an on his return to Beijing from the Great Contact: "As we walked in the mountains, nobody was around but a lone mountain man on a mountain path with a bundle of firewood on his back. In the distance someone sang 'Roving at Will' [a type of free-style Shanbei folk song]. It was poetic and picturesque."

Yes, there was indeed the "poetic and picturesque" side of Yan'an. If a painter decided to live there for a while, he or she would be able to produce an exotic painting. But to live there as a peasant and be part of the painting was another story.

THE PEASANTS

WHEN TALKING TO US, THE YAN'AN PEASANTS REFERRED to themselves as "we sufferers." At first I always laughed when I heard this expression. Only in the old society did poor peasants refer to themselves as sufferers. How could they use this term fifteen years after Liberation? But they weren't joking. This was the name their ancestors had given themselves long ago, and it was still in use today.

Sufferers. It was an appropriate name for the plateau peasants. True, Liberation had abolished the system of landlords and exploitation, controlled famine and epidemics, and provided peasants with basic foods, but it had not eliminated poverty. The peasants ate no luxury food, and few wore clothes without patches. Many had only one set of clothes. In winter they put cotton between the two layers, and in summer they took it out. They never changed clothes and seldom washed themselves. No wonder they were lice-ridden. Their homes were mere caves to sleep in with little, if any, furniture.

The plateau was beyond the stage of slash-and-burn — but not much. The land was still cultivated by oxen and humans, and the yield was low. There was no chemical fertilizer for the barren land, and the harvest depended solely on the mercy of heaven. All they could do was pray for rain, in the right amount. Mechanization was almost unknown and would have been next to impossible to use on the plateau anyway. No combine could climb mountains and work slopes, nor could water be led up to that height for irrigation.

Backward modes of production and poor materials made for a backward lifestyle. The peasants lived with outmoded customs that could not be uprooted even by the powerful Communist government. One of these was mercenary marriage. Raising children was a hardship, while raising a daughter was a hardship for nothing. On growing up she would marry a man, live with him, and help *his* family. Therefore, before passing their daughter to her future husband, parents would ask him for money. To them it seemed only fair.

All peasants in my village had paid for their wives. Even if a young man was educated and knew it to be wrong, he wouldn't be able to find parents with a daughter for him who also thought it was wrong. The price of a girl was set according to her looks and accomplishments. A cheap wife was a few hundred yuan, and in my brigade the most expensive one was 3,200 yuan — big money. Remember, we lived on ten yuan a month. Since wives were bought, they were thought of as more or less slaves. They lost their names in the marriage, and they treated their husbands as their masters after coming home from the fields.

When I had supper at Heitu's home, his wife never ate with us. She would put food in our bowls, stand on the side, and watch us eat. When our bowls were empty, she would refill them. "Come and join us," I invited her, but she never did. Later I visited other families and found the same thing. I thought this custom was ridiculous and at times urged the wives to join us, but they always turned me down. Finally, I gave up and let them do what they wanted.

Heitu, which means Black Baldhead, was an ugly man, one of the ugliest in the brigade. He had small eyes and a pointed head, wide jaw, jutting chin, and short, bent body. In comparison, his wife's round face was pleasant. She looked a bit dumb, but no dumber than Heitu himself. I thought Heitu didn't match up to his wife, and so he must treasure her at home.

One late afternoon in February when I was having supper outside our kitchen, Heitu's wife appeared and told me that her husband had just beaten her. I was astonished that Black Baldhead could be so barbaric. I gave her a lot of kind words and all my sympathy to comfort her, but that was not what she had come for. She kept talking anxiously and incoherently until I realized that she wanted me to go and teach her husband a lesson.

I didn't want to go. Who was I? A "capitalist half-intellectual" sent here to be re-educated! What gave me the right to teach a poor peasant a lesson? But she wouldn't leave. Standing there in a padded cotton coat that was too loose and too long for her, she stared at me pitifully. At length I gave in. She had chosen me to be her saviour, and I shouldn't let her down. After supper I went with her.

On the way I deliberated. Heitu must be impervious to reason. If he could be brutal to his wife, he could easily be rude to me, at the least. I was a woman, too. At the same time, I knew I had some advantages. The peasants seemed to consider us students, including females, as cadres. Heitu was no exception. Once he called me the big cadre from Beijing.

"No, I'm not even a small cadre," I argued. "I am an educated youth who is to be re-educated by you poor and lower-middle-class peasants."

"You are here only to be 'gilded'! Once that gold layer is thick you'll fly away!" He looked up, raised his right hand above his head, and then flipped all the fingers open, as if he were releasing a dove.

"You are mistaken. We come here to take root and stay. Really, this was what we were told."

Heitu didn't buy it. He persisted: "Tell me, how long are you going to stay? One year? Two years?"

I kept denying his speculations loudly, inwardly hoping he was right.

Heitu heard his wife and me coming and opened the cotton padded door curtain to see who it was. There was a tense look on his face. Pretending not to notice it, I entered and sat down cross-legged on their *kang*. His wife handed me half a bowl of boiling water and then moved agitatedly about in the dwelling.

"I heard that you have beaten your wife," I said to Heitu. "Don't you know it's wrong?"

"But she didn't have the meal ready. I was hungry!" He grumbled.

"Even so, you shouldn't beat her. If she did something wrong, you should just point it out. Think, how would you feel if someone stronger beat you when you did something a little wrong? You are a human being; she is a human being, too. Men and women are equal. Although men are physically stronger, women have other abilities men don't. Your wife cooks for you and sews for you, and she looks after you, isn't that true?" I looked at his wife. She nodded vigorously. Now, with me as her backer, she was ready to fight, but that was not my intention. If I became too bellicose, Black Baldhead might be provoked. Who knew what he might do to me if he got mad!

With great patience I told Heitu all the grand principles I knew, repeating my points at times, until he was no longer grumpy. Slowly he started to smirk, and I grabbed the chance. "So now you've realized your mistake?" I asked tentatively. He didn't answer but put on a big foolish smile. His big mouth looked bigger, and his tiny eyes became two short lines. I knew I had him. "Heitu, promise me never to beat your wife again!" I demanded. At first he wouldn't comply, but in the end he did.

The man kept his word, but not for long. Two months later his wife came to me again for the same reason. This time I refused to go. I was having a hard time myself and wasn't in the mood to play rescuer. If my last crusade, in which I had brought all my skill into play, didn't work, I didn't see how a second try was going to work. I was neither their leader nor a cadre sent here with power to lead a movement. And if this was their age-old tradition, how was I to change it alone in a few months? I told her to see the party secretary for help. She left crying.

TROUBLESOME STUDENTS
IN DATES GARDEN

THE COLLECTIVE LIFE OF THE THIRTY DATES GARDEN Beijing students was not harmonious. On the third morning after our arrival we had a meeting. It started all right, with some students expressing their wish to do well in the countryside. Then Shuli, the leader of the five boys from his school, spoke. He had drooping eyelids and the worst skin I had ever seen: purple, rough, and covered with pimples.

Shuli didn't talk like the others. He opened with a request for a water vat and other items from the brigade and then whined that the peasants hadn't got things ready for us. He and his pals were from the only other key school, and I expected them to do better than this. It wasn't my role to respond to him because I wasn't leader, but I couldn't hold my tongue: "How can we ask for more from the peasants? We're already so much trouble to them!"

"Maybe we are. But who can we ask for help, if not them? We were sent here and placed into their hands. They have to take care of us."

"No, they don't! They don't owe us anything! They didn't invite us here, and they don't want us. There's only limited land and limited work. Our unwanted help is just going to take food from their mouths. Isn't it obvious? We're a burden. They have to accept us because Chairman Mao told them to."

"The peasants don't suffer by having us." He narrowed his eyes and smiled faintly with disapproval. "The government gives them money for settling us in. Who knows how much they spend on us and how much they keep for themselves?"

"Are you saying they aren't trustworthy?"

"No. I just mean we don't know them. We have to be careful in our dealings with them. The peasants are one unit and we're another. Naturally there should be more trust between us than between us and them."

"I don't know the peasants _or_ you! What I do know is that the peasants have provided us with two meals a day and a cave dwelling to sleep in. They even carried our luggage all the way up. I think we should learn to appreciate them. Instead of being demanding and bitchy, we should thank them for what they have done."

My words were strong and acrimonious. His attitude towards the peasants provoked me. He had had a Communist education. How could he harbour such prejudice towards peasants and dare show it openly?

Before my clash with Shuli got worse, our group leader, Jiajun, interrupted and changed the subject. Shuli and I both shut up. A shadow had been cast, however. I thought Shuli and his bunch were backward. They thought I was a jerk.

By my analysis, roughly half of the thirty Dates Garden students were progressive. They worked hard in the fields, were friendly to the peasants, and watched how they behaved privately. Of the five girls from my school, Jinli and Tiancui were in this group. They were my friends. But the other two, Lanlan and Guoqing, were of a different stripe.

Lanlan was a chubby girl with wide lips, a short nose, and eyes that were not the same size and were never fully open. She always wore an army cotton-padded coat, hat, and pants. She was the only one whose father held a high position in the army, and I had been glad to have her in our Dates Garden. At least not all army officers were corrupt! But I did wonder why she hadn't joined the army like Xiaonan and Ping. How could she have resisted the temptation of privilege? Was she really different? Or would she leave us later anyway?

To find out, one afternoon I walked beside her on the way home from work. "What would you like to do in the future?"

She didn't answer but in her peculiar vibrating voice asked me back, "What would you like to do?"

"I know it may sound crazy, but I'd like to go to university some day."

"No way! Give up your dreams! Listen! China doesn't need more university graduates. It has too many already! There aren't enough places to put them even now! It makes no sense to use university graduates to operate machines in factories, right? The universities might be closed permanently."

"I don't believe it. I never heard of a country without universities."

"You don't believe me? Do you know what university graduates are doing now? Don't you see the six in our Dates Garden? Why would they be here farming, if the country had better places for them?"

I felt depressed. "Then what's our future? Surely you don't believe we will stay in the Dates Garden forever?"

Again she didn't answer. We walked in silence the rest of the journey. I realized she didn't want to talk with me about the matter. Maybe she hadn't made up her mind yet; maybe she didn't trust me. Whatever her reason, I didn't ask her about it again.

A week later there was another student meeting. Lanlan gave a nice speech about the necessity of the "Join the Brigade" campaign. I was delighted. She couldn't leave now. Having expressed this view in public, if she did, it would be like her slapping herself in the face.

In March 1969 Lanlan disappeared without a goodbye to any of us. She had joined the army. It turned out her nice speech about "Join the Brigade" was only meant for the others, not for "superior class citizens" like her. So much for my last illusions about honourable high-ranking army leaders!

Guoqing's father was a revolutionary martyr. She was a big girl, about five-foot-eight. Everyone expected a girl of that size to be able to work like a man, but in the quarry she joined the youngsters picking up small stones, and that was her performance at its best. Later she started to take off frequently, with or without an excuse.

She seldom talked. Nobody knew what she was up to, and nobody did "ideological work" on her. We were all grown-ups who should have known what we were doing. "She'll come around when she gets used to the new environment," I thought. But she never did.

Before coming to Yan'an, Guoqing must have believed the rumour that we were going to be guides for Mao's residence. Receiving visitors and moving her lips would be a tolerable life. Once she found that it wasn't true and that she really had to live like the peasants, she decided she couldn't put up with it. In April Guoqing also vanished. Later we learned from Tiancui, Guoqing's former classmate, that she had gone back to Beijing.

Following Lanlan and Guoqing, two more girls, Shuzhen and Yuemei, left the Dates Garden. Shuzhen was one of our two team leaders. She went through the official procedure for returning to Beijing because of "illness." I didn't know how ill she was or whether she was really ill at all. To me she looked as healthy as anybody else. Yuemei left for the army in the summer of 1969. Her father was only a middle-ranking officer and thus didn't have the rank to use "inside recruitment" directly, but he must have nevertheless found the contacts and got her in.

One summer day in 1969, Dates Garden was all atwitter: Jian and Xing, two boys from the same school as Shuli, exchanged blows because of Ying, the girl who earned the lowest number of points among the students. Jian and Ying, we learned, were "talking love," which is the Chinese equivalent of steady dating; casual dating is considered immoral in China. Ying had stayed home sick. When Jian left the fields early to visit her, he found Ying and Xing kissing. Jian hurled himself at Xing. The two of them fought, rolling from the *kang* to the ground and then back onto the *kang*. Ying, meanwhile, huddled in a corner shrieking. The noise alarmed the neighbouring women and children, who ran to the male commune members working nearby. They hurried back, pulled the two boys apart, and sent them to the hospital. When I saw Jian again he had a few bandages on his head, and Xing's head was completely swathed; he looked like a wounded soldier.

Afterwards Jian and Xing continued to get along like "fire and water." Whenever and wherever they met, their fists rose, and they threw themselves at each other. It was impossible for them to stay in the same brigade together. Shortly afterwards Xing was shifted to another brigade ten miles away. I never saw him again.

This event was more than bizarre, I thought. A love triangle and men fighting over a woman — these were the themes of novels about the old society. How could my generation, the "socialist new generation," be putting on such a farce? I couldn't understand.

The story of our thirty students wouldn't be complete without mentioning Wenqi and Xiaohu, two boys who had brought their bad names all the way from Beijing to Yan'an. Wenqi was thin, with a long nose, drooping eyes, and a mole-like profile. Xiaohu had a smooth, childish face and was as shy as a girl at times. They were both harmless-looking, especially Xiaohu. If the leaders hadn't told us that they had been troublemakers in Beijing, I would never have guessed.

Most of the time they weren't around. Where they went and when they left they didn't deign to say, and nobody dared ask. We were instructed to keep an eye on them to help them reform, but what could we do? We had no authority and were having enough problems of our own adjusting to country life.

One afternoon, coming home from the fields, I found Wenqi walking hastily away from my cave dwelling. He turned back to look at me once and blushed, his face as red as a beet. When I reached my door, I found it unlocked. Had we left it open? I became alarmed and quickly checked my belongings. With relief I found nothing missing but my army cap, a present from my half-sister Fuzhen.

Later on I saw Wenqi sporting a new army cap, which looked exactly like mine. I didn't do anything. There was no way I could prove the cap was mine. It didn't have any special marks on it, and I thought it would be dangerous to bring charges against him. If he lost face because of me, he might decide to take revenge. Who was going to protect me then?

Problems among Beijing students were widespread in Yan'an. Disputes occurred often, and some ended in fighting. Those who were already troublemakers felt free to do what they pleased. In Beijing they at least had parents to keep an eye on them; now who could constrain them? The peasants didn't know how, and their fellow students dared not.

To solve these difficulties, the Beijing government sent out "Beijing cadres" to each brigade to direct and take care of the youth. The one sent to our brigade was Old Li, a fifty-year-old gentleman. He laughed a lot and was very easy-going, but he never did succeed in establishing his authority. My contemporaries had been baptized by the Great Cultural Revolution and had little respect for anybody. All Old Li did was work, eat with us, and laugh.

Besides the thirty Beijing students, there were six university "graduates" in Dates Garden, three men and three women. They were also called the 1967 graduates because, if it hadn't been for the Cultural Revolution, they would have graduated from university that year. Although they lacked one year of university, they were treated as real university graduates and received a hefty state salary: forty-six yuan a month for the first year and fifty-six the second year, provided nothing went wrong. Compared with us, who had ten yuan a month for the first year and zero after that, they were plutocrats.

Since they did not earn work points, whether they worked for the peasants or not depended entirely on their fancy. Three turned out to be progressive and did their share in the fields, but the other three just loafed.

One of the three university graduates I lived with was Jijiu, a remarkable intellectual. She was a small woman with a small head, pursed mouth, terrible teeth, and fine, shining skin. When I heard she was the only child of two full professors in Beijing University I was very impressed, but she didn't like her parents. "They're bookworms," she scoffed. "They know nothing of life. We don't get along."

Jijiu was a Communist Party member, a true Communist. She loved the country, the people, the party, and life itself. And she was brilliant — so brilliant that she had studied in the mathematics department of Beijing University before the revolution started. Only the smartest people could study mathematics or physics in China, and in mathematics Beijing University had an outstanding reputation. Yet Jijiu was not pretentious. I admired her greatly.

She had a liquid voice and was very fond of singing. Before the Cultural Revolution, she had been in the university chorus and learned many songs, including Russian ones. I loved Russian songs, but I knew few. They were very popular in China until it broke with the Soviet Union in the early sixties. In my time they were seldom heard. So Jijiu taught me some. One was "The Communist League Member Song" from the Second World War:

Listen, the battle horn is blowing.
Put on uniforms, grab weapons.
League members get armed and move out.
We are ten thousand united to defend our country.

Dear Mother, farewell.
Please kiss your son goodbye.
Dear Mother, don't be woeful, don't be sad.
Please bless us for safe passage.

Dear hometown, farewell.
A victorious star will shine upon us.
Dear Mother, don't be woeful, don't be sad.
Please bless us for safe passage.

There were many evenings when we sang together. Our favourite Chinese songs came from the movies and were labelled "poisonous weeds" during the Cultural Revolution. Singing those old songs brought back memories of the good days before the revolution. We knew that they were banned, but now that the revolution was slowing, we thought it all right to be a bit daring in cultural matters. Besides, we sang only in our cave dwelling, where nobody would hear us, in isolated Yan'an, where nobody would take it seriously. We were wrong. Certain "revolutionary" men heard us when passing by our cave and sharply criticized Jijiu. "Fuck them!" I told her, but she couldn't treat it that way. After all, she was a party member. From then on Jijiu didn't want to sing any more.

Tianyun was a graduate of an engineering institute in Nanjing, a large city close to Shanghai. She was also from an intellectual family. In the beginning I respected her as much as Jijiu, but soon found that she didn't deserve it. Tianyun worked, on the average, no more than four afternoons a week in the fields. The rest of the time she stayed home reading or cooked special meals for herself. Jijiu ate the foods the peasants cooked, but Tianyun couldn't, or wouldn't. Every day when I returned dog-tired from work and saw her reclining on the *kang*, I'd get mad. She was a capitalist intellectual, I concluded, and treated her accordingly.

The *kang* was comfortable to sleep on in winter, but it could cause big trouble, too. If the mud on one part of it wasn't thick enough, letting the stove burn for a long time would start a fire. One day while we were all working in the fields, Tianyun ran to where I was working and reported that our *kang* had burned through all my blankets, quilts, and sheets. There was now a big hole, bigger than a person's head, in them. Her own belongings were untouched, of course! I was seething. "I'm sorry, I'll fix things for you," she said.

I didn't expect her to buy me a whole new set; that would be too expensive. But she would at least buy me a new sheet. It was entirely her fault, and she was so rich — forty-six yuan a month! But she just mended the big holes in all my bedcovers with two layers of white fabric, even my quilts with silk-worm floss inside and beautifully printed cotton on the outside. For the remaining two and a half years I stayed in Yan'an, I lived with this patchwork reminder of her.

Both Jijiu and Tianyun were engaged. Jijiu's fiancé was in Beijing, while Tianyun's, named Chengwei, had been assigned somewhere near Yan'an and came to visit her often. Each time, Tianyun would change into a new polyester jacket and matching pants. The two of them would go into town and enjoy themselves. By today's standards her clothes were not fashionable, but back then in the Dates Garden she looked trim and modern.

Tianyun must have been disturbed by my hostility and told Chengwei about it. On one of his visits he said, "I would like to talk with you. Let's make an appointment. Choose any time convenient for you."

"No time is convenient. I have no time, and there's nothing to talk about." With those words, I left for work. I didn't want to talk with him because he was Tianyun's boyfriend. I figured them to be birds of a feather!

He persisted, and the next time he came and caught me home, he began to talk right then and there. Grudgingly, I sat down on our *kang* and listened. "You and Tianyun are both having a difficult time. In such an environment, you should help each other. Don't you remember what Chairman Mao said? 'All the people in the revolutionary team should care for each other, love each other, and help each other.' Why don't you talk to Tianyun? What do you have against her? Why can't the two of you sit together and solve the problem, whatever it is?"

He sounded sincere, but I only turned my face aside and humphed. What I had against Tianyun was not just trivial personal matters but her whole philosophy. How could I change her attitude towards work, the peasants, and life, when the Communist educational system and even the Cultural Revolution hadn't succeeded? Funny that Tianyun should have a boyfriend who knew how to use Chairman Mao's words to lecture others!

SUMMER WORK AND NEWS

FOLLOWING SPRING SOWING CAME THINNING OUT THE seedlings, weeding, and building terraced fields. I was told that thinning and weeding were the lightest farm work there was. But to me, no farm work was light. In the fields, each of us had three rows to work on. I just couldn't keep up with the peasants, no matter how fast I moved my hoe. It was embarrassing. At first I had doubts about my dexterity. Was I really that much more clumsy than the peasants? Only after weeks did I realize that the problem was the hoe.

We students had no tools of our own. Each morning we took one from the brigade storage room and after work returned it there. The communal hoes in the storage were all in bad shape. They were blunt, because nobody sharpened them, and they were rusted, because the users didn't clean the dirt off on returning them. Every morning I carefully searched for a good hoe, but I never found one. With what I got, I usually had to strike two or more times to cut a weed.

The peasants had their own hoes, which they cleaned every day and sharpened often with stones. Their hoes were old, and the older the hoe, the better. The best hoe I saw was one-third the size of a new one. It was thin, light, and shiny. Mud didn't even stick to it. Its owner was so proud of it that he lent it to me for a few minutes so that I could appreciate it too. I could weed with practically no effort.

To build terraced fields in mountainous terrain was one of the "advanced experiences" of that model in agriculture, the Dazhai brigade of Shanxi province. Dazhai, a hilly village with poor soil, had been liberated in 1945 and collectivized in 1953. With incredible determination, the collective carried out a grand plan to alter the contour of the land. The peasants moved small hills, filled gullies, and created plains and terraced fields to prevent soil erosion and water loss. By 1963 the whole project was complete. With better land, their production rate increased sevenfold.

In Dates Garden, building terraced fields was a year-round activity, except in winter, when the soil was frozen. Whenever the farm work slackened, this work would keep the peasants busy. There were three stages in building a terraced field. The first step was to scrape the layer of rich soil off and pile it on the higher slope. The second step was to level the terrace and to make the terrace wall by slapping the dirt with the back of a spade. The third step was to put the rich soil back on top of the new terrace. The layer of medium-brown rich soil was only a couple of inches thick. Years later, when I saw the rich black soil of Canada and the United States and heard that it was often more than a foot deep, I was astonished.

After moving in with the university graduates in the spring, I noticed that all three of them, including my model, Jijiu, took off regularly to clean themselves, and I changed my piggish ways. Every two weeks I took half a day off, fetched a lot of water, heated it up on the stove, and washed myself with a towel in my little washbasin. Then I washed my clothes in my and my roommates' basins, and hung them in the yard.

When summer came, Tiancui and I took our clothes a half mile to the Yan River and washed them there. Like the countrywomen we'd seen in movies, we rolled up our sleeves and trouser legs, sat on big rocks with our feet firmly planted in the running water, hummed tunes, and kneaded clothes. The water was crystal clear. Multi-coloured pebbles on the bottom seemed to change shapes as the water undulated. In summer the river was much wider. It ran at a medium pace, its far surface reflecting the sunlight so brightly that I couldn't look at it directly. By then I had to admit the Yan River was beautiful. Winter or summer, its water was always a gorgeous jade green.

I was tempted to go swimming and take a real bath, but never dared. The male peasants had a spot to play and wash themselves. They let our male students share it, but nobody invited me. I guessed they were skinny-dipping. To my regret the female peasants didn't have their own place along the river. The feudalist tradition bound them so tightly that even with a river running by their doors they never swam or bathed in it.

In June 1969 the 1968 graduates received their assignments. They did not join the brigade in the countryside, nor did they become farm workers in the Corps. All were given jobs in factories or other workplaces in Beijing. I was stunned. What major differences were there, if any, between the graduates of one year and another? Why should we be plunged into hell and they lifted to heaven? How could one's fate depend only on one's birth year and have nothing to do with ability or performance? Could anything in the world be more irrational?

My middle brother, Weihua, was of better vintage, a year younger than me. He was a 1968 junior school graduate. That summer he was assigned a job as a lathe operator in a factory in Beijing that was involved in military research and production.

My eldest brother, Xinhua, was also a 1968 graduate, but from senior middle school. He could have become a worker in a linen textile mill in Beijing but, with four of his comrades, he went to the Production and Construction Corps in Inner Mongolia.

Xinhua's real desire was to become a writer. Beijing University had the best literature program in China, so he entered the Middle School Attached to Beijing University. It was also a key school. Xinhua was good at studies. I saw no reason why he shouldn't go on to Beijing University, but because of the Cultural Revolution, his dream became impossible. His second choice was politics. He had always liked people and had a special gift for stimulating them. As I said earlier, the way to excel in politics was to join the army. So that was what Xinhua decided to do — through not the back door but the front. He put his name down during a recruiting period, but as a result of high blood pressure failed the physical; he was too nervous.

Xinhua did not give up. The Corps in Inner Mongolia had a system close to the army's, although it was engaged mainly in agricultural production. He and his comrades rejected the offers of factory jobs in Beijing and applied for the Corps. Life there would be hard, but they didn't mind. Their blood was warmer than mine, and their sights higher. They weren't so enamoured of Beijing as I was.

Together with the 1968 graduates, the leftovers from 1966 and 1967 all got jobs in Beijing. Su'e wrote me that she was one of twenty students, most of them 1968 graduates, assigned to Yongdingmen train station in Beijing.* In the end, Su'e and her grandmother's brazenness paid off.

Su'e was my friend. I tried to be happy for her, but I couldn't suppress my resentment at the way the government had managed things. If we had known the cheeky ones would be rewarded like this, why should any of us have obeyed the order and come to Yan'an? No wonder the Chinese say that "people come to grief on account of their honesty."

Besides Su'e in Beijing, I corresponded with my friends Ping in Guangzhou, Guomei in Shunde County in Canton, and Xiangzhen and Yishu in Inner Mongolia.

*Yongdingmen train station was for slow trains only. Beijing has two train stations: Yongdingmen and the Beijing train station, the latter for fast and express trains.

Before leaving Beijing in October 1968, Ping wasn't even a Communist League member. By the summer of 1969 she had become a party member — that was indeed a fast political advancement. She was not necessarily the most progressive person of all my classmates, but she was the first to join the party. I was jealous. To have the right parents did make a big difference. Guomei, the other one with the right parents, was doing fine as well. In late 1969 her family got her back to Beijing and found her a job in a factory.

The circumstances of my friends Xiangzhen and Yishu in Inner Mongolia were not as good. As early as the end of 1968, the tone of their letters became sombre. By then they had finished their training. The three of them, Xiangzhen, Yishu, and Rongxi, were put in a yurt as one family. The herdsmen's yurts were so scattered that they seldom had visitors. The blue sky became grey and the grasslands covered with snow. The novelty and excitement faded away, and loneliness started to bite.

In spring of 1969 Rongxi left for her hometown in Sichuan Province, leaving Xiangzhen and Yishu behind. For days they didn't see another soul. Their only companions were the horses and sheep. In the summer, Xiangzhen fell off a horse and broke her leg. She was in bed alone for two months, with no television, no radio, and no novels to read. "Oh! You boundless grassland, lonely grassland!" she wrote. Her letters were sad.

INTERLUDE IN BEIJING

IN AUGUST MY CONTINUING GYNECOLOGICAL PROBLEMS became of serious concern to my parents. Since that spring my mother had sent me various herbal remedies, jars of herbal jelly, and boluses, which are soft balls made of Chinese medicine and honey. They are smaller than a ping-pong ball, and one can either chew them or dissolve them in water to take as a drink. I tried everything, but there was no improvement. Since my work was lighter, the time between my periods lengthened to once every sixteen or seventeen days. Finally my parents decided to get me back home to see doctors.

Their letter in hand, I went to see the brigade leaders for permission. They gave it to me immediately and told me not to hurry back before I was cured. I then went to the commune and got a recommendation letter, indicating my status as an educated youth in Yan'an, in case it was needed.

Those Beijing students who were close to me came to give their home addresses and invite me to visit their families. Jinli asked me to go to her home, too. She also gave me Guoqing's address so that I could pay her a visit. By then Guoqing had been gone for four months. "Go and see how she's doing. If she wants to come back, tell her she's always welcome," Jinli urged. Jinli was group leader for the five of us from my school. She wanted to be responsible for Guoqing. But I wasn't enthusiastic about this mission. The meeting with her would be awkward. What was there to say? I gave Jinli an ambiguous promise: "I will if I remember."

Travelling in China as a peasant was no easy matter. Years later, when I became a cadre, I could book train tickets through my institute and by means of its recommendation letter get a bed in a designated hotel. But as a peasant in Yan'an, there were no advance tickets or inn reservations for me. From Yan'an to Beijing I had to take a bus, a slow train, then a fast train. Knowing nothing about what awaited me on the way I got on an early morning bus. The ride was less dusty than my original ride into Yan'an, because the bus had windows, but the bumping and rocking were the same. In the afternoon I arrived in Tongchuan and managed to get the slow train to Xi'an. Around nine o'clock I reached Xi'an and found that the earliest train to Beijing wouldn't leave till noon the next day. I bought my ticket, but I didn't know where to find an inn. The long benches in the train station seemed the best and safest place to spend the night, so there I camped.

I got almost no sleep. Only when I was safely on the train the next day did I doze off fitfully. On the third morning, as our train approached Beijing, my heart beat faster.

Hello again, Beijing! I was excited as I walked with the jostling passengers towards the exit. Once into the square I turned back to view the Beijing train station. Under the sun its golden roof glittered splendidly, and its clocks chimed harmoniously. The station was one of the ten famous grand structures built in 1959 as a celebration of the republic's tenth birthday. It had golden glazed-tile roofs in classical Chinese style, and creamy tile walls in western style. On top of the wings were two towers, each with four huge clocks facing four directions. The station was said to have been deliberately designed to give all visitors to Beijing a good first impression, and it certainly impressed me that day. To my eyes, accustomed to cave dwellings, no building was taller or more sublime.

I was home again. I no longer had to get up early, climb mountains, and do hard labour. I didn't have to eat cornflour buns. Instead, I could enjoy my favourite food, rice, which is not grown in Yan'an. The peasants didn't know what rice was, and they never ate fish, saying they didn't like it. As to sweets, they were a luxury Yan'an was without. Now I could make up for everything. Each evening my mother brought home all kinds of food and goodies to feed her starving daughter. Oh, how I ate! Evenings I stayed home with my family. During the day I went to visit doctors and friends.

Medical care in China was inexpensive. Cadres, workers, and everyone who had jobs in the state-run enterprises needed only to pay the registration fee, five cents at the time. All expenses for tests and prescribed medicines were paid by the patient's work unit. As a peasant I didn't enjoy this privilege, and at every visit I had to pay a five-cent registration fee and a few yuan for herbal medicine.

The friend I visited most was Su'e. Since we had taken different roads in the Join the Brigade campaign, our friendship had weakened. Still, I spent a lot of time with her. She had a job at the Yongdingmen train station, and I went there to watch her work.

When Su'e and nineteen other girls from my school had started, they worked as loaders. Later, they were promoted to waiting-room attendants, then attendants on trains, and finally some were made booking-office clerks. To be a clerk was Su'e's goal. The work was the lightest, and it gave one some power, Su'e said. For a long time, train tickets, especially sleeper tickers, were hard to procure. People tried to get them through friends, friends' friends, even acquaintances' acquaintances. Those who controlled train tickets were much petitioned, and so had power. Su'e had changed. She was now transparently pragmatic. In 1973, she fulfilled her wish and became a booking-office clerk.

When I arrived in Beijing, Jijiu was for some reason also there. She had given me a dormitory number at Beijing University and asked me to visit her. A suave young man answered the door. He was tall and clean-shaven, with thick, low eyebrows and bright eyes. I told him I was looking for Jijiu; he stood aside, and I saw Jijiu inside. She stood up and introduced us: "This Zhenhua, my young comrade in the Dates Garden. This is Tongjun, my fiancé." I wasn't really surprised to see Tongjun because Jijiu had told me about him before. He was in the same university department as Jijiu, but one year behind her. He was now awaiting his assignment.

We chatted for a while, and then Jijiu suggested that Tongjun play the *xiao*, a vertical bamboo flute, for us. Tongjun took his *xiao* down from the wall and played an ancient tune from the twelfth century. He played well, but to my ear the sound of the solemn song on the low-pitched flute was a little too sad. It reminded me of someone sobbing in the night. For lunch they bought some steamed buns and two additional dishes from their refectory, and we ate together. Before I left Jijiu said: "I still have ten days left. Come again next week, and we'll take some photographs."

The next week I returned. Tongjun took photographs of us on the grounds of Beijing University. We went to their department, to the pagoda hill, and to the famous Weiminghu (No Name Lake). It was summer, and the lawn was green and the campus beautiful. I was happy to be in the university with intellectuals like Jijiu and Tongjun, but my happiness was tinged with sorrow. If it hadn't been for the Cultural Revolution, I too would have had a chance to study in this good university and live the life of an intellectual.

Despite my heavenly life in Beijing, I did not forget my comrades in the Dates Garden. Every few days I visited one of the families, as I had promised. Most turned out to be very kind. Rich or poor, all insisted on cooking me a good meal. In many of these families I sensed a worried feeling. All were very concerned for their children, but none said so explicitly. To comfort them I said that we were all living well and there were no troubles at all.

By mid-September I had visited all the ten families on my list. Jinli's words about seeing Guoqing started to nag at my conscience. No matter what, she had once been one of us. Perhaps she now regretted her defection and wanted to go back. In the end I paid her a call. If she was home, fine. If not, nobody could blame me for not having tried.

I arrived at her apartment at nine-thirty in the morning. She was home. Standing face to face at her door I felt embarrassed. She showed no feelings. With a faint smile she led me to a comfortable chair in their large living-room, made me a cup of tea, and then sat down on a huge bed at a considerable distance from me.

Obviously she hadn't got a job yet. The 1968 graduation assignments didn't seem to have benefited her as they had Su'e. I started to hope she might suggest going back to Yan'an with me. If she did, I was ready to relay what Jinli said. But she didn't even broach the subject. As before, she talked very little. While I kept the conversation going by telling her everything that had happened in the Dates Garden after she left, she knitted a sweater and listened half-heartedly. Occasionally she raised her head to say, "Is that right?" and even then her nimble fingers didn't stop.

After going on for about a half hour like that, I realized that she didn't give a damn about the people in the Dates Garden. I became ice-cold and decided to leave. "Come back to visit again when you have time," she said at the door, but it didn't sound sincere. I never went back, and she never returned to the Dates Garden.

Time flew too fast. In a blink it was October, and I was fully recovered. My problem had been caused mainly by extreme fatigue and lack of nutrition. With the help of medicines, rest, and good food, my period returned to normal and I felt well. I didn't want to leave, but I had no excuse to stay longer. For the second time, I left home for Yan'an.

BACK IN YAN'AN

WHEN I GOT BACK, THE HARVEST SEASON HAD ENDED. Jinli told me the work had been really hard. Every day, after cutting the crops, the workers had to travel back and forth two or three times to carry the bundled stalks back to the threshing ground. Some days the work ran so late that the last trip was made in complete darkness, with torches lighting the way. Jinli told me that her legs felt like jelly after galloping downhill so many times and that at some hairpin turns she could barely stop short before dropping off the edge.

In the past, during the "working in the countryside" periods, I had cut wheat and knew what it was like. Unlike westerners, the Chinese held the stalks in one hand and cut them with a sickle near the roots. This technique was very hard on the waist and back. Then you had to run with a big load on your back and work till after dark on those long summer days. I could easily imagine what my comrades had been through. Despite the pangs of guilt, I felt lucky to have gone home in time to miss the harvest.

When Jinli went on to tell me how well they had eaten during this period, I didn't mind at all that they had consumed my share. "We ate no cornflour at all, but newly harvested wheat. We had a large variety of fresh vegetables and were never short of meat. The peasants kept slaughtering pigs and we kept buying."

That autumn our brigade started to build cave dwellings for students. They were stone ones and were located right in the brigade centre. About half of the students, including me, were assigned to help in the construction. The peasants let us put our hands to almost all the field jobs, but they would not allow us to try laying stones for cave dwellings. These were expected to last for years, if not centuries. The work was too important to take any risks.

From beginning to end we were Xiaogong (Little Labour), or those who engaged in subordinate work. Male students carried stones on their backs to the spot; female students made mud with husks, soil, and water.

For a while, I was a "mud carrier," one who carried mud to the master builders in a cloth wrapper with two strings tied at its four corners. When some master shouted, "Mud!" I would reply, "Coming!" and quickly lift up the strings and run towards him. He took the strings, threw the mud into the space between stones and returned the wrapper to me. I then scurried back to the mound of mud and let other Xiaogongs fill my wrapper with a spadeful of mud. As soon as I was ready, someone else would shout, "Mud!" and I would be off again. It was non-stop running, but I didn't mind. The sense of being needed and useful was itself rewarding.

At the same time as the new cave dwellings were built, other groups of commune members were constructing underground tunnels to carry out Chairman Mao's instructions to "be prepared for war."

China had been invaded and reinvaded from time immemorial and was always vigilant against another invasion. When China broke with the Soviet Union in the early sixties, our former supporter turned into an enemy, and the smell of war in the air suddenly became very strong. This was the situation in which Mao proclaimed his slogan. In response, many military factories were dispersed to isolated areas, and the whole country dug underground tunnels and air-raid shelters. Even my middle school had them.

In 1969 many Chinese believed a war was imminent. I even heard that it was for our sake we were sent to Yan'an, since it would be the safest place in China if World War III were to break out. Indeed, if any country did have plans to invade China, the optimum time would have been during the chaos of the Cultural Revolution. Secretly I wished for war. War brings disaster but also opportunity. I would rather die heroically on the battlefield than live the hopeless life I had been given. And if I didn't die, things in China would definitely change for the better after the war, I thought. This was crazy, of course, but I was living in a crazy time.

I worked on two tunnels. One had just been started and at this stage was short and wide; the other was almost finished and was long and narrow. There were about half a dozen peasants with me in the wide tunnel. We picked the clay loose, shovelled it in the carts, and dumped the carts on the mountain slope. The narrow tunnel had been built a long time earlier but needed final touches near the second exit. Before entering it, I was warned that it wouldn't be easy for me to make my way through. It turned out to be an adventure. At the highest and widest part of the tunnel I had to walk with my back bent; at the lowest and narrowest part I crawled on my stomach and could barely squeeze myself through. The passage meandered to such an extent that I soon lost all sense of direction.

The three men who escorted me into the narrow tunnel were said to be the best labourers in the village. One was a migrant from Shandong, my home province, and two from Yan'an. I was most impressed by Tao'er, a sinewy, dynamic young man. He talked fast and walked fast, taking long strides. Others had to run to keep up with him. There was no job Tao'er couldn't handle. In the narrow tunnel where I thought it was impossible to dig, he did so at an amazing speed, keeping the rest of us busy carrying the dirt out. I had never seen anyone who worked like him.

Tao'er lived nearby. One day in November I saw him passing with a large bundle of firewood on his back. The weather was getting cold, and it was time to prepare for winter. The previous winter we had burned the peasants' firewood in our cave dwelling to heat water and the *kang*. This year we had to get our own. Seeing Tao'er's success, on a whim I decided to go out with him. He must know the best places to go. I trotted up behind him and called out, "Tao'er, are you going to gather wood again tomorrow?"

"Yes." His voice came from behind the small mountain of faggots on his back.

"Can I go with you?"

He thought for a moment, then turned back to face me. The firewood projected three feet on each side. "Fine. Do you have a chopper and rope?"

"No. Where can I get them?"

"I'll lend you my spares. Tomorrow morning I'll come and fetch you."

The next morning I waited for him in the yard. As soon as I saw him on the road, I jumped up to join him. We walked and walked. I tried to remember the road, but when we had passed over three mountains I gave up. Finally we arrived at a valley surrounded by cliffs. "This is our place," Tao'er said. "Late in the afternoon we'll meet here again." Without wasting a second he darted away and disappeared.

Looking around me, I saw only the barren loess and some tall weeds. These were no good, so I moved around the valley in widening circles. Here and there I found a few tiny bushes and chopped off their dried branches. Once in a while I saw a tree, but I had been told not to cut trees. The peasants had realized they were ruining the environment and were now trying to save whatever they still had. They did not have enough firewood to burn themselves, and now we thirty students had turned up, demanding our share.

Hours passed. I found very little and realized I wouldn't be able to collect even half of what Tao'er had gathered yesterday. On the way here I had worried whether I could carry it all back. I wondered how Tao'er was doing. Spotting him on a cliff far away, I watched him descend towards a big bush halfway down. "Oh, boy. I'd never be able to get that one in my life," I thought.

Long before sunset I was at our starting point. I preferred to waste time waiting than to miss Tao'er and not be able to find my way home. When he returned, he had a bundle as large as yesterday's. Beside his, my little bundle looked puny. I was afraid that Tao'er would laugh — he was often sarcastic — but he didn't. He squatted down and taught me how to tie a nice, tight bundle with the rope, then helped me to stand with it on my back.

I was not happy about my first firewood expedition, but I wasn't entirely discouraged. Maybe this was just an unlucky day. The following day I ventured out alone. My idea was to walk far, far away until I found a miracle valley full of big bushes. There I would hew as much as I could carry, and then announce my discovery to all the villagers. But after three mountains I saw no such valley and dared go no farther. The peasants said there were wolves in the mountains. I really didn't want to get lost and end up as wolf fodder. As on the day before, I wandered around a place with easily recognizable landmarks; and as on the day before, I gathered just a small bundle. With that on my back and my tail between my legs, I quietly returned to the village.

After that, I never bothered with wood gathering again. Fortunately, our "capitalist intellectual," Tianyun, was willing to do the job. She needed firewood if she wanted to keep her private kitchen running. Each time, she carried back less than I had, but the number of her trips made a difference. We didn't lack firewood that winter. No matter how selfish she was, I thought, she did help her roommates in one way.

Zhenhu was a progressive young peasant in the brigade, whom I got to know while digging in the wide tunnel. He was as ugly as a potato, as the Chinese say — stubby, with muddy skin, small, round eyes, a round nose, and deep wrinkles on his forehead. However, he was a primary school graduate and a "peasant poet." One of his revolutionary poems had even been published in a local magazine.

One day at work Zhenhu revealed to me the existence of his Youth Shock Team, composed of peasant children aged twelve to nineteen. They were "Lei Feng learners" who did volunteer work for the brigade in their spare time. He didn't propose anything, but I knew that he wanted me to join.

During the Cultural Revolution, Mao's instruction "Learn from Lei Feng" was heard no more, and doing good deeds was out of fashion. Rebelling was in. It was quite unexpected to encounter such a group in the Dates Garden. To be honest, I wished he hadn't mentioned his secret to me. One could do good only when one could afford to do so. The countryside had already taken its toll on me but I couldn't tell him that. He and his team thought I was as progressive as they were; I couldn't show them I wasn't. I applied and became a member.

After harvest, working hours were no longer from sunrise to sunset but were more flexible. Every few days we would be told to quit when an hour of daylight still remained. That was when the Youth Shock Team went to work. Carrying a spade on my shoulder, I would follow the teenagers to a gully to build a dam.

"What is this dam for?" I once asked Zhenhu.

"It's to stop the mud brought down by floodwaters," Zhenhu told me. "After a few years, a flat will form and the brigade will have an additional piece of land to cultivate."

Under Zhenhu's guidance, we piled the earth along a line across the mouth of the gully, rammed it down, and then laid on another layer until the dam reached the designated height — six feet. Then we moved on to another gully to start another dam. One after another, we diligently built three dams that fall. Unfortunately, none survived the next summer's floods. Later I read a book on the agricultural model, Dazhai, and learned that the dams they built for this purpose were all reinforced with large stones. Even then floods sometimes destroyed them. Our earthen ones didn't stand a chance.

Our Youth Shock Team was busy for one month. Then, after the completion of the three dams, our leader, Zhenhu, got married, and all its activities ceased.

The entire time I stayed in Dates Garden, there were three peasant marriages. Only Zhenhu's family made a big thing of it. They were better off than most peasants. Quite a few Beijing students, myself among them, received invitations. We heard that it was going to be a traditional wedding and wanted to go, but we were too poor to give Zhenhu a worthwhile gift. Turning our suitcases upside down, we found nothing but a few small metal Mao badges. With our "presents" in hand, we left for the wedding, promising ourselves just to look and not to eat anything.

When Jinli, Tiancui, and I reached Zhenhu's yard, the ceremony for the bride's arrival was already over and the banquet had begun. Too bad. We had missed the bride emerging from a sedan chair, dressed in red from her covered head to her toes — that was what we had come for. But now that we were there, we didn't leave right away. The yard bustled with activity. More than a hundred people were sitting at a dozen or so tables, laden with stewed pork, transparent bean noodles, tofu — a feast. Everything looked delicious.

Finally we decided to go, but Zhenhu came out from his cave dwelling, saw us, and came over. With a flush of embarrassment, we handed him our Mao badges and wished him a happy marriage. He smiled happily, and his heavily wrinkled forehead looked much smoother. "Sit down where you like," he said.

"No, no!" we protested. "We have to go back to work; we have no time."

"All right, have some noodles then." He waved to some peasants, who handed us big bowls of wheat noodles with meat sauce. We couldn't refuse, so we quickly and noisily slurped the noodles down and left. Had we stayed longer, more noodles would inevitably have arrived to make us feel even more guilty.

December brought winter to the plateau again. The majority of the students started to take off in twos and threes for New Year's reunions with their families. Before the year's end, all were gone except Shuzeng and me. I had just come back, so I couldn't leave again, and Shuzeng, one of the three senior middle school students who shouldn't have come but did, was having trouble with his parents.

Shuzeng's parents were both veteran revolutionaries, although neither was high-ranking. His father was an old Red Army soldier who had gone through the Long March of the thirties; his mother had been a party member since 1938; but they didn't act like revolutionaries. Joining the brigade in the countryside was considered progressive and encouraged by the party, but these two senior party members strongly opposed their own son coming to Yan'an. When I visited them in the summer, they groused non-stop about Shuzeng's filial impiety because he came without their blessing, repeatedly calling him a black-hearted wolf. At the end of the year they refused to send Shuzeng the money for a ticket home. I thought they were very strange. How could any parents treat a child like that?

There was no point in keeping our big kitchen with its huge wok running for the two of us. After a little discussion, Shuzeng agreed to be cook and use his cave dwelling as our temporary kitchen. Twice a day I climbed up for meals.

One day as we were eating, Shuzeng, with a flush, told me the peasants had begun to gossip about us. I thought this ridiculous. I had no plan to "talk love" with anybody in Yan'an. It was the wrong place and wrong environment. Besides, Shuzeng was far from my ideal as a husband. He was kind and progressive but also dumb and vulgar. He was no beauty either. His eyes were dark and bright, but his big protruding mouth spoiled the balance of his whole face. The peasants were wrong to have ideas about us, and Shuzeng too, if he was thinking so.

THE EASIER SECOND YEAR

AFTER THE NEW YEAR, THE BEIJING STUDENTS CAME BACK, our big kitchen reopened, and our new life on our own earnings from last year began. The fact that the male students had higher points and others, like Ying, lower points made no difference. As in the first year, all our income went to the kitchen. We continued to live as a half-communal collective.

In January 1970 the university graduates had been "re-educated" for a year. Improved or not, they had fulfilled this formal requirement and were now assigned real jobs. Tianyun became a teacher in a middle school in Yanchang County, and Jijiu became a teacher in the only key middle school in the whole area, the Yan'an Middle School in the town of Yan'an.

I once visited Jijiu in her school. Her dormitory there was an old, dark cave dwelling. She had cornflour noodles for lunch. During our talk I learned that her fiancé, Tongjun, had just graduated from Beijing University and had been assigned to a tractor factory in Tongchuan. One of them had to move if they wanted to live together. Tongchuan is a bigger city, which is very close to the provincial capital, Xi'an. It wouldn't have been too bad for them to live there. But the factory at the moment didn't need Jijiu, whereas the Yan'an Middle School welcomed Tongjun. So they decided that Tongjun should come to Yan'an.

It was common knowledge that if a couple were together in one place, the chance for them to leave was nil. Thus I knew Jijiu and Tongjun were prepared to spend the rest of their lives in the tiny and impoverished town of Yan'an. With their talents, I believed they were capable of achieving something in science, but they were destined to devote themselves to this little provincial school. What a pity, I thought, but Jijiu didn't seem to mind and, as she told me this, she was as jovial as ever.

During 1969 the number of Beijing students in the Dates Garden had decreased steadily. Each time another person left, I felt emptier. In late

January 1970, however, the current swung around. We had a newcomer. He was also a 1967 graduate and had come to Yan'an on the same day as we had. For the first year he had been in another brigade. Now, for some reason, he was joining us.

The day our newcomer appeared he was in a black padded cotton coat. It was so thick at the back that his shoulders looked rounded. I stood at our kitchen door and watched him approach, shaking hands with whomever he met and introducing himself repeatedly, "Zhou Binghe from the 35th School." A polite smile never left his face. This was odd to me. Nobody in my generation was so courteous and formal. We hadn't been brought up this way, not even the children from wealthy families.

His unusual manner and sudden appearance in our midst aroused people's curiosity. Some people, Shuzeng among them, even made a special trip to town to investigate his background. They came back with the news that Binghe was Premier Zhou's nephew! He had been harassed by some ne'er-do-wells in his former brigade and so was transferred here. I was skeptical, but the next time I met him I paid a little more attention. To my surprise, his features actually did resemble Premier Zhou's!

The previous year we had heard that a couple of Beijing students went to see Premier Zhou and told him about the poverty in Yan'an. He felt so sad that tears flowed from his eyes. "I didn't know that life was so hard for folks in the old liberated area," he sighed. Soon after that, Yan'an received extra funds to aid in its modernization and to enlarge it from a town to a city. We hadn't been able to figure out who the two Beijing students were. Now everything seemed to fall into place.

All other students lived in groups, but Zhou Binghe had a cave dwelling to himself. One day on my way home after work, I passed by and saw him standing at his door. We exchanged a few words, and then I asked if I could come in and have a look at his home. "Certainly," he said.

His home, lit by a five-watt light, was as simple as ours — nothing special. However, he did have a huge trunk, large enough to hold who knows what treasures. As soon as I sat down on the edge of his *kang*, he scrabbled in the trunk far away in the shadows and took something out. He then walked over and handed it to me. It was a chocolate bar. I tried hard to refuse. Sweets were a great luxury in Yan'an. In the garden where Mao had lived a tiny store sold inferior biscuits and primitive, poor-quality candies that were nearly inedible. After visits home to Beijing, we brought back some sweets, but they were soon gone. Nobody would offer even a little piece of candy to anyone else, much less a whole chocolate bar. But Binghe persisted and in the end I accepted it.

As I ate the chocolate, he dove into his trunk again and this time took out a photo album containing the most beautiful photographs I had ever seen. They were all 8" x 10" black and whites with sharp contrast and focus and exquisite settings. Most were winter scenes. In some Binghe stood on a snowy field under a pine tree with outstretched branches, and in others he was standing on the ice of a big lake in front of a high arched bridge or some other structure. He wore a wool overcoat and leather gloves and shoes, similar to Chairman Mao's. His pose was also like Mao's, with his head raised and slightly tilted and his hands clasped behind his back. He looked very handsome and gallant.

"Who took these for you? They are so professional and perfect!"

"My friends took them, and I developed them myself during the unfettered period. To develop photographs like these is very time-consuming, you know. I had to shade here and partially cover there and experiment all possible ways. Back then, fortunately, time was something we had plenty of."

I liked him. He was unassuming and generous, and I was happy that he had come to join us. Finally I saw that one high-ranking officer, a really high one, was incorruptible.

The summer of 1970 brought a special army recruitment to Yan'an. Only two Beijing youths were taken. Binghe was one. Everybody knew what was happening, but nobody complained. He had been "tempered" in the countryside for a year and a half and had done much better than children from corrupt high-ranking families. But Premier Zhou surprised us all. After two months, he had Binghe demobilized and flown from Xinjiang Autonomic Region all the way back to Yan'an. To avoid gossip, he wasn't returned to my brigade, but to another.

Later I read in a book about Binghe's sister, Bingjian. She was a 1968 graduate but went to the grasslands in Inner Mongolia in the autumn of 1968. At the end of 1970 she joined the army like Binghe, and shortly afterwards Premier Zhou had her demobilized and returned to the grasslands.

Zhou didn't have children of his own. His nephews and nieces were his closest young blood relatives. He didn't allow any of them to take advantage of his special position. I wished that China had more leaders like Zhou Enlai.

My second year was physically a much easier one. In January and February I worked with one brigade leader, one accountant, and one work point recorder to check accounts back for five years. Finally I had a chance to use my knowledge and brains.

As the cold plateau wind blew and snow fell outside, we sat cosily on the warm *kang*, flipping through receipts and clicking away at our abacuses. It had been a long time since I had learned to use an abacus in primary school, but it didn't take me long to recall all the formulas. On the second day my fingers could move as fast as the accountant's.

I loved the job. I scrutinized every receipt with enthusiasm and earnestly hoped to find errors to demonstrate how useful I could be to the peasants. And I did find one from two years before. When the brigade had sold some goods to a company in Yan'an town, it didn't receive the forty yuan it should have. I showed my findings to my three co-workers, and after studying it carefully, they agreed there was indeed a mistake. The next day the brigade sent a person to the company and got the money.

This coup and my speed in calculation so impressed my three co-workers that it soon became known among the peasants that my brain was "very sharp." I began to fantasize: why shouldn't the brigade make me their accountant, or better yet, their school teacher, so that my abilities could be put to use? But months passed and I was still a peasant. My desire was unrealistic. They already had a good accountant who had also graduated from junior middle school like me. In the preceding five years there had been no mistakes except the one I had found. And the school had enough teachers. Unless it fired them, it would never need me or any of the thirty of us.

In March I did miscellaneous jobs. One was to feed oxen in the cowshed. There I saw the old peasant in charge force-feeding the two dozen oxen with a thick liquid made of bean-curd. This was done every year before spring sowing to make them strong. When time for spring sowing came, I was sent to the team that carried manure to the fields.

There were seven of us. The other six were men, but they were small and weak, and their work points ranged from only seven to nine. We worked shorter hours than the other workers, leaving home after breakfast, when others had already finished their early work, coming home for lunch, and occasionally packing up as early as an hour before sunset.

Our job was to carry manure to the fields, but the actual carrying was done by the poor donkeys. We only shovelled the manure into long, slender gunnysacks, put them on the donkeys' backs, and drove them to the croplands, which were scattered all over the mountains. There we dumped the manure out, came back to the manure piles near the brigade centre, and started all over again. We usually made seven trips a day, but the number of trips varied depending on how far away our destinations were. Most of our time was spent climbing mountains.

In our team the heavy work was to lift the gunnysacks onto the donkeys' backs. Each sack weighed 110 pounds — I knew because I weighed them myself. Our team leader, Sanhu, told me not to lift them. "It's good enough as long as you do all the rest of the work with us," he said with a nasal twang. But I didn't want to be relegated to a minor role. To earn my seven points, I thought I should do some heavy work. If I didn't, someone else would have to do it in my place. They were only weak, small men, and they all could do it!

Whenever Sanhu wasn't around I would try. I could lift the bags high above the ground, but never quite as high as a donkey's back. I tried to do it slowly, I tried to do it fast, and I tried in all different positions. The sack always ended up a few inches lower than the donkey's back! Finally I had to admit that I wasn't even as capable as these small men.

Once the sacks were on the donkeys' backs, the climbing began. From the brigade centre to the croplands was mainly uphill because the village sat on lowland. With one person behind a string of several donkeys, our team filed up the winding mountain paths.

When I began, I was given two donkeys to drive; later the number increased to three or four. Usually I just followed them with my hands clasped behind my back like a peasant, but every once in a while a donkey would get tired and stand still. It wasn't easy to climb a mountain with a 110-pound load on one's back, even for a donkey. To get the beast moving again, I would have to hit it with a clod of dirt. If after two clods it still wouldn't move, I would step off the narrow road to approach it from the side on the mountain slope. Beating and pushing, I would try everything to get it going. While slapping it on the buttock, I sometimes imagined what an angry donkey might do. If it kicked, I would definitely lose my balance. How would it feel to roll down a steep mountain?

The trip home was mainly downhill and pleasant. The donkeys needed no prodding — they ran faster than we did. At one point, close to the top of our mountain, Mao's old residence in the Dates Garden came into view. Surrounded by the vast, drab loess, the apricot, peach, and pear trees were in full spring blossom, forming an island of white, pink, and green. It was heavenly.

Sanhu was a smart and considerate man. Very soon after we met, I came to like him and ultimately took him as my poor and lower-middle-class peasant teacher. Before him I had another teacher, Dahu, Sanhu's older

brother, who was one of the brigade leaders. He was assigned to me by
the brigade after our arrival. We students had proposed the idea so that we
could be better "re-educated" in the countryside. But to my disappointment Dahu didn't pay much attention to me. In the field he never worked
with me, and after work he never invited me home. I didn't know
whether he was too busy or had simply forgotten I was his student.

Sanhu took his role seriously and was a good teacher. One day while
we were filling the sacks with manure, he noticed that my way of shovelling was wrong: "You are trying to push the spade into the manure with
the strength of your arms. It is much easier if you use your whole body."
In the beginning I ignored him. I couldn't imagine that there was a skill
to shovelling and thought I was doing all right. My back and arms did get
sore, but all physical labour causes some pain. Still Sanhu kept at me and
in the end I asked him to teach me. He demonstrated, explained, and corrected me until I really caught on.

What a difference! From then on I could shovel as much as the peasants without pain or great effort. I came to a sudden realization that there
probably was a skill to every farm job. Sanhu probably had a way of
dealing with all the painful jobs I had done. It was a pity that I hadn't met
him earlier.

Despite his cleverness, he was an unhappy man. His smile was always
wan, and he never laughed. "Aye! What is the meaning of life?" he would
ask. "It is suffering piled on suffering, year round, all for nothing but to
feed ourselves. This year we work hard to grow crops. Next year we eat
them and grow more for the year after. Aye! Why should we live?"

I wanted to change his view, but I couldn't think of any convincing arguments. One's life can be beautiful if only one can dream. My dream was to
go to university. What could I tell Sanhu to dream? He would probably
spend all his life like his ancestors in this little village growing crops just as
he claimed. The farthest he could travel would be the town of Yan'an.

After Sanhu became my teacher, he often invited me home to eat
supper. There I met his wife, a legendary woman, the most expensive
wife in the village.

The first time I saw her I tried to find some faults. I thought her parents
black-hearted to ask so much money from poor Sanhu. How could
anybody be worth 3,200 yuan? But as I got to know her, I had to admit
she was a lovely woman. Her half-moon-shaped eyes were like black
gems, her oval face was expressive and vivid, and she was clever. She
spoke well, kept a snug home, and made delicious food. A dish made by
her hands tasted much better than the same thing made by Heitu's wife.

"Is it true that your parents asked three thousand two hundred yuan from Sanhu?"

She only smiled in response.

"Why did they ask so much money?"

"Because they're poor."

"Now they've made you poor, too. Have you paid off the debt?"

"No, we're still paying."

"Why don't you ask your parents to forgive Sanhu some of the debt? What do they do with all that money?"

"They have no money now. It's all gone. Several cave dwellings easily cost a few thousand yuan," she said softly. She seemed to have no hard feelings towards her parents, who had put her and her husband deeply in debt. Even someone as clever as she couldn't see that mercenary marriage was wrong.

"Let's not talk about that any more." She changed the subject. "Tell me something about your life in Beijing. What do you wear in Beijing?"

"Nothing special. We wear the same clothes we do now, except cleaner."

"No. That can't be true. Tell me really. What do you wear in Beijing?" She just didn't believe me. In her mind Beijing must be paradise, where all people wear beautiful clothes of silk and wool. We knew little about the peasants' ways of life and their ways of thinking, but they knew nothing about ours.

"When one of our sons grows up, we'll send him to the army," she confided, "so that he can wear many layers of clothes like you."

"Many layers!" I was amused. "Do we wear many layers of clothes? Is that what you think?" I couldn't help laughing. Then I remembered that last spring, when the peasants took off their cotton-padded coats to catch lice, there was nothing underneath. They probably wore no undershorts, either. Our underwear, blouses, sweaters, jackets, and overcoats were indeed many layers.

"How many children do you have?"

"Three, two boys and a girl."

"That sounds perfect. I suppose you don't want more?"

She didn't answer me at once. Although the government had not yet become serious about the policy of one child per couple, it had long before stopped advocating large families.

"For your sake as well as your children's you shouldn't have more. You must know the more children you have, the harder your lives will become."

"Just one more. One more would be nice," she finally said.

"Why?"

She wouldn't explain. But I knew why. It was tradition that prosperity was proportional to the size of a family. The peasants had no pensions. When the inevitable time came that they could no longer work the fields, they had to depend on their children. They thought that it was worth it to work hard when they were young to raise enough children in exchange for security in their later years.

I enjoyed working with Sanhu, but we had to part company when the spring sowing was over. Our team was disbanded, and its members went off in all directions. Sanhu went to herd sheep alone, and I to the brigade's vegetable field in the lowlands along the Yan River.

Growing vegetables was for the most part a job for old people. There was no lighter job in the brigade. There were no mountains to climb and no early work to do. I hadn't wanted that job, but there was no choice. Although I had been cured the previous summer in Beijing, once I was back to manual labour on the plateau, my period again began to give me trouble. Besides that, I started to have flu and stomachaches. My resistance to disease was collapsing, and I felt feeble. I didn't hesitate any more to take sick leave. The peasants saw this and starting from the second year arranged light jobs for me. Carrying manure was light, but climbing the mountains all day long still seemed to be too much. As a last resort they put me in the vegetable field. There I hoed weeds, cut Chinese chives, and watered and manured vegetables.

The sale of vegetables and fruit from the Dates Garden was an important source of income for the brigade. In summer and autumn our tractor transported tons of fresh vegetables and fruit to the town of Yan'an and returned with cash. In mid-August, when the majority of Beijing students left the countryside for factories, the brigade was able to pay for our second year of work in cash. I received sixty yuan.

THE ONE CRACKDOWN AND
THREE COMBATS CAMPAIGN

IN JUNE 1970, THE YAN'AN MUNICIPALITY ASKED MY brigade to recommend a Beijing student to help the One Crackdown and Three Combats Campaign, a sub-movement of the Cultural Revolution, in town. The One Crackdown was to crack down on counter-revolutionaries and the Three Combats were to combat graft, waste, and corruption. The brigade recommended me for the job. It was better for me and for the peasants as well. They wanted to keep me away from heavy work, but their vegetable field didn't really need me. By lending me to the municipality, they would receive forty cents cash a day, which was more than I was worth to them. There was no better place to put me to use.

The revolution in Yan'an was not intense, but it was there. Since we had arrived in the beginning of 1969, every few days the brigade would hold a meeting in the evening — in slack seasons more, in busy seasons fewer. Willingly or unwillingly, after a day's work and supper, we all had to go down to the conference hall to listen to Cultural Revolution trash. I was never absent, but I hardly heard anything. If I was in a mood to talk, I sat beside somebody at the back in the dark. If I wanted to be alone, I moved to the front and tuned out.

There were no chairs in the huge hall and no central heating. In the winter, as at camp, we sat on huge logs around fires. While Zhifu gave his oration in a flow of eloquence up on the stage, the peasants below went about their business. The fire crackled, some peasants smoked their pipes, some spun wool, and some tucked their hands in their sleeves and dozed off. Ears perked up at the end, however, when Dahu or some other brigade leader announced the next day's production plans.

The peasants weren't enthusiastic about the revolution. They couldn't avoid meetings, but the whole time I was there they never held one to "denounce and criticize." All their meetings were so general and innocuous that nobody felt pressure. I was glad to live in political peace. Yet when the brigade told me to aid the One Crackdown and Three Combats Campaign in town, I didn't say no. The brigade had chosen me from all its twenty-some students. I felt honoured. Also, after the primitive life I'd led for sixteen months, I really didn't mind living in a town for a while, however small it was.

More than three years had passed since I was criticized and ousted from the Red Guard. My bitterness had ebbed, and my vow about staying away from politics had almost washed away. I was ready to make more mistakes. Accompanied by a bit of luggage, I took a ride on our brigade tractor to a compound in town to register. There I was assigned a room all to myself.

My working group had four members. Two, including our group leader, Qun, a red-faced man in his early forties, were cadres from the province. They lived in a room a few doors from mine. The other member was a native from Yan'an who went back to his family every day. The objects of our campaign were the Yan'an town catering and service trades, about which none of us knew anything.

Our work started with a mobilization meeting of all the managers of restaurants and bathhouses. There were about ten. After Qun's opening speech, Xiuchun, who was the manager of the biggest restaurant and was always appraised as "advanced," responded. She said a few words of support for this campaign and then began to sing the praises of her restaurant, recounting how active they had been in past campaigns. As she smiled smugly, her silver front tooth glittered.

I couldn't stand her. As she went on, the fighting spirit in me woke up and rose higher and higher. Forgetting my own advice to myself about not getting too serious about this campaign, I erupted. "Hold it! This is not a meeting to elect a model unit. This is a mobilization to start the One Crackdown and Three Combats Campaign. Are you trying to tell us your unit is so perfect that this campaign should not take place at all? As an advanced cadre, what example are you setting? If all of you have such an attitude, how are we going to carry out our task? I suggest that you, and you all," I nodded to all of them, "cooperate with us and don't try to play tricks. Otherwise you will face the consequences!"

Xiuchun's long face purpled. She was embarrassed, but I didn't care. Even though I had experienced the mortification of being publicly criticized, I hadn't learned to sympathize with others who were in a similar situation. I simply didn't see the connection between Xiuchun and myself. In my case, I was so well intentioned, trying so hard to do well; whereas in her case, who knew if she wasn't a grafter or embezzler? Some of these managers must be corrupt, I thought, and it was my job to suspect and catch them.

After the meeting Qun patted me on the back: "Well done! Surprising that a young girl like you could be so incisive!"

I smiled modestly. "I only did what I should have."

Although I sounded tough, like everyone else I had no idea about how we were going to crack down and combat, and what we were supposed to achieve in the end. The municipality didn't give us any concrete instructions — maybe they didn't know either. All they did was to pass on to us piles of dossiers detailing the problems of all the units that had been denounced in the past. Qun decided that we should start by reading the dossiers. After that we would improvise and probe our way forward.

Most of the problems concerned graft or "lifestyle." There was not a single case of counter-revolutionary activity. Even so, some of the files were interesting. I remember one man's confession that he committed adultery in the Yan'an Bathhouse. His handwriting was big and ugly, but his description was vivid. The man had been a worker in the bathhouse and the woman was temporary help. They liked each other and flirted a lot, causing the other workers to gossip. One day he hugged the woman from behind, pulled at her pants, and said, "They already say we do the thing; why don't we just make them happy?" The woman didn't object, and they completed their project on one of the beds for people to rest on after bathing. From the report that followed the confession I learned that the man had been publicly criticized, but the woman was fired! Yan'an was no place for women, in the country or in town.

Every morning our group got together to discuss what we had read. If someone had doubts about a point, Qun would send one of us to the unit to investigate. I went out to talk to the workers a number of times. I found them cool. They answered all my questions as succinctly as possible, and no one ever came to me on his or her own initiative to expose hidden crimes in a unit. People often did this in movies and I wished to experience it in real life.

The service workers might not like me, but they "respected" me. As a matter of fact they "respected" me so much that for this one and only short period of my life, I found my portions of noodles larger than those of other customers, and there was no need for me to stand in line. Someone always signalled me ahead. I wasn't sure about their motives. Was it because they were afraid of being framed by me or the working group, or because they had a guilty conscience, or because they simply did this to all people in authority? I was only a tiny fish who temporarily held a bit of power. What happened when the big fish in government patronized their restaurants?

Our campaign lasted two months. When we were ordered to stop, I felt we hadn't accomplished anything. No new "bad elements" or "class enemies" had been discovered, no new crimes had been uncovered, and no old wrongs had been righted. Were there problems in the system or not? I didn't know. Nor did I know the right way to find them if there were. Should we check all the accounts? Should we work in the restaurants to pick up gossip? What I did know was that the way we went about it was a pure waste of time.

In August I returned to the brigade and found that big changes had taken place. The brigade was also having its own One Crackdown and Three Combats Campaign. The person in charge was a cadre from the province, Comrade Liu, a tall, dark, and thin middle-aged man. Not only did he have power over the brigade leaders, he had power over the Beijing students as well. That wouldn't have mattered if our lives were to go on as before, but we were again at a crucial stage. That month Shanxi Province decided that the Beijing youth had had enough re-education, although as far as I could tell everyone was exactly the way they had been before coming to Yan'an. It was time for the students to contribute to Shanxi's industries.

Our reaction to this varied. Some students were happy to go for a better life, and others, including me, had other, even more extravagant desires. Although the universities were still shut, the resourceful ones knew they would soon reopen and take new students. They also knew that those who could manage to stay in the countryside would have a much better chance to get into one. Despite the fact that our official residence was no longer registered in Beijing, it wasn't yet settled in Shanxi Province. Only if we became workers or cadres would we become permanent residents. Then it would be extremely difficult to get permission to move again. Therefore, if one wanted to go to university or to leave open the possibility of living in Beijing one day, the optimum strategy was to stay on in the countryside.

With my mind set on staying, I went to see Comrade Liu, yet another person who held my fate in his hands. He didn't like me. While I was away he had already become acquainted with the students and made his choices, mostly from workers' families. After I returned from town, he hardly paid any attention to me. As I talked to him, I tried to be sincere, but he wouldn't be serious. He didn't want to hear my statement or my wishes.

When his list was posted, I was on it. Shuzeng, Yuzhen, and I were assigned to a new knitting mill in Yan'an; Shuli, the one I clashed with in the beginning, and two other boys from his school were assigned to the local taxation office, and the bulk of the students, fifteen of them, were assigned to a big armaments factory in Hanzhong, the richest part of Shanxi Province to the south. Only four, Liu's favourites, were allowed to stay in the brigade. My friend Jinli was one.

Happily or unhappily, all of us obeyed the order and went to our new units, except for Shuzeng. In mid-August he joined the army through a backdoor located by his Red Army–soldier father. For a year and a half I had thought him courageous to stand up against his crooked parents. In the end he yielded and swerved onto the same corrupt path.

A DREAM SHARED
BY TWO GENERATIONS

THAT AUGUST MY FATHER WAS APPOINTED COMMERCIAL consul in the Chinese embassy in Albania. Before leaving, he asked to see me again. I had another excuse to go home!

When I got home, Weihua was gone. During a recent recruitment, he had succeeded in enlisting in an army regiment in Wuhan, a big city in central China. Even for someone like Weihua, who had a good job in Beijing, the attraction of the army was very strong.

My youngest brother, Jianhua, was now the only one who remained with my parents in Beijing. Before the Cultural Revolution he was in the fifth grade of primary school. Recently he had entered a middle school, which was close to home. It had not been a key school, but that didn't matter any more. No schools had ratings nowadays. They were all at the same level — the lowest. One day I asked Jianhua how his studies were going.

"Who studies these days? What's the use when, in the end, everybody has to go to the countryside to grow crops?"

The middle school graduates who followed us had been dealt with similarly. Some went to join the brigade in the countryside, and some were assigned to units in Beijing. However, the policy became more lenient in one way. If a graduate was the only one remaining with his parents, he would be exempted from leaving Beijing. Also, because of the discipline problems some Beijing students had in Yan'an, students were for the most part sent to suburb communes of Beijing. This way their parents could keep an eye on them.

From Jianhua I learned that my father had gone to Europe with a delegation of import and export company directors and associates, headed by a vice-minister of foreign trade. As we were talking, he took out an album of pictures from the trip. They were the best photographs of my father I ever saw, mostly in colour, which was very rare at the time. Many were group photographs taken indoors. I couldn't see any features of the country my father was visiting — it seemed he did not seek out scenic spots. However, he had paid his respects to Karl Marx's grave in High-gate Cemetery. In one black-and-white picture, Father stood small and alone at the base of the gigantic bust of Marx.

Many Chinese thought it a great honour to visit foreign places, but in his letters my father hadn't even mentioned his trip to me. To him, it was just a job assigned him by the party. He was not a vain man. In all the years after Liberation his rank had hardly changed, whereas his friends rose higher and higher. Every one of his job changes could have been a promotion, had he wanted one, but he insisted on staying at the same level. "How big one's ability is — that's how much responsibility one should take. One has to know one's limits." That was his philosophy.

My father's position in the trade ministry required him to attend banquets hosted by foreign businessmen from time to time. On the invitation card, my mother's name was always included, but she never accompanied him. When we asked her why, she explained that she felt uneasy in front of foreigners and didn't like western food. Now my father was taking a long-term position in the embassy in Albania. Mother could have gone with him, but again she chose not to.

One day, when she was sewing a silk floss padded coat for me, I lay down on her bed to watch her working, and we talked. "Aren't you curious about foreign countries? Don't you even want to have a look?" I asked her.

"Not really. I'm not too curious about them. I don't believe there are other countries better than ours. I like what we have here."

"Don't you mind living apart from Father for such a long time? How long is he going to be away?"

"Four years. He can visit us in China only once after two years. This is a problem. Your father and I did discuss it. After balancing everything, though, we thought it best for me to stay. If I go, Jianhua will be the only one at home. He's hardly sixteen. What if he falls in with bad company? And who worries about you and your three siblings who are away from home? Especially you. Although you are in a mill now, you're still in Yan'an. We never know what help you'll need from us. I really can't go away and leave all this behind."

"Do you still worry about me? I think I'm all right now. How can things go wrong in a factory? The work won't be too hard, and I won't get sick again. After the three-year apprenticeship, I'll be able to support myself and visit you each year. Yan'an is not the best place in the world, but I can put up with it now that I'm a factory worker. The countryside was really too hard. I don't know how long I would have been able to sustain myself if I were still there. Even so, I didn't want to leave the brigade. They say one has a better chance of getting into university if one stays."

"If only you could get into university! That is what we wish for. Once you're in, we can put our minds to rest."

"Don't bet on it. Who knows whether the universities will start to function again? And who knows, if and when they do, whether I will then be too old to qualify? You know how much I want to get to university. There's nothing I want more in this world. But some dreams never come true." I heaved a sigh. "I am prepared."

"Talking about universities, I almost got in one."

"Really? Which?"

"Shandong University in Qingdao. It's on a mountain slope facing the ocean. Very beautiful."

"How come you never told me? When was that?"

"Back in the fifties when I'd just finished the speeded-up middle school. Believe it or not, I was a very good student. I was the monitor of my class and got straight 5s."

"I believe you," I said earnestly. With the way she treated her work and studies, what else could she have been?

"My teachers and school all liked me. After graduation they recommended me for Shandong University."

"So you did get into the university! Why did you say almost?" I was excited and propped myself up on the bed.

"Let me finish! I had pneumonia. The university would never have admitted me had they known, but my school and teachers covered it up for me. They wanted me to try my luck anyway. One month later, at a physical examination, the truth came out. I was dismissed."

"No! They can't do that!"

"You don't know how I regretted it! I cried for three days and nights! Even today I can feel the pain. Oh, did I ever want to go to a university!"

I could not find words to comfort her. She had missed her own chance to go to a university, and now she couldn't even see her children get into one. All five of us were born at the wrong time. None of us seemed to have a chance. Soon after my visit home, however, a letter reached me from my older brother, Xinhua, with the great news that he had entered Hebei University in the city of Shijiazhuang.

In 1970 the universities had taken some tentative steps towards reopening and admitted a small number of students, Xinhua among them. He did not choose the university or his specialty, chemistry. I didn't think Xinhua liked chemistry, but under those circumstances who was going to be choosy? Hebei University couldn't compare with Beijing University, but it *was* a university. At last there was one university student in the family! I was thrilled!

Xinhua had done well in the corps in Inner Mongolia. From a plain soldier he was promoted to squad leader, then platoon leader. Nothing came easily, though. Once he told me that while inspecting the crops at night, he fainted in the field. He was working too hard. Hard work, plus his skills in organizing and motivating people, turned out to be Xinhua's key to success.

THE KNITTING MILL

MY MILL WAS THE FIRST OF ITS KIND IN YAN'AN. THE grand plan was to start by knitting socks and eventually to produce a whole line of knitwear. Its mother mill, the Twelfth State-Run Cotton Mill, was in Xianyang, an industrialized city close to Xi'an. All of the hosiery machines at the Yan'an mill were borrowed from Xianyang, and the mill's sixty workers were trained there.

In October Yuzhen and I left Beijing for Xianyang. When we arrived, the first batch of thirty workers had finished their training and left for Yan'an to start the mill. We were put in the second batch, whose program had already been running eleven days. The one in charge of us in Xianyang was a technician, Meili, a graduate of a textile college. Even though Meili means "beautiful," there was nothing beautiful about her. She was ugly, with a gorilla mouth and a terrible hoarse voice. From her we learned that Yuzhen was assigned to sew the socks closed at the toes; I was to run hosiery knitting machines.

The next morning Meili took us to the workshop. It was spacious, with more than fifty thousand square feet of floor area, and as bright as the outdoors. We walked along a passage, and passed by lines and lines of running machines and workers moving around them. The machines were painted green; the workers wore snow-white aprons and hats. I was fascinated. This was a big industry! It was fabulous. In one step I had jumped from the Stone Age to the Industrial Era.

All the machines were imported from Japan. They seemed modern and impressive to me, but in fact they were out of date. They could knit socks only from below the ribs. The new model the Japanese were now producing could knit the whole sock. Naturally these were more expensive. China had plenty of labour, but not much money; so we used cheaper machines and more workers.

That day I was taught how to put the ribs onto a special tray and I was given an out-of-order machine to practise on. With zeal I put the ribs on, took them off, and put them on again. After work I chatted with other workers in the dormitory and found they had all progressed past this stage. They were now running their own machines, some one, some two. (The masters in the Twelfth Mill ran four, even five machines.) Suddenly I realized how far behind I was and became anxious. I put my all into learning my trade and the gap between me and the rest quickly narrowed. In eleven days I could run two hosiery machines and had reached the proficiency of most workers. My masters praised me, as did my fellow workers.

In the beginning I felt spoiled to be a factory worker. Running the machines was cushy, and after work I had time to enjoy city life. I roamed the streets, went window shopping, and tried out the restaurants. Xianyang was a much bigger city than Yan'an; there were more goods in the department stores and better food in the restaurants. The most famous local dish was bun in mutton, a toasted bun torn into pieces, put in a bowl, and covered lavishly with a sauce containing stewed mutton. It was spicy and tasty.

Xianyang was an ancient city. Twenty-two hundred years earlier it had been the capital of the powerful Qin Dynasty. Today it was industrialized and polluted. There were many coal mines and large factories in Xianyang. When it rained, the streets were thick with a black mire that looked like a slurry of coal powder. From its present state, one could hardly see the city's past glory.

While I was in Xianyang, my brother Jianhua wrote me a letter. He had just learned the famous ci "Shuitiaogetou" by Su Dongpo (1037-1102), from the Song Dynasty. Jianhua like it so much that he decided to share it with me.

Dongpo wrote this ci on the night of a mid-autumn festival, which is on the fifteenth of August in the Chinese calendar and occurs in September in the western calendar. The moon is supposedly at its fullest that day. To the Chinese, it is a festival for family reunions. In the evening the entire family sits together under the moon to eat moon cakes and fruit, and absent family members are thought of with longing. That night, after a big party with his friends, Dongpo wrote this ci to express his great love for life and fond wishes for his younger brother who lived far away.

Since when did the bright moon start to shine?
Holding up the liquor, I ask the blue sky.
I wonder in all the heaven,
What year it is tonight.

I want to fly away with the wind,
But fear that in the jade palaces of immortals,
It will be too cold when it is so high.
To dance with only my shadow
Is worse than staying with mankind.

Illuminating the vermilion pavilions,
Penetrating through window panels,
The moonlight shifts and keeps me awake.
Towards people the moon should bear no resentment.
Why does it always become full when they are apart?
Humans have sorrows and joys, partings and reunions,
The moon can be cloudy and clear, half and full,
It has been so since ancient times.
I only wish we both live long
And share the moon from a thousand li apart.

I had never heard this *ci* before, and it greatly moved me. I couldn't let it go. I memorized it and quoted it often. In all the many years I have been away from my family, it has given me immense comfort.

By the end of November we could all run three machines and our training was finished. We returned to Yan'an. For the first time I saw our own mill, which was just under two miles from the town of Yan'an. It had two workshops of over two thousand square feet each, one for hosiery machines, another for sock-top sewing machines, and rows of offices and workers' dormitories in cave dwellings on the mountain slope behind. Compared with the grand Twelfth Mill in Xianyang, my little Yan'an Knitting Mill was humble.

When our group of thirty new workers joined the mill, the leaders decided to mix the old and new, and to reorganize everyone into four squads. Two leaders were to be elected for each squad. Among the thirty old workers was a small clique of three Beijing girls. One was a squad leader. All three were fast learners and acted in a haughty manner. Seeing them act this way made me want to compete and show them how one should behave. I began working harder, spoke actively in squad meetings, and befriended many workers. While some Beijing students looked down on the locals, I treated them as equals. The local girls might not have seen much of the world but it wasn't their fault. They were kind, unsophisticated people.

In the end I was elected squad leader. After that I did an even better job, kept production shipshape, organized lively study meetings, and made my squad a harmonious unit. If two workers quarrelled, I mediated and helped them make up. If someone shouted at me I didn't get mad, but talked with her and let her pour out her grievances. With calmness and self-restraint I kept myself above trifles and factions — before long I was popular.

In February 1971 my mill began to establish its revolutionary committee. There would be five members. Three were appointed: Old Wang, the associate director, Old Lei, the associate party secretary, and Boge, the only political cadre in the mill. The other two were to be elected by the workers. Through nomination, lengthy discussion, and voting, Yan'an, a local boy and a machine maintenance worker, and I emerged with an overwhelming majority. Yan'an was one grade higher and one year older than I. He had many wrinkles on his face, though, and looked much older. I had heard he was good at his job and was starting to make innovations to our hosiery machines.

After the election the leaders stalled. Then a rumour circulated that they had preselected the two remaining members of the committee: Zhang, another local boy and a machine maintenance worker, and Shifen, one of our two accountants and the only Beijing student to enter the mill as a cadre. When the leaders did make up their minds and announced their decision, Zhang and I became committee members, and Yan'an, who had been legitimately elected, was discarded! That was how our leaders worked. Indeed, Old Wang and Old Lei were not the sort of leaders I looked up to.

Old Wang was forty, a demobilized army leader of low rank. He was sallow and gaunt with triangular-shaped eyes and a face that never smiled. He always wore a faded army uniform. Old Lei had joined the revolution in 1949, just before Liberation. He was a fifty-year-old fat man of medium height with a reddish-brown face, big eyes, and a big nose. He was always smiling. In my mind, neither of them looked like revolutionary cadres. Old Wang was something like a peremptory warlord, and Old Lei a slick merchant from the old society.

These two men detested each other and were forever engaged in open or veiled warfare. All the workers in the mill knew it. During my entire stay at the mill, there was no director or party secretary. That was the position they were both after. Incompetent as they were, both wanted more power. What did they care about the workers, or the mill?

TREADING THE BOARDS

ONE DAY, IN EARLY APRIL 1971, THE WORKERS OF OUR mill all went out to plant trees on a mountain close to Yangjialing, another wartime home of the party leaders in Yan'an. When we arrived I saw many fish-scale-shaped pits on the bare mountain slopes — I knew it had been planted before, but futilely. Afforestation was a yearly routine and even in primary school we had planted trees. The effort was great, but the trees had a low survival rate. Sometimes they were planted improperly, or the weather was too dry, or the seedling trees were stolen by the peasants for firewood. As we dug into the hard loess, I wondered who would be here next year doing the same thing all over again.

As we planted, the workers asked me to sing. "You don't have to work. Just sing for us," a few of them said. So I began singing loudly, quite unaware that a university graduate from Shanghai, Failuo, was passing by the foot of the mountain. Failuo turned out to be the organizer of the Mao Zedong Thought Performing Arts Propaganda Team in the Yan'an region. His interest piqued, he climbed up and asked some workers what my name was. A couple of days later an order came from the local government to transfer me to the team.

After running the hosiery machines for six months, I had lost my enthusiasm. It was now drudgery. The working class may be the "leading class" in China, but workers' jobs were repetitive and monotonous. I happily abandoned ship. I knew that if and when I returned to the knitting mill my skills would lag behind my fellow workers', but I wasn't overly concerned. Life had been unpredictable so far. Who knew what the future would bring?

I was with the Mao Zedong Thought Performing Arts Propaganda Team for seven months. I had expected to be formally trained in singing but I got nothing of the sort. The members of the propaganda team were all amateurs, save for one director, Old Guo, from the Yan'an Cultural Troupe. He directed our chorus and band. For the remainder of the program the performers served as their own directors.

The programs were a potpourri. Choruses were copied from the radio, group dances were transplanted from the Yan'an Cultural Troupe, and other acts were brought by the actors and actresses, or created by team members.

In July I started playing in a mini-opera about the Beijing students in Yan'an. I didn't know who the playwright was, but Failuo was the composer. The opera had three characters: a Beijing girl, Hongyun; her younger brother, Hongsheng; and the old party secretary of the brigade they were in. It began with Hongsheng wavering in his resolve to take root in Yan'an. He told Hongyun he was leaving and threw away the sheep-tending whip that the old secretary had put into his hand when they had arrived. Hongyun was greatly worried. She came to the old party secretary for help, and he recalled his sufferings in the old society, telling Hongsheng how he had been beaten by a landlord with that exact whip. Hongsheng was moved. He repented his mistake and decided to stay.

I didn't think much of the script. Most shows were phoney in those days, but this was one of the worst I had ever read. No peasants in my brigade had ever told us their sufferings. Even if they had, Lanlan and Guoqing would never have stayed in Dates Garden just because of that. Before Liberation "recalling past sufferings" worked well to motivate the soldiers in the fight against the Kuomintang reactionaries — before the Cultural Revolution it also worked to persuade people to behave themselves — but today, to convince people that despite people's personal desires or physical capabilities they should spend their whole lives in the countryside, better reasons must be offered.

I didn't like the cast either. I was to be Hongyun, and the role of Hongsheng, a Beijing student in Yan'an, was assigned to a local boy who spoke Mandarin with a definite accent. It wasn't that there were no Beijing boys around: the role of the native old party secretary was given to a Beijing student. The whole thing was absurd, yet I played Hongyun for months. In China people didn't do things because they wanted to.

From July to October our team with its mediocre programs travelled all over the Yan'an region to "propagate Mao Zedong Thought." On crude stages in open fields, we presented our shows to factory workers, commune peasants, and university students in the only university created by the party in the 1930s. All shows were free. The audience was usually large but applause was scarce. The opera was never really welcomed anywhere except, believe it or not, at Yan'an University. I never knew what the intellectuals saw in it.

On September 13, 1971 Lin Biao tried to escape from China to the Soviet Union after his plot to assassinate Mao failed. His plane crashed in Mongolia. All Chinese were shocked. They thought this kind of treachery only happened in ancient China, not under Communism.

What astonished me the most was that Mao hadn't seen through Lin. As shrewd as Mao was, he had let Lin climb all the way to the second chair. This time it was clear that Mao had made a mistake. No sophistry could help him make it vanish.

A few days after this event our leaders held a meeting to convey the central party's documents detailing how vicious Lin and his family (except his daughter, who was not implicated) were. As usual, when a person fell, his whole history reeked of evil. In the end we had a discussion, but no one knew what to say. Only I was all eager to open my mouth: "Lin Biao was vicious to play a double-dealer," I exclaimed. "But, on the other hand, Chairman Mao and the party centre made a mistake. They didn't recognize Lin's real nature and wrongly chose him to be Chairman Mao's successor. It's good that the mistake has now been corrected. It's good Lin gave himself away before it was too late." After my speech everyone was deadly quiet, but I didn't feel there was anything amiss.

When the meeting ended, the leaders found me. The party secretary, a small man with eye glasses, grey hair, and a small face, said agitatedly: "You'd better be more careful about what you say! Just now you said that Chairman Mao made a mistake. How can Chairman Mao make mistakes? If you weren't from a good family, you could have been interpreted as being anti–Chairman Mao!"

I thought those stuffy antediluvian old men ridiculous. Me? A counter-revolutionary? I tried to laugh it off, but they were all grave-faced and very serious. The small man pursed his mouth. Another man, tall and thin, with a long, lean face and a damaged eye, fixed me with his good eye. Under their stares I got scared. What if they reported my words to their superiors? No one knew what consequences might follow. To keep out of prison, I decided a bit of bending was appropriate. I thanked them for their kind warning and promised to watch my mouth from now on. Only then did they let me go.

While frittering away seven more months in the propaganda team, I made a wonderful friend: Yuehua, another singer. She was clever, sensible, and very generous. Her salary was thirty-one yuan because she was a senior middle school graduate; mine was a mere twenty-one. But she mixed her food coupons for our refectory with mine, and so, thanks to her, during that period I ate decently.

In November I returned to the mill, and Yuehua became a cadre in the Cultural Centre of Yan'an. Every Sunday I walked into town to visit her. We would put a wok on top of Yuehua's burner, sit on little stools, and cook eggs sunny-side-up. The food served in my mill was poor. The staples were cornflour buns and noodles with very little meat, eggs, and oil. Stuffing in six or eight eggs once a week in Yuehua's little room was the height of luxury.

One Sunday morning, when I was waiting outside the Cultural Centre for Yuehua, I caught sight of a familiar figure, Liu Wenhui, my best friend from primary school. We had not seen each other since the start of the Cultural Revolution in 1966.

"Liu Wenhui!" I called out loudly.

She heard me and turned back. She was in plain, dark men's clothes, no shape, no style, with her jacket buttoned to the collar. But she was just as pretty as ever.

"How are you? It's been years! I didn't even know you were in Yan'an, and I bump into you on the street! Am I glad to see you!" I brimmed with memories and nostalgia.

We stood on the street and chatted, and I learned she was still in the countryside and so were some other of my classmates. According to her, Jiamei, the class beauty, who had wanted to be a professional dancer but couldn't in Beijing, was now in the provincial ballet company in Xi'an.

"Now that we've found each other, let's not lose contact again, okay?" Wenhui said seriously. "By the way," she remarked, "my name is now Liu Kai."

I asked her which Kai, since the spoken word "kai" has several meanings. "Triumph."

This was one of the common names people used during the Cultural Revolution. Wenhui must have changed her name when it was in fashion during the Destroy the Old Four Campaign. I didn't like her new name and told her so. "The old one, Liu Wenhui, sounds better to me. I'll keep calling you that."

"As you like. But if you write to me put Liu Kai on the envelope. I'm known as Liu Kai now; if you put down Liu Wenhui, I won't receive the letter."

Wenhui's change of name reminded me of the early, crazy days of the Cultural Revolution. I was curious about her part in the revolution but I never asked her. I was afraid to hear that she had been maltreated as a

Son of a Bitch, which was a distinct possibility since she came from an intellectual family. Besides, she might in turn ask about my own activities. I had no desire to recall any of that ugly business. How fortunate it was that Wenhui and I had not been in the same class! Otherwise our friendship would never have survived.

FIGHTING FOR UNIVERSITY

At THE END OF 1971, AFTER DRIFTING IN THE CULTURAL Revolution for five and a half years, universities began to enroll students on a large scale. There were to be no examinations. Students would be recommended — that is, elected by the masses and then sanctioned by the leaders. They had to have a junior middle school education and be under twenty-five years of age, healthy, and "politically sound." All had to be workers, peasants, PLA soldiers, or cadres for at least three years. They were called worker-peasant-soldier students. First of all, however, quotas had to be allocated from above to regions and then to work units within the regions. Most units got no quota at all.

As a small city with a low level of education, Yan'an received a quota of a dozen or so places, but the Beijing Municipality donated five hundred additional places for the Beijing students sent here since 1969. It was said that there were twenty thousand of us!

The local government did not want to release any of the Beijing students like me who had been absorbed into industries. Only those who were still in the countryside were classified as Beijing students, and all five hundred positions went to them. Had I stayed in the Dates Garden, there would have been no problem. I would have been recommended by the peasants. I knew they liked me. As things evolved, however, I found my luck was not completely exhausted. By then my mill had one hundred young workers and it was asked to nominate one candidate.

According to the stated conditions, all the workers in my mill were eligible. However, intimidated by the competition, only four applied. My only real rival, the popular boy, Yan'an, didn't apply. I thought it a pity for him but I felt relieved. During the recommendation stage I got an easy majority, Baoyuan, a Yan'an student, got some votes, and Xiangyun, another Yan'an student, got a few. The fourth candidate got nothing. I thought I was a shoo-in.

One day our new associate party secretary, Huang, wanted to talk with me. The previous associate party secretary, Old Lei, had been transferred to some other unit by then. Secretary Huang was a short, plump woman about forty-five years old. She didn't take me into her office but to a stone bench outside the kitchen. Luckily, the winter's day wasn't cold and the sun shone generously down on us.

"Zhai Zhenhua, I want to talk about your application for university. You have behaved well, and we think you should study in a university, but we would like you to take a broader view and consider some factors that might not have occurred to you. First, let's talk about Xiangyun. She only wants to go to a medical institute." Xiangyun's father was a local doctor of Chinese medicine. We all knew she wanted to become a doctor too. "I guess neither you or Baoyuan is interested in medical institute?"

She was right, I didn't want to be a medical doctor. Medical doctors in China do not have the prestige or the exceptional incomes they do in the West. The hierarchy in Chinese universities, ranked by perceived difficulty and not potential earnings, is mathematics, physics, engineering, literature and the arts, and lastly medicine.

"If our quota turns out to involve a medical college, the place should be Xiangyun's. But if it isn't, would you be kind enough to concede your place to Baoyuan? He is twenty-five years old. This is his last year to apply. You are young and have many chances ahead. You can go to the university next year, I promise you! We know you want to join the party. Give us another year to foster you, then you can go as a party member. Isn't that better?"

Of course it was better to enter the university as a party member. Ever since I was eighteen, I had applied to join the party. Party membership was, at that time, still held in esteem. I had tried in the Dates Garden brigade, but no Beijing youth had been admitted. I had tried in the mill, but in the mill no workers were admitted. The door was tightly closed. Now Huang was promising me party membership in one year! How could I not be tempted?

Besides, what she said about Baoyuan was true. If the rules for universities didn't change, this was his last chance. He had been in the third grade of senior middle school before the Cultural Revolution. I heard he was a good student and ranked sixth best in Yan'an. He had even been put on the list to study in the Soviet Union. I didn't like to see talent being stifled. I could wait until next year, couldn't I? Normal recruitment had now started; why should it stop next year?

"All right, I withdraw," I told Huang, who was staring at me intensely. On hearing that, she broke into a smile. She left contented and so did I. I had just sacrificed my deserved right to someone else who needed it more — wasn't I noble?

In my dormitory a large group of my friends were waiting for me to tell them what Huang had said. They thought she was going to tell me my application was approved. Pleased with myself, I told them what I had just done. "What!" They raised a ruckus: "Don't be so foolish!" "Don't believe those promises. Who knows what it will be like next year. Maybe our mill will never get another place in the quota. Maybe Huang won't be here! How can she keep her promises then?" "Maybe they'd already decided on Baoyuan before the competition opened." "Why should you give way to anyone? Whoever is good should go! Whoever gets recommended should go!"

I suddenly sobered up. Their words jarred on my ears, but they smacked of the truth. Having experienced so much in life, I should have had more sense about the uncertainty of the future. Next year there might be no university recruitment. Even if there was, Beijing might not keep on giving part of its quota to Yan'an. In one year's time Old Lei had been replaced by Secretary Huang. Who knew how long she was going to be around? This could well be my last chance too, not only Baoyuan's. I was now having second thoughts but it was too late. "What's done can't be undone. What can I do now?"

"Go see her. Take it back!" answered Zhongcheng, a dark girl with a mouth of crooked teeth. She was a very upright person and never toadied to or feared the mill leaders.

"Go back on my word so soon? I can't do that!"

"But you have to, or you'll regret it the rest of your life!"

"All right, just leave me alone now. I have to think things over." I pushed them out and closed the door.

I was chagrined. I blamed myself for being gullible and overly pliant. "You always wanted to go to university. You had your chance and now you've blown it!" I then blamed Huang for putting me through all this. Going to university was a competition. Baoyuan lost the competition, so he shouldn't go. It should have been as simple as that. Why should Huang complicate things and hang a yoke of moral responsibility around my neck? Why couldn't the leaders in my mill respect the workers' will and carry out the party's policy for once in their lives! Maybe Huang had hidden motives. Maybe she was partial to Baoyuan because he was male, or a native Yan'aner. Maybe she was even a friend of Baoyuan's family. Otherwise why should she go out of her way to have that embarrassing talk with me?

The next morning I went to see her. "Secretary Huang, I've come to tell you I've changed my mind. I am not going to give my place to

Baoyuan. The masses recommended me, so I should go. I heard you leaders already selected Baoyuan before the mass recommendation."

"Who said that? In no way did we preselect Baoyuan!" Her face fell.

"It's not important who said it. What is important is what you do. You can prove they're wrong with your actions."

"It is too bad you feel this way. Now we have to reconsider the whole matter!"

My warning had little effect. Three days later the leaders handed three names to their superiors instead of one, as required. I was angry. I told everything to Yuehua, and she suggested that I go to see the person in the municipal administration who was in charge of recruitment. Because of her work, Yuehua was more familiar with the municipal government. She took me to the compound, and there we inquired and found out that Limin was our man.

I went to Limin's office twice. The first time he wasn't in but the second time I caught him. He was sitting behind his desk, a sheaf of reading material in his hand, his body turned to the side. As I walked to the front of the desk he didn't change his position, nor did he invite me to sit down on the nearby chair. So I stood. "What can I do for you?" He looked askance at me. Besides his stolid eyes, the next thing I noticed was his shapeless nose with a wart on the side. I guessed his age to be thirty-five.

"You can uphold justice! I'm from the Yan'an Knitting Mill. I'm the one who got all the votes to go to university, but the leaders want me to give my place to Baoyuan. That isn't fair!"

Instead of asking me more about the situation as I had expected, he said, "You should wait for the result in your mill. Why do you come here to disturb our work?"

"I had to come. If I don't speak for myself, who will? My leaders in the mill certainly won't."

"Do you really want to get into a university?"

"With all my heart!"

I was all passion but he wasn't paying attention. We talked at cross purposes for a while, and then he stood up and headed towards the door, saying that he had a meeting to attend. Unwillingly, I followed him out. While locking up he commented, "It seems that everyone likes university. You want to go and Baoyuan wants to go too. He has already paid me two visits."

"What did he say? Do you know Baoyuan?"

"Yes," he said and turned away. I stared at his back as he walked swiftly to the end of the corridor, descended the stairs, and crossed the yard. My heart sank. Baoyuan was a local. Naturally he and his family would know people. Who did I know? With a blank mind, I plodded the two miles back to the mill.

The war was over. I had lost, my mind told me, but my heart refused to quit. Day and night I dwelt on it. Limin didn't like me. Could I turn to someone else? No, he was the only one. Why on earth didn't he like me? Was it because he had been in a bad mood that day? Or because my manner was too official and serious? Or because I didn't offer him anything? Suddenly a new light went on. Until now I hadn't met a cadre corrupt enough to seek bribes, but Limin might be one. I abhorred back doors and bribery, but now was not the time to protest. I wanted to get the position, which, after all, belonged to me in the first place. I wanted to go to university.

Three days later I was in his office again. Instead of claiming my rights, this time I abased myself and begged for his help. Suppressing my aversion to him, I put on my sweetest smile and told him I would ask my mother to send me a package of expensive candies from Beijing as a thank-you present for him if I did get the position. I fawned and he began to defrost. He listened to me with interest and then even invited me to sit down. Eventually, he said what I wanted to hear: "I'll see what I can do, but no promises!"

The decision was made a week later, and our political cadre, Boge, was summoned to the municipal administrative offices to receive it. Boge had been friendly to me in the past because of the reports I wrote for him, which summarized how well our mill was performing and improving. About the time he was to return, I went out of the mill to meet him. He was late. I had almost reached the town when, at the end of the bridge that crossed the Yan River, I spotted him on his bicycle. Before he got off his bike, I shot out, "Am I ratified?"

"Why should you be?" He tried to put on a straight face, but instead he cracked a big smile. His red eyes twinkled.

"You know why! Come on, please, no jokes. I'm dying to know!"

He finally nodded. "You got it."

"Really? Which university?"

"Zhongshan University in Guangzhou." Zhongshan was one of the top ten universities in China, although not as good as Qinghua or Beijing University. I jumped for joy like a child. I had never been happier in my life. My dearest dream had finally come true!

Boge remounted his bicycle and rode towards the mill. I didn't want to go back right away, so I walked to the centre of the bridge. Leaning on the carved stone balustrade, I looked around in excitement. The air was clean and the visibility high. Above me was the clear, bright blue sky with no trace of cloud. Under my feet ran the Yan River, its water a buoyant jade green. In front of me was the Pagoda Mountain, now towering and majestic, on the left were the yellow loess mountains shimmering in sunlight. I didn't know Yan'an could be so beautiful! I didn't know life could be so wonderful!

How could I ever thank my friends in the mill enough? If it weren't for them, I might have lost the chance to get into university forever. In the years that followed, Beijing never gave Yan'an part of its quota again, and my mill never received another university place. In my hardest years I had made my best friends.

Now that I had gotten in, I started to feel guilty about Baoyuan. I was too selfish, too cruel to have fought him like that. But then I argued to myself that it was not really me who had deprived him of a university education — it was the Cultural Revolution. The local leaders were to blame too. If they had given our mill two positions instead of one, both of us could have gone. I later learned that another unit with only ten people in it got one position, all because the future daughter-in-law of a top leader in the Yan'an region worked there. In proportion my mill got one per cent, whereas hers got ten per cent. Yan'an, the "sacred shrine of the revolution," was rife with nepotism and injustice.

Later my mother did send me almost five pounds of high-quality candies. I stole a little for myself and took the rest to Limin. "Will you tell me what happened?" I asked.

"Sure. It was very hard!" he exaggerated. "Since this was a matter of controversy, I couldn't make the decision alone. A meeting of the leaders of the municipality had to be held. Beforehand I talked to a couple of people, but at the meeting nobody wanted to take the lead. I couldn't speak first. It would be too obvious. We sat there for a long time in silence until Secretary XXX broke the deadlock: 'I think it is better to let the younger one go,' he said. After a while, I supported him. Then, one by one, all agreed."

"Thank you very much!"

"Don't thank me now. In the future when you become a big leader, don't forget me!"

"Of course not!" I forced myself to say. Before I was securely ensconced inside the university gate I wouldn't dare cross anybody. My dream was still fragile. At any moment it could break like "the moon in water" or "the flower in the mirror." I had no political ambitions, but even if I did achieve power some day, Limin could rest assured that he wouldn't profit.

MY NEW LIFE BEGINS

THERE WAS SIGNIFICANT UNIVERSITY RECRUITMENT THAT year, and quite a number of my friends and acquaintances benefited. Because of the special status of my brigade, three of the four Beijing students remaining there went on to university: two to Qinghua University and one to the Second Foreign Language Institute in Beijing. Premier Zhou's nephew, Binghe, got into Qinghua University from another brigade. This time our premier didn't step in to stop him. The two privileged classmates of mine, Ping and Xiaonan, entered military medical institutes from the army, and my friend Yishu in Inner Mongolia entered Beijing University.

After our reunion, Wenhui and I had kept up regular correspondence. In a letter I told her about my good fortune, but I didn't hear any great news from her. In January 1972 Yan'an held an assembly of ten thousand people in a big open gymnasium for something — I can't remember what. I attended and so did she. After the meeting I stayed in the bleachers of the stadium to wait for her as we had agreed. Ten minutes later, when all the people were on the field below, she came up. "I am going to a university too, Qinghua University!" she shouted when she was still a fair distance away.

"Wow! Good for you!" I was happily surprised. Wenhui certainly deserved it. "What are you going to study?"

"Telecommunication. It is a classified specialty. My department isn't in Beijing, but in Sichuan Province."

"That's fine. I'm sure you don't mind about that."

"No. I don't."

"When do you leave?"

"Right away. The term starts in February. How about you?"

"I don't know anything yet!"

"Don't worry. You'll soon know!" she assured me. We stood and talked on the bleachers, anticipating our new university lives. After all the nightmare years, it was hard to believe we could end up so well.

Wenhui and I were the lucky ones. Unfortunately, in my generation there were far more unlucky ones. Of the twenty thousand Beijing students who went to Yan'an only five hundred, or two and a half per cent, were granted a university education. Most of those who had been absorbed into the industry of Shanxi Province were excluded, as were those who, for whatever reasons, left Yan'an a bit early. My friend Jinli, one of the four who remained in my brigade, had left Yan'an in the summer of 1971 and missed the boat. She had held out for two and a half hard years and was short just six months.

Jinli was ill when she left. She also had gynecological troubles, except hers were much more serious than mine. She had metrorrhagia and her womb bled all the time*. Because of that her family shifted her to a factory in Tongchuan, where her father had a demobilized comrade-in-arms in a mid-level position — both Jinli's parents worked in the army, teaching in an artillery institute in a suburb of Beijing. Had Jinli stayed in the brigade I was sure she would have been chosen. She was the only one from a priority school and the nicest of the four that remained. Yet she alone had to be the one left out.

Another unlucky friend was Xiangzhen, who had accompanied Yishu to the grasslands in Inner Mongolia. At the end of 1971 the brigade they were in received a quota of one. The herdsmen didn't want to hurt either of them. They told the two to discuss the matter and decide between themselves. Naturally both Xiangzhen and Yishu wanted to go, but each tried hard to sacrifice her own desires for the other. In the end, Xiangzhen lost out and Yishu went to study chemistry at Beijing University.

Xiangzhen lived in solitude on the grassland for two more years. In 1974 she returned to Beijing and got a job in a small factory. When we met in the summer of 1974, she was no longer the Xiangzhen I knew. Before she had been warm and full of life; now she was gloomy and forlorn.

By February most candidates had been interviewed by their future universities and had left Yan'an, but I had heard nothing. "What's wrong? Have they changed their minds? Has Zhongshan University cancelled its quota?" I was on tenterhooks. At last, at the close of the month, I was

---

*I seemed to be the weakest of the thirty at the beginning, but in the end none of the girls who worked concientiously survived well. Jinli was ill, and the other two girls who went on to university in 1972 also had gynecological problems when they left. I couldn't understand why none of us could make a healthy transition to plateau life, but that was how things were.

informed that Zhongshan University was going to start its academic year in September 1972, although other universities had started theirs in February. After fighting so hard for university, I had to wait and fret for six more months before getting in.

During the waiting period I managed to borrow some middle-school textbooks and started to review what I had once learned. With surprise, I found it came back fairly easily. Had I foreseen this day, I would have kept at my studies all these years.

In April two teachers from Zhongshan University visited Yan'an to check their student allotment. One morning I was called to an office in our mill to meet them. They were both men in their late twenties, urbane and amicable. They began by saying, "We would like you to know that our university has been entrusted by the Second Machinery Building Ministry to train you. After graduation you will work for them. As you know, this is a classified ministry. We know very little about their plans for you or where you will be assigned at graduation. It could be anywhere, even where conditions are the hardest. Are you sure you want to enroll?"

"Yes, I am." To work in a classified ministry had prestige in China — only those from good families were allowed. As to the assignment, I didn't want to think about it. It was too early. I hadn't even gotten into university yet! And where on earth could there be a place worse than Yan'an? After living here, I could take anything.

"Then be prepared for the assignment. Now let's talk about your specialty. Your department will be mathematics and mechanics and your specialty mechanical engineering. Do you have any objection to this?"

"No, none whatever!" I didn't really know what mechanical engineering was. It was not one of the frontier disciplines in science like nuclear physics or mathematics, but it didn't sound too awful. Aside from medicine, the other specialty I wanted to avoid was Chinese literature. The lives of the literati were too dangerous. Even before the Cultural Revolution writers often made "political mistakes" and were publicly criticized. There were so many rules, taboos, and petty things to watch out for in writing. How could one produce anything of quality under such conditions? If I decided to write what I really wanted, my life would be nothing but fear and trouble.

Following the talk was a simple test. The two teachers wrote a few questions on a piece of paper and handed it to me. The questions all covered material I had recently reviewed. It seemed to me they only wanted to make sure I had reached the level of the first middle school grade. In no time I finished the questions and gave the paper back to them. They seemed surprised at my speed.

The formal notice of university acceptance arrived at the mill in June. On receiving it the leaders weren't thoughtful enough to deliver it to me so I could put my heart back where it belonged. They kept it for a month and a half longer, until the end of July. Then there was a farewell meeting. One or two representatives of each squad were summoned by the leaders to comment on my past performance and express their wishes for me for the future. Based on these comments and the leaders' opinions, our political cadre, Boge, wrote an official memorandum about me. It was put in my dossier and from then on would accompany me wherever life took me.

At last I was allowed to go home. Yuehua, Zhongcheng, and some other friends came to see me off at the bus station. When there were only a few minutes to go I boarded the bus, found my seat at the back, and sat down. There was no sadness in me. However, my emotions were stirred by the thought that I was leaving Yan'an forever. Three years and eight months ago I had arrived, bitter and depressed, swearing to myself I would never come back if one day I could just make my escape. Today I was succeeding and my resentment towards the place had lessened. Although my life here had been filled with hardship and disappointment, it had a happy ending and I had made wonderful friends. I looked out of the window and saw them standing in the early morning sun. Then I looked out towards the Dates Garden, home of my peasant friends. They had been very kind to me while I lived with them. Perhaps someday in the future I might like to return for a visit. Who knows?

Say goodbye to Yan'an
Leave the misery behind.
My heart flies to the future,
My new life has begun.

Once I was the country's flower,
Once I was full of hope.
Then I was thrown into fire,
Then I was thrown into water.

Today I am reborn,
Miseries I won't dwell on.
Life's path is still long.
Gather courage and spirit, move on!

POSTSCRIPT

T HE NEWLY REOPENED UNIVERSITY WAS A MESS. THE "worker-peasant-soldier university students" ranged in educational level from the first year of junior middle school to the third year of senior middle school, and most had "returned their knowledge to their teachers," or forgotten what they had learned six years earlier. Before anything else, the university professors spent a semester teaching them middle school mathematics, physics, and chemistry.

In ability, in culture, and in temperament these "elected" (or chosen by whatever other means) students couldn't compare with the old ones, who were selected through rigorous exams. As a matter of fact, some students were so ignorant they should never have come. I had hoped to find a good husband in the university but I found no one. Apart from that, however, university life was pleasant. I enjoyed my studies and living in metropolitan Guangzhou. It was subtropical, clean, and pleasant.

The campus of Zhongshan University was especially famous for its beauty. Every other day after supper I took a walk with my classmates to the west gate where the Pearl River flowed. Along the way we passed buildings of classic Chinese beauty with glazed tile roofs, palm trees, banana jungles, and countless flowering plants, camellia bushes, and yulan and magnolia trees. The magnolia were especially breathtaking, tall with crimson flowers bigger than one's hand.

In former times, one attended university for five years, but we spent only three and a half, including the preparatory six months. Like it or not, this was the new educational system of the Great Cultural Revolution. I graduated in January 1976. Completely out of the blue, I was assigned an engineering job in Beijing. After seven years of exile, I returned home. My unit, the Second Research and Design Institute of Nuclear Engineering, was only half a mile away from my parents' home. My colleagues and leaders there were good-natured and life could not have been better.

In January 1976 Premier Zhou Enlai died. He was a man truly loved by the Chinese. In late March and on into April, Beijingers spontaneously gathered in Tiananmen Square in memory of Zhou. On April 4 I went to the square to pay him my respects. There were people and wreaths everywhere. The walls of the Monument to the People's Heroes were covered by layers of essays and poems. Most praised Zhou's life, but a few also made veiled attacks on the Gang of Four. I even saw a speaker but I could not get close enough to hear him.

These attacks, which were mild to my eyes, greatly offended the party leftists. On the night of April 5, 1976 the police assaulted hundreds of people massed in the square, beat them with clubs, and arrested them. The square was stained with blood. The next morning the police had to wash it off with water and mops. On April 7 the practice of mourning Zhou in Tiananmen Square was labelled counter-revolutionary by the newspapers. All units in Beijing were ordered to denounce those who took part. I was incredulous — I wasn't the same naïve girl who, ten years earlier, had believed all she was told. If anyone who wrote a memorial poem to Premier Zhou could be counter-revolutionary, then China had no revolutionaries left. Many other Beijingers reacted similarly. In my unit not one counter-revolutionary was ferreted out.

In September 1976 Mao Zedong died. I felt less bitterness towards him by then, but still secretly rejoiced at his death. China could finally move ahead without him.

The newspapers were crammed with articles singing his praises, but the Chinese wanted a more objective assessment of his life. They made up their own last will and testament for him. Mao, they said, had two regrets: that he had started the Cultural Revolution, and that he couldn't live to see Taiwan liberated. When I heard this, I believed it and wished to see it confirmed in the newspapers. Indeed, had Mao recanted at the last moment, I would have forgiven him.

The Gang of Four was smashed in October, less than a month after Mao died, and the Cultural Revolution ended. Like all Chinese, I was overjoyed. However, while studying the documents detailing the crimes of the Gang of Four, I learned they had tried to criticize "walking through the back door" into the army. This measure was said to be aimed at General Yie Jianying, who had been in charge of the military committee. Even Mao had scolded the Gang of Four for that: "By criticizing 'walking through the back door,' you direct your fire at millions in the Liberation Army. There are soldiers who joined through the back door, but are you saying that among them none is any good?" Thus "walking through the back door" never did get criticized.

I couldn't for the life of me understand this. The Gang of Four might have committed a thousand wrongs, ten thousand wrongs, but to criticize the privileged for sending their children into the army through the back door was absolutely right. Whereas all their extremist ideas, all their wrong ideas, had been put into practice, this one good idea had been thwarted by Mao. Then, when they were overthrown, it became one of their crimes. Why on earth could nobody touch the army leaders? Why should everybody fear them? Were they leaders of the People's Liberation Army or the warlords of the new China?

Deng Xiaoping came to power in 1977. The Cultural Revolution was then dismantled step by step, and all the old policies he and Liu Shaoqi instituted before the Cultural Revolution were restored. The educated who had "joined the brigade" were finally allowed to return to their home cities, provided they hadn't married. Universities resumed the traditional strict entrance exam system and five-year course of study. My two younger brothers, Weihua and Jianhua, both took the exams in 1977 and passed.

When Shuzeng left the Dates Garden for the army in the summer of 1970, I didn't hear from him for five years. At the end of 1975 he was demobilized and, with the help of his family, returned to Beijing. From my parents he got my address in Guangzhou and we started to correspond. We remained casual friends in Beijing for a year. Then, in 1977, he asked Jinli to convey his wish to "talk love" with me.

By then I was twenty-six years old. I hadn't met a suitable man, and I saw no possibility of meeting one in the future given the mess made by the Cultural Revolution. Although I felt no passion for Shuzeng, I married him in September of that year. We lived together in disharmony for a year, and then he was sent for four years to the embassy in Algeria as an accountant. From that time on we lived separately.

In 1978, for the first time in its history, the People's Republic began to send scholars and graduate students to study in the West. I wanted to come out. Since the old educational system was fully restored, the worker-peasant-soldier university graduates, who had once been welcomed by the work-units to which they were assigned, were now out of favour. I didn't want to be looked upon as inferior. I passed two qualifying English exams, the first given by the institute for which I worked and the second a country-wide examination. In 1980 I came to study in Canada, and eight years later I received a Ph.D. in mechanical engineering from McGill University.

Eventually, I divorced Shuzeng. While in Montreal I met Professor Charles B. Daniels of the University of Victoria, fell in love and remarried happily, and moved to Victoria, British Columbia, where I now live and work.

I am now a Canadian. I love Canada because it is a free country. I also love China, but I love her ambivalently. She wasted my youth and put me through many ordeals for nothing, but she also gave me life, educated me, and made me who I am today. She has corrupt cadres and army leaders, but she also has masses of kind, honest people. She is scourged by one catastrophe after another, but through her pain and misfortune she moves forward. Slowly, she is changing for the better. China, my homeland. China, my sorrow, my regret, my hope, my love.